Qualitative Studies in Social Work Research

For students—who want meaning and lives in research

Qualitative Studies in Social Work Research

editor

Catherine Kohler Riessman

SAGE Publications
International Educational and Professional Publisher
Thousand Oaks   London   New Delhi

For information address:

 SAGE Publications, Inc.
2455 Teller Road
Thousand Oaks, California 91320

SAGE Publications Ltd.
6 Bonhill Street
London EC2A 4PU
United Kingdom

SAGE Publications India Pvt. Ltd.
M-32 Market
Greater Kailash I
New Delhi 110 048 India

Printed in the United States of America

Library of Congress Cataloging-in-Publication Data

Main entry under title:

Qualitative studies in social work research / edited by Catherine
   Kohler Riessman
        p.   cm.
   Includes bibliographical references and index.
   ISBN 0-8039-5451-4 — ISBN 0-8039-5452-2 (pbk.)
   1. Social service—Research.   I. Riessman, Catherine Kohler,
1939-
HV11.Q   1993
361—dc20   93-31227

94 95 96 97   10 9 8 7 6 5 4 3 2 1

Sage Production Editor: Diane S. Foster

Contents

Preface: Making Room for Diversity in Social Work Research

This book features studies of a variety of problems that use a variety of qualitative methods. Building on the challenge by social work to empiricism educators[1] (Heineman, 1981; Pieper, 1985, 1989; Rodwell, 1987; Witkin, 1992), the collection provides alternatives. Chapters "go beyond the stage of suggesting that other . . . technologies and methods are available" (Blythe, 1992a, p. 268); they detail what alternative methods actually look like, and the kind of knowledge they produce.

Our field has witnessed polarized debates about the relative value of quantitative versus qualitative methods. In this extended preface I go beyond criticizing the dominant paradigm in social work research. Based on research experience with both methods, I argue for diversity: equal time for qualitative approaches in research training. I compare recent developments in the social sciences with current practices and critiques in social work. Drawing on recent scholarship about philosophical underpinnings of different orientations to practice (Dean, 1993; Dean & Fenby, 1989), I use the metaphor of maps to argue for different orientations to research. Locating myself and a description of how the book was created places the 10 empirical studies in context.

Extending Diversity in Research

A virtual explosion is occurring in the social sciences around methodology. Psychology is witnessing a "textual turn," with increased attention to interpretive work, narrative studies, and discourse analysis (Bruner, 1986, 1990; Mishler, 1984, 1986; Packer & Addison, 1989; Rosenwald & Ochberg, 1992). Case studies are enjoying reconsideration in sociology (Feagin, Orum & Sjoberg, 1991; Ragin & Becker, 1992). Anthropology never abandoned its adherence to participant observation, and thick description, but anthropologists are experimenting with new forms of ethnographic writing, and asking difficult questions about power in ethnographic texts (Clifford, 1988; Clifford & Marcus, 1986; Rosaldo, 1989). Feminist scholars from a variety of disciplines are modeling new ways to do social science to benefit women (Behar, 1993; DeVault, 1990; Fonow & Cook, 1991; Gluck & Patai, 1991; Reinharz, 1992; Stivers, 1993). Placing themselves in their research, feminists for some time have been postmodern, that is, questioning objectivity, rejecting detachment, and accepting contradictory readings of a text (Wolf, 1992). Stimulated by these intellectual developments, social science is entering a period of reflection: What is our relationship to those we study? How do we represent the experiences of informants? For whom are we writing, and how?

Social work draws its research methods from the social sciences, but the field has been reluctant to ask such questions, and to embrace methodological diversity. Many act as if particular research approaches are superior, not only for a given project, but for *all* research projects. Polarized arguments about the relative value of qualitative, compared to quantitative, methods obscure what each has to offer (Gambrill, 1992). Both sides of the debate have contributed to lack of mutual respect. Quantitative researchers imply only their methods are "empirical," other kinds of data are "anecdotal" or "descriptive," suitable perhaps for generating hypotheses but not for "testing" them. Proponents of qualitative methods engage in science-bashing, imply their methods are better, and label anything they don't like as "positivist," sometimes incorrectly. Technology, especially the computer, has magnified the dichotomy between methods; it facilitates large numbers of observations and their statistical manipulation (Rein, 1991).

Organizations also bear some responsibility for polarized discussions by coupling the profession with a particular view of science. *Empirical* has been equated with representative samples and objective measurement although, as Blythe (1992a) observes, there are many forms of empirical data. "Over time, the number of quantitative research reports has increased in social work journals. However, Gambrill (1992) continues, "quantitative research is not synonymous with scientific reasoning" (p. 25). In applied settings particularly, not all problems lend themselves to quantification and computer manipulation. Yet population-based and variable-centered models dominate research courses at both master's and doctoral levels, research reports in the profession and program evaluation in agencies. The Council on Social Work Education (CSWE, 1992) mandates the teaching of qualitative *and* quantitative methods (but provides no specifics about the former, in contrast to repeated mention of statistical procedures for the latter).

It is ironic that the profession lags behind the social sciences in methodological diversity. The theories that clinical practitioners of diverse persuasions use in their daily work were developed through the intensive study of individual cases by Freud, Erikson, Piaget, and Skinner (Mishler, 1993). Social workers deal with living human beings, in clinical and community settings and in policy analysis; human experience, initiative, and emotion need greater attention in our research reports. Practitioners are taught to respect the person-in-situation and foster individual agency —the self-determination of the client; yet we privilege the abstract, statistical aggregate in social work research: average tendencies, not individual lives in context. Most published work emphasizes product—findings—not the process of investigation.

As a consequence perhaps, the field has witnessed a schism between practice and research. According to practitioners, social work research presents depersonalized accounts that do not help "in the trenches." According to researchers, workers do not use empirical findings to select interventions, or evaluate them. (On the debate, see Blythe, 1992b; Ivanoff, Blythe, & Briar, 1987; Imre, 1984; Peile, 1988; Witkin, 1992.) The two communities speak different languages, they construct reality from different standpoints, contributing further to divisions within the field and lack of productive collaboration.

The Task Force on Social Work Research (1991) identifies the lack of connection between practice and research as a major problem in the field and recommends strengthening research training at all levels. Methodological diversity might also help. Different forms of practice are suited to different forms of research. Behaviorism fits well with quantification; it is possible to operationalize concepts and count behaviors. Interpretive forms of practice (such as psychoanalytic or constructivist forms) are better suited to textual approaches that focus on interaction. There is a sympathetic connection between certain kinds of social work and qualitative kinds of data—talk, therapeutic conversation, agency records, narratives about experiences with organizations and macro systems.

Why has social work given such authority to the quantitative, population-based model of research? Perhaps it has to do with the quest for professional status, a response to Flexner's challenge (Austin, 1983; Fraser et al., 1991). Professionalization has isolated many from major intellectual currents of the last decade in the social sciences. Perhaps as women workers (primarily), we "talk numbers" and present rates to be taken seriously; research on human experience and meaning is seen as "soft" in male-dominated settings. There are institutional pressures on academics who depend for tenure, even for hiring, on dominant notions of "good science," and related constraints from funding agencies who value particular ways of doing science. Social work is not alone, of course, in emphasizing quantification, but few in leadership positions are modeling other ways to do research, as many in the social sciences are.

To locate my position on the issues, I have employed quantitative and qualitative methods to address questions about gender, health, and illness. Typically, I've used them in separate investigations, but occasionally I've combined methods. This is not as easy as it would seem, for methods can rest on very different philosophical assumptions (to be discussed later). Integration is not always possible or desirable. But where methods are compatible, research about a problem is strengthened when various kinds of data are brought to bear (Allen-Meares & Lane, 1990; Denzin, 1978).

In a project on gender and divorce, for example, I wanted to understand the psychological distress experienced by women compared to men. Quantitative comparisons using an established scale suggested women carry a considerable psychological burden when marriage ends; men, by contrast, appeared to experience little distress. However, these findings were challenged when I examined men's responses to open-ended questions about their emotions, and other spontaneous statements during the research interview. Close analysis of one man's discourse—how he constructed his account of emotions—illuminated patterns that helped me understand others too. The kinds of distress were missed entirely by the scale. Qualitative data, in this case, provided a check on quantitative results, suggested gender bias in psychological measurement, and uncovered men's unique idioms of distress following marital dissolution (Riessman, 1990).

As a result of cumulative experiences in various research contexts, my methodological preference has shifted over time. I now do qualitative research almost exclusively. The research problems I have become interested in, and the interpretive perspective I find compelling, fit better with qualitative work.

It is a common belief that the research problem should determine the method of investigation. There are also other determinants, which I'll turn to shortly. But presumably methods are selected for their appropriateness to the area of study, and choices made only after considerable theoretical specification. If, for example, I want to study the impact of a program of prenatal care on infant mortality, I would be well-advised to select a quantitative health indicator for the dependent variable, track it longitudinally, and secure a large enough sample of allow for subgroup comparisons. If, on the other hand, I want to study how families construct meaning after an infant death, it would be best to understand the situation in family members' terms—in their own words—and data over time would not necessarily be required. Topics could be initiated by subjects themselves and pursued in open-ended questions that might vary from interview to interview. Intensive study of a small number of cases (people, not variables) would be appropriate.

The ideal sequence is often violated in practice: Methods dictate the way research questions are framed, rather than the reverse (Reinharz, 1979/1991). Research problems get forced into a priori schemes. To meet the expectations of funding agencies, for example, variable-centered models and technologies of abstracted empiricism take hold (Mills, 1959). My study of the meaning of infant death might be transformed into a survey of family outcomes, with an instrument composed of predetermined, forced-choice items and established scales. Although rarely discussed in print, political contexts often shape the methods chosen. Certain ones "become icons because they're powerful, because they're rewarded by institutions" (Vizenor, as quoted in Stivers, 1993, p. 424). Any research method is limited in the kinds of questions it can address, but when particular methods are privileged over others, questions suited to alternative methods may not get asked.

Despite the tendency to polarize, social work journals of the last decade have provided excellent critiques of traditional methods and pointed to some alternatives (Heineman, 1981; Pieper, 1985, 1989; Rodwell, 1987; Ruckdeschel, 1985; Witkin, 1992; Zimmerman, 1989). A moderating voice, Ann Hartman (1990) offers a plea for the "many ways of knowing." Often missing from the debate, however, are detailed descriptions by social work investigators working systematically with data in nonnumeric ways. This anthology is designed to fill the gap. It provides a resource for teachers, scholars and human service practitioners who want to think about and incorporate a variety of methods into their research programs.

The studies featured here—all by social workers—demonstrate that there are many ways to be "empirical"; that is, ways to develop knowledge from systematic analysis of observations. Personal lived experience can provide empirical data, just as interviews, field, or laboratory studies can. Diversity within qualitative research—in kinds of data and in their treatment—is the organizing principle of the book.

Deconstructing Dichotomies

The research literature is full of dichotomies: qualitative/quantitative; descriptive/analytic; etic/emic; and positivist/post-positivist. Although language is all we have to communicate distinctions, it is limiting, and fails to represent nuance and complexity.

There is no good word, for example, to refer to the range of research in this volume. *Qualitative* was invented by quantitative researchers to describe data that are nonnumeric. Yet the term refers to a family of approaches with very loose and extended kinship, even divorces (Glaser, 1992). Beyond focus on text—which some investigators combine with numeric data—it is hard sometimes to see the relationship between what various qualitative scholars do. They use *very* different kinds of texts, in this volume for example: field observations, a sample of interviews, a single case, organizational documents, and literary narratives. They also treat texts in radically different ways, ranging from the examination of surface content to analysis of deep structures of discourse. Qualitative research is not a unified tradition, like conventional research derived from the experimental model is.

Although true, it is not sufficient to say that quantitative methods are suited to certain kinds of research questions, and qualitative ones to others. I put forward that position earlier, but now add philosophy to the brew. Beliefs about the nature of social reality and how we are to know it (ontology and epistemology) shape which method we chose, which questions we ask, and what counts as knowledge. Philosophical positions about reality and knowing are critically different for positivist and post-positivist research.

It is beyond my scope to trace developments in positivism (see Kolakowski, 1993; Phillips, 1987; Heineman, 1981; Pieper, 1985), but it is crucial to realize that the quantitative model dominant in social work research today was derived from the natural sciences and is based in positivist thinking. Human behavior is understood similarly to the way we understand physical phenomena. The explanatory framework assumes a realist ontology, that is, reality consists of a world of objectively defined facts, distinct from interpretations. Put simply, there is a world "out there," separate from us, and we can know it through observable qualities—sensory data that can be isolated, measured and related causally. Stivers (1993) summarizes key assumptions of positivism:

> That the subject matter of interest to social science—that is, social reality— is as hard or concrete as the physical objects studied by botanists or geologists and is "out there" waiting to be revealed; that social science acquires systematic knowledge by adhering to rules of hypothesis testing, controlled (unbiased) observation, and the replication of previous research results; and that by using the prescribed methodology, social science arrives at Truth, which consists of lawlike generalizations that take the form, "Given conditions A, B, and C, when X occurs, Y will follow," laws that make possible the prediction—hence, the control—of events. (p. 408)

The possibility of objectivity is assumed in positivism; the distorting influences of a researcher's personal perspective (subjectivity) can be eliminated by detachment. Not all approaches to empirical social research make such claims and, ironically, they are increasingly questioned in the physical sciences.

Philosophy forces us to locate the assumptions about reality and knowing that undergird the research methods we choose. Methods are like maps: They focus inquiry and lay out paths that, if followed, are supposed to lead to valid knowledge of how the world works. But like maps we consult in everyday life, they contain assumptions about what is important. Different maps make certain features of the terrain visible, and obscure others.

When hiking along the coast, I consult a topographic map because it represents the trails, elevation, and ridges from which to view the sea. When sailing, I use a navigational chart that represents rocks and depth, and buoys that mark a channel into the harbor. The same coastline could be mapped in yet another way, to represent a world of property lines, taxation districts, and political divisions. Not objective pictures, maps are instead representations of reality that reflect the interests of the mapmaker, a point of view.

> Consensual assumptions, hypotheses, and interests direct our attention in certain ways, thereby making possible the constitution of a meaningful world from a welter of otherwise meaningless phenomena. (Stivers, 1993, p. 420)

Like research methods, maps are powerful tools for making statements about social life. Different ones connect us to realities we could not know without the map. Many question whether the positivist/natural science map is even appropriate for human studies; others find it useful. "Seeing social realities as 'things' makes them appear susceptible to research based on the natural science approach" (Stivers, 1993, p. 418). A number of post-positivist maps exist to guide inquiry. Each makes distinctive features of the terrain visible. Two (often used in combination) contrast with the map of the natural sciences. They are particularly appropriate for studying certain kinds of social work practice.

Phenomenologists begin with human experience. Rather than locating worldly objects "out there," the map privileges human awareness, because our capacity to know any object depends on awareness. Based in 20th-century developments in philosophy (Husserl, 1939/1973; Merleau-Ponty, 1962/1989; Schutz, 1932/1967), psychologists and sociologists are examining consciousness with phenomenological research methods, focusing on subjects' experienced meaning instead of their overt actions or behavior (for a review, see Polkinghorne, 1989).

Interpretive social scientists add that our capacity to know any object in the world is rooted in our definitions, so their map privileges language and how we construct experience (for example, an informant's definition of her situation). Rabinow and Sullivan (1979/1987) summarize an aspect of the interpretivist position:

> We are fundamentally self-interpreting and self-defining, living always in a cultural environment, inside a "web of signification we ourselves have spun." There is no outside, detached standpoint from which we gather and present brute data. When we try to understand the cultural world, we are dealing with interpretations and interpretations of interpretations. (p. 7)

In a word, there is no view from nowhere, no way to see the world as it really is, separate from ourselves and language (Ford, 1975; Nagel, 1986). *Facts* are interpretive, because they are grounded in the consensual rules of the relevant knowledge (research) community, not in transcendent standards. "Facts and interpretations require and shape one another; they constitute a continuum rather than a dichotomy" (Stivers, 1993, p. 421).

Assumptions about reality and knowing that underly the map of phenomenology/interpretive research are distinct from the assumptions that underly the methods derived from positivism. One map is not sufficient for all research problems, kinds of practice, or all investigators. Contemporary social work requires diverse modes of inquiry.

Locating Myself: Background and Organization of Book

The construction of any work always bears the mark of the person who created it. I have what my colleague Judith Gonyea calls DDS—Different Drummer Syndrome. It often leads me to be suspicious of received categories, established conventions and, especially, one dogma. No doubt my early Catholic upbringing is implicated. A kind of scientific thinking (Phillips, 1987), core values define who I am and therefore this book: skepticism about universalizing generalizations; respect for particularity and context; appreciation of reflexivity and standpoint; and the need for empirical evidence. I firmly believe students should be taught a variety of research methods. I also think that deconstructing the rhetoric of science can open up new ways to think about and do research.

This book is situated in the politics of knowledge. I have an explicit purpose: to reduce the monopoly of numeric methods on the production of ideas in social work, to expand the rules of knowledge development, and to correct the present imbalance in research education. Because qualitative approaches offer the potential for representing human agency—initiative, language, emotion—they provide support for the liberatory project of social work. I want to assist a birth happening in the social sciences and, because of critiques by social work scholars before me, beginning in our field.

> The edifice of positivist epistemology was never as solid as it once looked and today the social sciences encompass, albeit uneasily, several diverse paradigms, each with its accompanying methodology. (Stivers, 1993, p. 409)

If we believe in paradigms, social work too must make way for methodological diversity, however uneasy it makes us. Having the most inclusive possible knowledge community is consistent with the values of the profession.

The idea for this specific book emerged from my frustration with the limited attention in social work research to philosophies of science and recent intellectual developments in the social sciences. As a teacher of research methods at the master's and doctoral levels (Riessman, in press),

I searched for accounts of how research is actually done. The literature is dominated by dry, "scientistic" reports that may be useful to experts perhaps, but are difficult for research novices to learn from. Research textbooks give short shrift to nonnumeric approaches, ignore complexity within qualitative work, and simplify philosophical issues. I searched in vain for empirical work in social work that discussed the positive role of subjectivity in research, like that which is available in clinical and feminist scholarship.

I knew from the onset I wanted to construct a book that featured various kinds of qualitative research done by social workers, but I had no idea what the response would be when I mailed a "Call for Papers." Looking back, I secretly feared I was throwing a party and no one would come. Because research in the profession is so identified with quantification (Fraser et al., 1991; Glisson, 1990), I worried there wouldn't be enough good work to include that explicated method—how a qualitative study was done. I called friends and colleagues, and "beat the bushes" to locate social workers who were doing alternative kinds of research.

My fears were ill-founded. Thirty-five proposals for papers were submitted, and several more papers found their way to me later, thanks to colleagues. There was an outpouring of enthusiasm for the project. Scholars knowledgeable about qualitative methods reviewed the papers, and those selected were revised. In true inductive fashion, I constructed the book from the ground up, and selected papers that reflected substantive and methodological diversity. When I began I was not sure what form the organization of the book would take, but papers "naturally" grouped themselves into three sections.

As I look at the completed volume, I am pleased so many papers from junior investigators made it into the final set. Younger scholars are clearly interested in alternative models of research. Perhaps the group was also willing to persevere through multiple revisions because of academic pressure to publish, and maybe they needed the money (contributors were paid for chapters). Seriously, younger scholars seem to be getting stronger training in qualitative methods than their predecessors in social work did. The Group for the Advancement of Doctoral Education in Social Work (GADE) now recommends training in qualitative approaches (GADE, 1993), such as grounded theory, ethnography, narrative analysis, and other textual approaches. As in the past, however, students in some programs have to fight to do qualitative dissertations; some must learn the methods on their own or take courses in social science departments that support the perspective. Several contributors to this volume speak to these issues.

Like any text, the book can be read in several ways and, I hope, by multiple audiences. First and most obviously, it offers a place for beginning students to discover the world of qualitative research. The chapters showcase work being done by social workers at varying points in professional careers. Second, the book can be read by practitioners looking for empirically-based insights—about the isolation of the chronically ill, the meaning of abuse for women and girls, what happens when the homeless apply for public assistance. Research methods, whatever kind, provide investigators with ways to systematically examine substantive problems, and readers can learn about important social work issues here. Third, the book can (and should) be read to learn about diversity *across* research approaches. Different methods come under the rubric we call qualitative.

Finally, the book can be read by the methodologically inclined to learn about diversity *within* a particular qualitative method. Not everyone uses grounded theory or narrative analysis in the same way. Philosophical positions differ among qualitative researchers. These are reflected in the chapters, how they are sequenced and discussed in my introduction to each section, which places each chapter in context.

The book is organized into three parts. The first includes studies that use a well-established qualitative tradition, grounded theory, to study health and illness. The second presents an emerging tradition, the analysis of personal narratives, here about sexual and physical trauma. The third part does not represent a tradition but mixes methods and topics to reveal how subjectivity matters in social work research. Chapters examine long-term care, welfare application by the homeless, conservatism and feminist organizing, Alzheimer's disease and caregiving. Despite topical diversity, all investigators in the last section show how reflexivity can be a source of knowledge.

Many individuals made this book a better one and I thank them. Authors put up with repeated requests for revision, usually with good humor. Reviewers evaluated the chapters thoughtfully, and wrote detailed comments that helped make for tighter chapters. Marquita Flemming and Diane Foster were patient editors who understood the delays but also pushed me to let go of the manuscript. Cathie Rocheleau did the clerical work with care, and Michelle Huber and Karen Bullock tracked down and carefully compiled references. Elliot Mishler, my mentor, critic, and friend, reviewed the introductions and talked endlessly with me about the ideas. My Philosophical Friends, a study group composed of clinical and research faculty from several Massachusetts schools of social work, supported the idea for the book. Babs Fenby, Ann Fleck-Henderson, and Carol Swenson from the group provided helpful criticism of a draft at the end of a busy semester; Ruth Dean looked over several drafts, and her pointed criticism made this a better Preface. Nick Warren read a draft with supportive and critical eyes and pushed me to elaborate metaphors. Cheryl Hyde helped clarify ideas and provided badly needed humor. Last but by no means least, I thank my students. They pushed me in classes to depart from the canon in the textbook and teach about doing research in other ways.

CATHERINE KOHLER RIESSMAN
Wellfleet, Massachusetts

Note

1. Drawing from C. W. Mills (1959), I use the term *empiricism* to refer to a style of work that adopts "philosophies of natural science . . . to form a program and a canon for work in social science" (p. 57). Social work debates about methodology typically equate *empirical* and *empiricism*, a confusion I clarify in the Preface.

References

Allen-Meares, P., & Lane, B. A. (1990). Social work practice: Integrating qualitative and quantitative data collection techniques. *Social Work, 35*(5), 452-458.

Austin, D. M. (1983). The Flexner myth and the history of social work. *Social Service Review, 57*(3), 357-377.

Behar, R. (1993). *Translated woman: Crossing the border with Esperanza's story.* Boston: Beacon Press.

Blythe, B. (1992a). Reply to Dr. Witkin. *Journal of Social Work Education, 28*(3), 268-269.

Blythe, B. (1992b). Should undergraduate and graduate social work students be taught to conduct empirically-based practice? Yes! *Journal of Social Work Education, 28*(3), 260-263.

Bruner, J. (1986). *Actual minds, possible words.* Cambridge, MA: Harvard University Press.

Bruner, J. (1990). *Acts of meaning.* Cambridge, MA: Harvard University Press.

Clifford, J. (1988). *The predicament of culture: Twentieth-century ethnography, literature, and art.* Cambridge, MA: Harvard University Press.

Clifford, J., & Marcus, G. E. (Eds.). (1986). *Writing culture: The poetics and politics of ethnography.* Berkeley: University of California Press.

Council on Social Work Education (CSWE). (1992). *Curriculum policy statement for master's degree programs in social work education.*

Dean, R. G. (1993). Constructivism: An approach to clinical practice. *Smith College Studies in Social Work, 63*(2), 127-146.

Dean, R. G., & Fenby, B. L. (1989). Exploring epistemologies: Social work action as a reflection of philosophical assumptions. *Journal of Social Work Education, 25*(1), 46-54.

Denzin, N. (1978). *Research act: A theoretical introduction to sociological methods.* New York: McGraw-Hill.

DeVault, M. L. (1990). Talking and listening from women's standpoint: Feminist strategies for interviewing and analysis. *Social Problems, 37*(1), 96-116.

Feagin, J. R., Orum, A. M., & Sjoberg, G. (Eds.). (1991). *A case for the case study.* Chapel Hill: North Carolina University Press.

Fonow, M. M., & Cook, J. A. (Eds.). (1991). *Beyond methodology: Feminist scholarship as lived research.* Bloomington: Indiana University Press.

Ford, J. (1975). *Paradigms and fairytales: An introduction to the science of meanings.* Boston: Routledge & Kegan Paul.

Fraser, M., Taylor, M. J., Jackson, R., & O'Jack, J. (1991). Social work and science: Many ways of knowing? *Social Work Research and Abstracts, 27*(4), 5-15.

Gambrill, E. (1992, October 1). *Social work research: Priorities and obstacles.* Keynote address, Group for the Advancement of Doctoral Education in Social Work Conference, University of Pittsburgh, PA.

Glaser, B. G. (1992). *Basics of grounded theory analysis.* Mill Valley, CA: Sociology Press.

Glisson, C. (1990). *A systematic assessment of the social work literature: Trends in social work research.* Knoxville: University of Tennessee College of Social Work.

Gluck, S. B., & Patai, D. (Eds.). (1991). *Women's words: The feminist practice of oral history.* New York: Routledge & Kegan Paul.

Group for the Advancement of Doctoral Education in Social Work (GADE). (1993). *Guidelines for quality in social work doctoral programs.*

Hartman, A. (1990). Many ways of knowing. *Social Work, 35*(1), 3-4.

Heineman, M. B. (1981). The obsolete scientific imperative in social work research. *Social Service Review, 55*(3), 371-397.

Husserl, E. (1939/1973). *Experience and judgement: Investigation in a genealogy of logic* (J. S. Churchill and K. Ameriks, Trans.). Evanston, IL: Northwestern University Press.

Imre, R. W. (1984). The nature of knowledge in social work. *Social Work, 29*(1), 41-45.

Ivanoff, A., Blythe, B., & Briar, S. (1987). The empirical clinical practice debate. *Social Casework: The Journal of Contemporary Social Work, 68*(5), 290-298.

Kolakowski, L. (1993). An overall view of positivism. In M. Hammersley (Ed.), *Social research: Philosophy, politics, and practice* (pp. 1-8). Newbury Park, CA: Sage.

Merleau-Ponty, M. (1962/1989). *Phenomenology of perception* (C. Smith, Trans.). London: Routledge & Kegan Paul.

Mills, C. W. (1959). *The sociological imagination.* New York: Oxford University Press.

Mishler, E. G. (1984). *The discourse of medicine: Dialectics of medical interviews.* Norwood, NJ: Ablex.

Mishler, E. G. (1986). The analysis of interview-narratives. In T. R. Sarbin (Ed.), *Narrative psychology: The storied nature of human conduct* (pp. 233-255). New York: Praeger.

Mishler, E. G. (1993, June 9). *Missing persons: Recovering developmental stories/histories.* Paper presented at Conference on Ethnographic Approaches to the Study of Human Development, Oakland, CA.

Nagel, T. (1986). *The view from nowhere.* New York: Oxford University Press.

Packer, M. J., & Addison, R. B. (Eds.). (1989). *Entering the circle: Hermaneutic investigation in psychology.* Albany: State University of New York.

Peile, C. (1988). Research paradigms in social work: From stalemate to creative synthesis. *Social Service Review, 62*(1), 1-19.

Phillips, D. C. (1987). *Philosophy, science, and social inquiry: Contemporary methodological controversies in social science and related applied fields of research.* New York: Pergamon.

Pieper, M. H. (1985). The future of social work research. *Social work research and abstracts, 21*(4), 3-11.

Pieper, M. H. (1989). The heuristic paradigm: A unifying and comprehensive approach to social work research. *Smith College Studies in Social Work, 60* (1), 8-34.

Polkinghorne, D. E. (1989). Phenomenological research methods. In R. Valle & S. Halling (Ed.), *Existential-phenomenological perspectives in psychology* (pp. 41-60). New York: Plenum.

Rabinow, P., & Sullivan, W. M. (1979/1987). *Interpretive social science: A second look.* Berkeley: University of California Press.

Ragin, C. C., & Becker, H. S. (Eds.). (1992). *What is a case? Exploring the foundations of social inquiry.* New York: Cambridge University Press.

Rein, M. (1991). Technology's stranglehold. *Boston Globe,* January 1, 1991, p. 62.

Reinharz, S. (1979/1991). *On becoming a social scientist.* New Brunswick, NJ: Transaction.

Reinharz, S. (1992). *Feminist research methods.* New York: Oxford University Press.

Riessman, C. K. (1990). *Divorce talk: Women and men make sense of personal relationships.* New Brunswick, NJ: Rutgers University Press.

Riessman, C. K. (in press). Teaching research: Beyond the storybook image of positivist science. *Journal of Teaching in Social Work.*

Rodwell, M. K. (1987). Naturalistic inquiry: An alternative model for social work assessment. *Social Service Review, 61*(2), 231-246.

Rosaldo, R. (1989). *Culture and truth: The remaking of social analysis.* Boston: Beacon Press.

Rosenwald, G. C., & Ochberg, R. (Eds.). (1992). *Storied lives: The cultural politics of self-understanding.* New Haven, CT: Yale University Press.

Ruckdeschel, R. (1985). Qualitative research as a perspective. *Social work research and abstracts, 22*(2), (17-21).

Schutz, A. (1932/1967). *The phenomenology of the social world* (G. Walsh & F. Lehnert, Trans.). New York: Northwestern University Press.

Stivers, C. (1993). Reflections on the role of personal narrative in social sciences. *Signs: Journal of Women in Culture and Society, 18*(2), 408-425.

Task Force on Social Work Research. (1991). *Building social work knowledge for effective services and policies: A plan for research development.* Austin, TX: Capital Printing.

Witkin, S. (1992). Should empirically-based practice be taught in BSW and MSW programs? No! *Journal of Social Work Education, 28*(3), 265-268.

Wolf, M. (1992). *A thrice told tale: Feminism, postmodernism, and ethnographic responsibility.* Stanford, CA: Stanford University Press.

Zimmerman, J. H. (1989). Determinism, science, and social work. *Social Service Review, 63*(1), 52-62.

PART I

Grounded Theory and Health

Grounded theory originated in sociology, but the method has been widely applied by a variety of disciplines and professions. It is perhaps the best-known qualitative approach, besides ethnography, in the social sciences. A corpus of work on the method is available to investigators, including debates about fundamental premises and ways to do this form of qualitative research. Grounded theorists do not all agree. Investigators have philosophical positions and preferred standpoints. Some are represented in the chapters by social workers to follow, which all examine health topics.

To place the studies in context, the term describing the method was coined by Barney Glaser and Anselm Strauss in their path-breaking book, *The Discovery of Grounded Theory* (1967). Challenging the dominant methodological paradigm—logical deduction and verification of prior theory through hypothesis testing—Glaser and Strauss advocate an inductive approach: the purposeful discovery of concepts from data. Urging scholars to "theorize from the data rather than the armchair" (p. 14), they argue for constant comparison of cases to create a dense network of theoretical concepts. From the ground up, the investigator builds conceptual categories that "fit" the data and "work," that is, are meaningful and able to explain the behavior in question. Sampling decisions and data collection in grounded theory are driven by the evolving analytic concepts.

As initially conceived, the book provided a language (and legitimation) for a generation of investigators. It offered a systematic, phenomenologically based method for social research, an alternative to the dominant natural science paradigm of knowledge. It is often forgotten that Glaser and Strauss rejected the sharp distinction usually drawn between quantitative and qualitative research, arguing instead for "different forms of data on the same subject" (p. 18) that can be compared. The original authors and others have applied, amended and extended grounded theory, but virtually all use qualitative data. Philosophical premises vary, however. Kathy Charmaz (1983) explicates aspects of the method that remain opaque in Glaser and Strauss's original work. Later, she challenges their "discovery" epistemology—the idea that an external reality can be uncovered by an outside observer. She offers an interpretive, social constructionist reframing of the method (Charmaz, 1990). As Mary Catherine Bateson (1990) says in another context: It is invention that we do "not discovery, for what we search for does not exist until we find it" (p. 28). Anselm Strauss and Juliet Corbin, by contrast, assume a realist ontology. Their recent manual, *Basics of Qualitative Research* (1990), represents a positivistic explication of grounded theory.

Turning to the specific studies in Part I, each investigator examines an important health problem and each uses the grounded theory approach to make sense of her data. But the method is applied in somewhat different ways in the three examples. Differences reflect some of the tensions and crosscurrents in contemporary debates in grounded theory.

Denise Burnette describes the experiences of 20 chronically ill elders, chosen from a larger sample of 540 Medicare beneficiaries on whom she has extensive quantitative data. In repeated interviews with the carefully drawn subsample, and observations in their natural settings (meals, housing meetings, bowling tournaments, even the aftermath of an earthquake), Burnette documents the cognitive and behavioral work people do to manage chronic illness—a process initially identified by Glaser and Strauss (1975). Adopting an interpretive and explicitly partisan standpoint, she celebrates the ways old people struggle to live independently and persevere despite formidable odds and multiple losses, including their health. Regarding methods, the study illustrates how extended engagement with informants (a hallmark of grounded theory) can produce knowledge about psychosocial *process,* adding depth and texture to quantitative analysis—a *static* portrait of the population.

Julie Abramson and Terry Mizrahi examine collaboration between physicians and social workers, but from the standpoint of the traditional unbiased, objective, value-neutral researcher. An ongoing project that also includes quantitative data on more than 100 professionals in 12 hospital settings, they describe in considerable detail here their inductive work—from the ground up—to develop a conceptual framework. They create a typology of the role of the social worker, one dimension of an evolving categorization of collaborative relationships. Although any typology is, by definition, static, it gets constructed through a process. We see how coding of initial interviews shapes subsequent sampling decisions and interview topics. This recursive process is a defining feature of the grounded theory method, in sharp contrast to the "fixed" designs of traditional quantitative (and some qualitative) research, where sampling, interviewing, and analysis are distinct, unrelated stages. The authors have considerable "insider" knowledge about hospital practices, yet their inductive strategy leads to discoveries that challenge prior assumptions about physicians and social workers, and about how they work together.

Robin Gregg examines the experience of pregnancy, specifically, identity transformation in a group of 31 women. Although the sample is limited to white, middle-class women, the interpretive treatment and the reflexive approach generate original insights about pregnancy. The findings challenge the biomedical model and raise questions about how prenatal care is provided to women in the United States. Women in Gregg's sample define pregnancy differently than doctors do (it is possible to be "a little bit pregnant"), and understandings of risk also vary from medical definitions. Regarding methods, preliminary analysis of early interviews leads to major refocusing of the study, new research questions, an expanded set of items for subsequent interviews, and emergent analytic categories. Gregg extends grounded theory principles in important ways, coupling it with research from a feminist standpoint so she can move beyond assumptions of positivism and objectivity. Reality is being interpreted and constructed, not merely reflected. Gregg attends to context often missing from grounded theory research: complex and evolving relationships with informants; how pregnancy stories emerge in interview conversations; ways the research empowers subjects, and herself. Gregg's subjectivity becomes a source of knowledge, it is brought into the work, not viewed as something to be controlled, or defined as bias. (I return to the uses of subjectivity in the final section of the book, where Gregg's chapter could equally well be placed.)

Taken together, the chapters provide substantive findings about health topics of concern to practitioners and policymakers—chronic illness among the elderly, collaboration between doctors and social workers, and

4 QUALITATIVE STUDIES IN SOCIAL WORK RESEARCH

pregnancy for women in a high-tech age. The studies illustrate how the grounded theory method, in all its diversity, can generate useful knowledge for social work practice.

References

Bateson, M. C. (1990). *Composing a life*. New York: Penguin.
Charmaz, K. (1983). The grounded theory method: An explication and interpretation. In R. M. Emerson (Ed.), *Contemporary field research: A collection of readings* (pp. 109-126). Prospect Heights, IL: Waveland Press.
Charmaz, K. (1990). "Discovering" chronic illness: Using grounded theory. *Social Science and Medicine, 30*(11), 1161-1172.
Glaser, B. G., & Strauss, A. (1967). *The discovery of grounded theory*. Chicago: Aldine.
Glaser, B. G., & Strauss, A. (1975). *Chronic illness and the quality of life*. St. Louis: C. V. Mosby.
Strauss, A., & Corbin, J. (1990). *Basics of qualitative research: Grounded theory procedures and techniques*. Newbury Park, CA: Sage.

1. Managing Chronic Illness Alone in Late Life: Sisyphus at Work

DENISE BURNETTE

The struggle alone is enough to fill man's heart.

—Albert Camus,
"The Myth of Sisphysus"

This chapter describes individual adaptation to profound shifts in disease epidemiology and social demography during the 20th century—notably the increased prevalence of chronic illness and a growing propensity to live alone. I explore how 20 older people work to synthesize the convergent processes of aging and long-term illness and to incorporate these changes into their personal lives. An initial overview of shifts in health and social trends situates the individual lives in a broad, structural context. Then, after a brief discussion of the research methods, the chapter examines the complex and reciprocal cognitive, behavioral, and social processes that informants use to organize the experience and manage the exigencies of illness in their day-to-day lives.

AUTHOR'S NOTE: This research, from the author's doctoral dissertation at the School of Social Welfare, University of California at Berkeley, was supported in part by the Jane B. Aron Memorial Fellowship Award, NASW National Center for Social Policy and Practice. The author wishes to acknowledge the good will and guidance of Anselm Strauss, Professor Emeritus of Sociology, and members of the Qualitative Methods working seminar, Department of Social and Behavioral Sciences, University of California at San Francisco, for their valuable contribution to the formulation and development of this project.

Sociohistorical Context

In 1900 there were 3.8 million persons aged 65 and over. In 1990 this figure was estimated at 31.8 million; by 2020, it will increase by another 62% to 51.4 million elderly (Gilford, 1988). The dramatic aging of the population, one of the most influential sociodemographic trends of the modern era, stems from the confluence of social, political, and economic trends with advances in public health, and more recently in biomedicine, that have virtually doubled life expectancy during the 20th century.

The unprecedented scope and pace of progress yield longer, fuller life spans for many. But for others, genetics, environmental factors, and medical technology add years of lengthy, incurable illnesses (Gruenberg, 1977; Rice & Feldman, 1983; Verbrugge, 1984). At this time, 80% of persons aged 65 and over have at least one chronic illness (National Center for Health Statistics, 1989), and multiple conditions are common (Rice & LePlante, 1988). And like other health problems, these conditions are not equitably distributed, even among the older population. Due to advanced age, widowhood, and poverty, prevalence rates are highest among the aged who live alone, and more than half of poor elderly who have chronic health problems live alone (Kasper, 1988).

The societal impact of these figures lies in the rapid rise of single-person headed-households (Kobrin, 1976; Michael, Fuchs, & Scott, 1980; Wall, 1989). The number of these households more than doubled between 1960 and 1978, from 7.1 to 16.7 million (U.S. Bureau of the Census, 1979) and now stands at 23 million (U.S. Bureau of the Census, 1991). Although population aging accounts for a relatively small proportion of this phenomenon, about one in three (10 million) elderly people now live alone, including 47.1% (more than 1 million) who are aged 85 or older, up from 38.8% in 1980 (U.S. Bureau of the Census, 1991). And, though the proportion of older persons living alone is not expected to change much, their numbers will nearly double over the next generation (Kasper, 1988).

Research has confirmed that older persons prefer to live independently rather than with friends or relatives (Beland, 1987; Beyer, 1980; Bishop, 1986), primarily for the privacy and autonomy the arrangement affords (Beresford & Rivlin, 1966; Schwartz, Danziger, & Smolensky, 1984). But such advantages are countered by risks of economic deprivation, social and psychologic problems such as loneliness and depression, and a greater need for community and institutional long-term care (Kovar, 1986; Mui & Burnette, 1991).

Description of the Study

Data are from a two-part project (Burnette, 1991).[1] The first part used survey data from a study of older Medicare beneficiaries ($N = 540$) at the Institute for Health and Aging, University of California at San Francisco (Benjamin, Feigenbaum, Newcomer, & Fox, 1989) to examine factors associated with the likelihood of living alone at hospital discharge. The second part, reported here, used field methods to gather data from interviews, observations, and interactions with a subsample ($N = 20$) of the survey respondents who lived alone.

Selection of Participants

Interviewees were selected from referrals to a hospital-affiliated home health agency based on the following criteria:

1. Participated in the post-hospitalization Medicare study
2. Had one or more significant chronic illnesses, such as cancer, heart disease, emphysema, or diabetes
3. Lived alone
4. Had reasonable geographic proximity to one another and to me

Of the 145 persons who met the first two criteria, 58 lived alone. After reviewing the 52 available charts, I eliminated 10 persons, 4 that were too cognitively impaired and 6 that had died. Large-print descriptions of the study were then sent to the remaining 42 persons, followed by telephone calls 2 weeks later to schedule initial interviews. Five individuals were too ill or confused, 2 no longer lived alone, and 2 could not be located.

I selected 20 of the final 33 persons using selective sampling strategies common to field research, whereby a sample is chosen for its representativeness of a population (Schatzman & Strauss, 1973). I used statistically nonrepresentative stratified sampling (Trost, 1986) to ensure variation by gender, ethnicity, housing status, and functioning (see Table 1.1). The method achieves variability in salient "independent variables" (chosen for their relevance to the purpose) and provides an alternative to snowball and constant comparison techniques for creating a varied sample.

Initial in-home interviews lasted about 2 hours and moved from a semi-structured format to more open-ended discussion about general and health-related circumstances. I audiotaped interviews, transcribed and coded

TABLE 1.1 Statistically Nonrepresentative Stratified Sampling (N = 20)[a]

Gender	Male (5)				Female (15)			
Race	White (3)		Black (2)		White (11)		Black (4)	
Housing	Senior Apartment	Own Home	Senior Apartment	Own Home	Senior Apartment	Own Home	Senior Apartment	Own Home
	(1)	(2)	(2)	(0)	(4)	(7)	(1)	(3)
ADL Status[b] 1	1(1)	1(1)	1(1)	1(0)	1(1)	1(3)	1(0)	1(1)
2	2(0)	2(1)	2(1)	2(0)	2(3)	2(4)	2(1)	2(2)

a. Numbers in parentheses indicate the number of individuals in the sample that fit the category.
b. Due to small numbers in cells, functional status (ADL) was treated as either (1) performs personal ADLs independently or (2) needs assistance with at least one personal ADL.

them according to grounded theory protocol, then used these data in conjunction with information from medical and social service records and contacts with families, friends and neighbors, and various professionals to guide subsequent data collection, with an eye to increasing variability and verification.

Grounded Teory

Grounded theory, a field method described more fully elsewhere in this volume, has been refined and extended since its original conceptualization (Glaser & Strauss, 1967) and is now among the most developed methods available for systematic analysis of qualitative data (Glaser, 1978; Strauss, 1987; Strauss & Corbin, 1990). Charmaz (1983) briefly summarizes the method as follows:

First, data collection and analysis proceed simultaneously. Theory is constructed directly from the data, which are gathered on the basis of analytic interpretations and discoveries of the researcher. Second, both the processes and products of research emerge from the data, rather than from some preconceived, logically deduced theoretical framework, thus helping to avoid perpetuation of ideas that could be refined, transcended, or discarded.

Third, respectable research standards, such as significance, comparability, generalizability, reproducibility, precision, and rigor, are considered essential, but they must be defined within the qualitative research tradition (Kirk & Miller, 1986; LeCompte & Goetz, 1982; Strauss, 1987). Rather than ascribing to quantitative canons of verification, grounded theorists check developing ideas with further observations, making systematic comparisons between them. Finally, in addition to studying process, these researchers recognize that making theoretical sense of social life is itself a process, and thus seek fresh theoretical interpretations rather than definitive explanations of the data.

Context of the Data Collection

Although ascribing to general tenets and prescribed injunctions of grounded theory methods in analyzing transcribed texts and field notes, I deliberately intended to use these data to substantiate, enhance, refine, and/or qualify already categorically defined quantitative data. Accordingly, I initially coded and presented the data categorically as (a) sociodemographic; (b) medical, cognitive, and functional status; and (c) informal and formal supports. Realizing the potential violation of the proscription against approaching the data with preconceived notions, I worked assiduously to keep the categories from governing subsequent analyses—efforts that were facilitated by substantial overlap.

I collected data for 9 months and averaged three encounters per interviewee. Scheduling alterations were due mostly to the demands of theoretical sampling to gather data in a variety of settings and to seek interviews that could contribute most substantially to developing theory. About two thirds of the interviews occurred in or near informants' homes during the day, but I also joined several informants and their families for meals, observed senior housing meetings, and participated in a sewing circle and a bowling tournament during evening hours. To extend the range of experiences, I interviewed three homebound individuals three to four times each.

The only problem with accessibility was that informants often wanted more time than I could afford (see Reinharz & Rowles, 1988). Thirteen friends and family members (of 11 informants) were very accessible and provided valuable information, including insight into their own vital roles, that extended and added depth to the data. A few informants had minor health and/or family-related problems, but I observed no major individual maturational changes.

Of historical note, though, the devastating Loma Prieta earthquake struck the San Francisco Bay area 2 months into the study. By then I was interviewing eight people, and I observed marked shifts in their affect, thought content, and behavior as they became temporarily preoccupied with vulnerability, loss, and death; a few were reluctant to leave home for several months afterward. I, on the other hand, not being a native Californian, was extremely anxious to hasten interviews punctuated by the bold swaying of senior highrises during the aftershocks.

I was almost half the mean age of my informants, in excellent health, and living in a close-knit family, so there was little danger of "going native" in the sense of becoming "one of them." However, the universality of the aging process and its concomitant declines in health and the preponderance of women in the study did create an "anticipatory identification" with informants for me.

Emotional proximity to interviewees grew considerably over the course of the study. An articulated personal and professional commitment to understand their experiences, to assist them when possible, and to redress social inequities that could compromise the quality of their lives did pose substantial problems for maintaining "sufficient distance." Ongoing cognizance of the issue and discussion with colleagues helped, but it remains a critical question for much qualitative research in social work.

Sociodemographics

Distributions of age, gender, marital status, race/ethnicity, education, income, housing, and Medicaid status in the subsample closely mirrored those of the larger survey sample. The mean age of the subsample was 78 years. Three quarters of the sample were female, and a similar proportion was white. More than half had completed high school, and about the same percentage had midrange annual incomes of $7,500 to $20,000 (another third were below $7,500). Two thirds lived in an apartment or a rented room, 44% received public aid for housing, and one third had Medicaid benefits.

The most salient demographic factor was marital status—specifically, the personal, social, and economic sequelae of being unmarried in late life. Five interviewees had never married, 13 were widowed, and 2 were divorced. All had lived with family or friends until postretirement age. The women had lived alone an average of 16.6 years, and the men 8.1 years. The path to living alone, whether by choice or circumstance, was often strewn with stressful losses that substantially affected their own health.

Recently widowed persons described Herculean efforts to simultaneously care for themselves and an ill spouse. Most were gradually assuming full responsibility for themselves, but a few longed to join the decedents. These lengthy interviews focused on the absent spouse and the effects of a visceral, pervasive grief on their own health. An 80-year-old woman, alone 4 months after the death of her husband of 59 years, was disconsolate:

> My husband had leukemia and the doctor gave him bad blood. I would sue him, but it wouldn't bring my husband back. . . . It's funny, but the thing is that we were not simply together all those years. We were together in the sense that we were part of each other. I guess nowadays that isn't looked on so favorably. But it was a unique companionship. My daughter calls me and asks if I'm "better." I ask you, what does that mean? I say, "No, it's not that I can't get over losing him, I have no desire to get over it." I see it as the beginning of the end. Most days I pray I'll join him soon.

The irrevocable nature of such losses, the time and energy needed to recuperate, and detrimental repercussions on survivors' health were prominent features in this and other interviews. Distraught and adrift, this woman did not plan to move closer to her family, despite her own serious health problems. As a long-time, insulin-dependent diabetic with peripheral neuropathy, her husband had administered her insulin, walked with her daily on the nearby marina, and adhered to a diabetic diet, all and only to support her. When we met, she had eaten and taken her insulin sporadically, failed to fill an antihypertensive prescription for 2 months, and not left her apartment since the funeral. Interruption of the vital link between care of self and others, maintained through shared, habitual routine, can create both instrumental and emotional needs during acute grief.

Long-widowed persons also spoke freely of losses, recalling hardships of solo navigation in a world where they had been paired, in their eyes and those of others, their entire adult lives. An 83-year-old widow of 12 years recollects:

> My husband died of a massive heart attack unexpectedly while he was shaving one morning. I heard him hit the floor and by the time I got to him he was already gone. . . . I used to go to summer camp in Carmel when I was a girl, and I met him there when I was 11 and he was 12 years old. Hard to believe, huh? The irony is that it seems so long but so short. It's always hard. It just happens. It's never easy. Don't ever let anyone tell you different. You lose such a part of yourself. But you have to go on. There is no other choice.

A college-educated, 80-year-old widow who stayed home to raise her children describes her adjustment when her husband died 21 years ago, leaving her with three of the children still in high school:

> I find that you have to keep yourself busy. I had to mourn my husband, make sure my children adjusted OK to his death, and go out and get a job for the first time in my life when I was almost 60 years old. I look back on it now and I think that life was somebody else's. There was just so much heartbreak in there that uh . . . it was like I was just acting the part. I don't recall it as a hard, bad time. I just see it as if it were written in a book and someone else had lived it.

Approaching their eighth decade, other informants also linked losses, directly and indirectly, to their own health. A 78-year-old woman identified a move from her extended family in 1946 as the first in a series of losses. She then developed arthritis, had two miscarriages, and lost an infant before having five more children. Both parents died in 1973, and her husband suffered a fatal heart attack the next year. She then lived and worked with her youngest son until he died of cancer 5 years ago, an event that she deemed her own coup de grace. They had operated an upholstery business for many years. She describes the pleasure of his company, the reciprocity of their relationship, a conspiracy of silence around his illness, and its devastating effects on her own health:

> He'd get up at 7 o'clock to help me at the shop, even at his sickest. It was our life, our livelihood, you see. I'd say, "I don't want you to work today, son." I'd say, "You're not feeling good, I can tell. Why don't you jest sit here and jest be wi' mama." And you know we never did speak straight about it. He got a car and run all the errands. It broke my heart he had to do that 'cause I learned to drive but never did get me a license. . . . It was jest a joy to have him here singin' and jokin' around. . . . When I saw he was going down, I prayed every day for the Lord to take me, too. I didn't have no more reasons to keep goin' and I wasn't a bit worried to die. I wished I could have died for him. But God took him and you see here He left me here with a broken heart and a shoebox full of pills. . . . I ain't never got over it, and I knows now that's the biggest part of my troubles.

According to her daughter, this woman's health had degenerated steadily since her son's death. When I met her she was struggling to manage uncontrolled hypertension and cardiac arrhythmias in her body while generating a credible rationale for living in her mind.

The anguish and confusion expressed by the recently bereaved were tempered for long-time "aloners," but their memories remain vivid. Sixteen interviewees prominently displayed photographs of their deceased spouses and/or family portraits—visual cues that symbolized coherence and loyalty. A 76-year-old widower, nodding to a photograph of his wife of 42 years, explains:

> You see her there. She's gone pretty near 8 years now. She was something else, though. Mind you, we didn't see eye-to-eye on a lot of things, but she was an awful good woman. It might be hard to tell, but if you look up close at her face, I think you can see somethin' of it. . . . We were pretty wild when we were young and yeah, we probably deserved each other. I look over at her near about every day now and I say to her, "Yep, I ain't never gonna get over losin' you." That was the biggest thing I had, my wife. I didn't know it but now I know it good.

Three women widowed in very old age worked actively to perpetuate memories, maintaining that the limited time left in their own lives precluded the urgency and even the need to seek closure on their losses. The emotional and existential presence of a lifelong companion still provided the critical sense of an "other." With an affect of fortitude and resolve that in no way indicated "pathological grief," their explanations provided a reasonable reconciliation with a deep and abiding void. Death thus figured prominently in accounts of how informants came to live alone. They invoked various agents and analogues of fate, including physicians, diseases, luck, and the simple passage of time to work out probable causes, reasonable explanations, and acceptable adaptations for their current circumstances. Most informants had integrated losses into the ongoing procession of life, with a gradually renewed sense of personal and social self, and had acquired new knowledge and mastered new skills to meet ongoing demands, including health problems that mounted in inverse proportion to physical, social, and economic resources.

Health and Functional Status

In a study of 60 chronically ill persons and their spouses, Corbin and Strauss (1985; Strauss & Corbin, 1988) identify three major lines of "work" for managing chronic conditions in the home: illness work, everyday life work, and biographical work. Illness work refers to activities directed toward, for example, regimen care, prevention, and management of symptoms and crises. This type of work is then closely related to the everyday work and biographical work that maintain the ongoing flow of daily activities and integrate the experience of illness into one's personal biography, respectively.

The framework provides a useful vantage for examining the experiences of the sample, who had at least one long-term illness for a median of 13 years. Informants obliged my probing about these conditions, but they were far more concerned with related issues down the spiral of failing health, functional impairment that begets powerlessness, helplessness, and social isolation, and the attendant dependency and depression that renew the cycle.

Unconscious denial of illness is distinguished here from deliberate efforts to reframe the experience to fit the context of daily life (for a discussion of awareness contexts in social interaction, see Glaser & Strauss, 1964). No one denied the existence or effects of disease. But most refused to ruminate about it, working instead to alter negative ideas and activities. Consider the remarks of a woman with complex, longstanding, life-threatening problems, including multiple minor surgeries, a heart attack, removal of a cancerous kidney, hypertension, and diabetes:

No. I don't really feel 83. That's the good thing about age. You always feel
OK about it . . . as long as your health's all right. Well the fact is I don't feel
any different than I did when I was 20. The ladies here like to get together
and talk about their illnesses, but I don't like that. Don't like to dwell on
that. It's of no use. Like when I had the cancer. A lot of people would be
worried to death, would take to their bed. I didn't like it, but I just couldn't
worry about it. You can't just hole up and worry. No use. None.

This woman's awareness and defiance of illness may be colored by her
lengthy experience with it, but she did not deny it. She related a detailed
health history and asked me to check her blood pressure on each visit.
While acknowledging her problems and monitoring potentially serious
side effects, for now she can defy their debilitating effects on her life by
disallowing their dominion over her thoughts, self-image, and movement
in the world. Indeed, the onset of illness was so distant ("I can't remember
when I didn't have something wrong with me") and its occurrence so
much anticipated ("You've got to expect it at my age") that most had come
to regard it as a steady if not constant companion. Chronic conditions were
thus so intimately woven into the fabric of everyday life and personal
biography that recognition had become practically subliminal—common
knowledge, rarely acknowledged.

Cognitive reframing is a valuable strategy for managing many of the
effects of illness, but perceptible functional decline and acute crises
require other tactics. Symptom exacerbation and acute episodes, signaled
by a wide range of internal and external cues, augment anxiety about
emergencies. The following excerpts show an awareness of portentous
cues and the vulnerability of "close calls." The first incident involves a
fortuitous rescue and the latter two describe crisis management alone.

A 76-year-old woman with uncontrolled hypertension, of which she is
usually unaware, was rescued in a daughter's daily visit:

Yeah it [blood pressure] gets real high. Now about 3 weeks ago it had rose
real high unbeknownst to me. I didn't know what was my trouble, but I just
got real sick. I got so I couldn't hardly walk, you know I was just here and
I couldn't. I was on the verge of going down when my daughter came and
swept me off to the doctor. He said to me, "You know you just about died."
But you know me, I just puts up with things.

A 91-year-old widower describes the ultimate responsibility for preserving his own life during his last heart attack:

I had already had one heart attack, so I pretty much knew what was going on. I managed . . . to get over to the phone and call 911. Then I sat down and waited. I knew from the pain I'd be gone before they got here. Then I went back over all these scenes from my life . . . like a film rolling. Then I passed out.

Finally, a 76-year-old never-married woman with asthma, cardiac arrhythmias, and hypertension relates:

Well you know it's up to you what happens. I mean it is and it isn't. You have to be totally responsible, but if you're too sick you can't be. Well, when I went into this terrible asthma attack one night I didn't know what to do. I couldn't breathe. My brother is in town, but he's 10 times worse off than me. My closest friend is 95 and of no use here—confined to her own home, you see. It was so frightening. I tried to beat on the wall. I thought I would die. But my neighbor heard me. She broke the glass in the door and called the ambulance.

Crises can crystallize the potentially fatal outcomes of conditions that usually run as undercurrents in the subconscious stream of everyday life. The gravity of each of these incidents was readily apparent, but in other cases poor outcomes were more insidious, manifested through a progressive diminution of functioning and/or chronic pain. An 81-year-old man explains:

I worked with underprivileged children here in our community for some years. I headed up their athletic program. You know tennis and basketball, especially basketball. . . . Then I got to where I couldn't keep up, my heart you know and even worse my lungs. Finally, one day I fainted on the golf course and that was it. I went back down for a while, but it was no good.

In extreme cases, progressive decline can encroach upon and gradually usurp daily life and one's sense of self. A 78-year-old woman with debilitative arthritis, a severe heart condition, and untreatable cataracts, seated in a wheelchair at a lake near her home and outside for the first time in 3 months laments:

I wish that there was some way I could tell you what I feels like. I wouldn't want you or nobody else to be in this bad a shape. But how else could you know? I don't feels like myself, but I don't know what happened to me. Like on this beautiful day, this warm day. I don't even belong here on this day . . . . I feels like my life is over, but it won't stop. What I mean to say is my life as I see it is over. You see I can't walk, and I can't hardly see a thing. I can't hardly even get up. I'm just trapped here in a body that ain't even mine.

This poignant commentary on how illness ravages the self exemplifies lived experiences that are most accessible to others in qualitative accounts; statistical aggregate data conveys only the skeletal structure of phenomena. Notably, though, severe disruption of domains of daily life that are essential to managing illness was also evident in nurses' and social workers' composite ratings of medical, cognitive, and functional status.

All 20 informants were deemed cognitively intact; two thirds needed no supervision, and the rest could manage most decisions or needed help only with major decisions or occasional reminders. Medical and functional ratings were less favorable, with no one in the sample judged in excellent or good health. Five had acute, resolving medical problems, 11 had moderately acute problems, and 4 had major and/or multiple conditions that severely limited functioning. Ratings of functional status (ADL) were similar: Three persons were independent in all ADLs, two required minimal assistance, and the rest needed a moderate amount of help.

Thus about a quarter of the interviewees were in reasonably good health, able to care for themselves, seek appropriate assistance when needed, and maintain social contacts. Health conditions posed periodic troubles but were not on balance excessively problematic. But what of the other three fourths, especially those in the lowest quartile or quintile in both types of data, for whom pain and/or disability had become a way of life?

The inability to leave home (three persons had been confined for 3 to 6 months and two others rarely ventured out) or to engage in meaningful activities and relationships caused extreme isolation and depression. Exhausted and removed from the mainstream of life, they spent most of their waking (and many sleeping) hours watching television. The devastating interaction of psychological despair and social isolation prompted candid talk of suicide and death. A long-confined, 73-year-old woman describes her course:

After my stroke I started using a cane, just on my left side and I was getting by fine after I moved in here with the cane. Then some months after I moved in I started losing the use of my hands, first my left than my right. My doctor put me in for a CAT scan and found out I had pressure on my spine that was causing my hands not to move, so I had a, what was it, a cervical laminectomy, yeah. Then I was on the walker and my son was still taking me out once a week. But it got harder to get around and I was afraid of falling. He

came every other week for a while, then once a month. He last came about
2 months ago, but we didn't go out. He feels kind of bad but I say, "Heh, it
doesn't matter." I mean it. It doesn't matter.

She goes on to exonerate her son, then explains,

It's like I told the doctor, just give me one pill, no pain, and I'd take it in a
minute. I think I've lived long enough. Suicide, once you've lived long
enough, should be a choice.

Asked to delimit the circumstances of this choice, she (and all other
informants, eight of whom had filed advance directives for care in case
of incapacitation) cited quality of life criteria, such as capacity for self-
care and ability to remain meaningfully engaged in life (see Strauss,
1984). She explains:

I don't consider it living, what I'm doing. I mean there's a lot of people in
this building who go out to the store and they can walk without help and
bring their groceries home. If I could do that, I wouldn't say this. But I can't
take care of myself. That's why I feel like I've lived long enough.

In regarding functional ability as intrinsic to an acceptable quality of
life, informants saw it less as a safeguard from actual death than as protection
from a painful, protracted dwindling toward death and a very real Damo-
clean sword of nursing-home care. Two veteran caregivers address this
issue. The first is a 76-year-old woman who spent 2 years caring for a
beloved husband. His life followed a tortuous, grueling route to its end
through prostate cancer, including iatrogenic irradiation damage to his
intestines and bladder, a colostomy and an indwelling suprapubic catheter
that worked briefly, intravenous feedings, and two strokes that left him
aphasic and paralyzed. She tearfully relates their story:

It wasn't worth it. Not to either of us. All the X-rays, and tests, and pain and
crap they put him through. I consider myself a fairly intelligent woman. But
when you get the call. When you get the call that it's malignant, you're
already caught up in it, and what do you do? You never know. You want to
believe them. You know, the next time whatever they come up with might
work. . . . The last stroke, which he had in the hospital, was his undoing. I
was hospitalized from exhaustion, right down the hall from him. The powers
that be sent him on to the nursing home while I was still there, and he died
3 days later. By that time he had already died a dozen deaths. I never saw

him again. Yeah, uh, that's right. I never saw him again. I wasn't released until after his funeral.

A lengthy conversation between an 80-year-old woman who cared for her ailing mother for her last 18 months and her long-time hairdresser elicited similar sentiments. The beautician and another customer were discussing a client, now comatose and sustained on a ventilator, when the woman interjected:

> You see that's the thing that frightens me. You just don't die. The lucky ones do. I think we start dying when we are about 35 or so. Things weaken incrementally and gradually. But how long does it take? You have to have a roof over your head and food until the end. I have an affidavit on file. If I'm no longer able to take care of myself I don't want any extra heroics. But of course that doesn't mean they won't do it. And then once they do, look at the lawsuits and everything to get you off. What scares me is that they'll take me to the emergency room and put me on it and then try to get me off.

An 81-year-old man who lived with his sister until recently relates the dread of nursing home placement:

> I moved out of my sister's house about a year ago. I was with her and her husband but he got so sick that it was too hard for her to take care of both of us. And well, we were taking care of Mother, too. We finally had to carry her to a home. . . . Well, we hoped she'd go on, she was so sick. But she lasted almost 5 years. So I say to my sister . . . if it gets that way for me, I want you to help me do away with myself. We agreed it would be better to help each other out here. Better to go to hell for dying than 5 years in purgatory like Mother had.

In summary, illness, like age, becomes an integral and, in some cases, a defining aspect of life. Its salience vacillates between field and ground depending on how deeply and persistently it affects routines of daily life. When the flow of life is steady and predictable and disease processes quiescent, bodily changes are monitored subliminally and the experience of illness settles fixedly, if not comfortably, into the broad, undifferentiated field of everyday existence.

The deliberate relegation of illness and its detrimental effects to the field are adaptive and effective to a point, but perceptible functional decline and acute crises that threaten daily activities and social or psychological integrity, bring it into sharp focus. Additional knowledge, motivation, and emotional and instrumental resources are then needed, especially by those few persons whose illness seeps into the field of everyday life, overwhelming the capacity to cope.

Coping Strategies:
Knowledge, Motivation, and Resources

Strategies to manage the routines and exigencies of illness depend upon knowledge, motivation, ability, and support for self-care activities, and illness work is guided by both internal and external cues. Impending or actual crises and threats to functional integrity prompted informants to rally to reestablish equilibrium using a remarkably complex mix of objective knowledge about the cause, type, duration, severity, and expected outcome of disease; physiologic measures of disease status such as blood pressure, glucose level, and cardiac rhythms; subjective symptoms like lethargy or fever; and professional and lay advice.

Ongoing collection and evaluation of these data are grist for an often painstaking weighting process in which decisions in favor of a regimen are balanced with costs and available resources. A close friend of an informant, who met us at a local fast-food restaurant for breakfast, provides an example. Salting his fried eggs, he explains that 6 months ago his physician had recommended bypass surgery and prescribed a low-salt, low-fat diet. He refused surgery and tried the diet, but within a few months, physical, financial, and social constraints defeated his resolve:

> It seemed like a good idea at the time. I was in the hospital and this diet lady came and gave me a booklet of recipes and diagrams. I listened and wrote notes . . . but it was kind of confusing. So then I went down to the Safeway and . . . you know my eyes are bad and you have to read all that small stuff, you know. And when my son went with me he ended up having to pay for part of it because I didn't have enough money. That told me something. Then when I got it all home I had to figure out what to do with it and the worst part was I had to eat it [they laughed good-naturedly]. My friend, here, he was still coming down here for breakfast, so I finally said, "What the hell." I know my heart's bad. I don't blame the doc or the diet lady. I can't see it being all such a big deal.

Informants worked actively to synthesize empirical information with subjective appraisals, including perceptions and beliefs about health and illness and judgments about their medical, functional, social, emotional, and financial conditions to arrive at a "working diagnosis." This assessment was the core of developing, choosing, implementing, and evaluating self-care strategies, and it bore directly on decisions about the nature, difficulty, and expected outcomes of choices. The modus operandi of the working diagnosis is discretion. Initial disequilibrium prompts questions about whether, how much, and in what ways to pursue treatment. Informants usually solicit and heed professional advice in impending crises, but they nearly always filter and dilute it first with input from neighbors, bowling or bridge partners, hairdressers, or adult children, for example. And when a crisis abates, they ascribe amazingly little credence to medical expertise, as each described instances of mistrusting, discounting, or patently ignoring medical advice.

Illness is essentially self-managed, although not always optimally. Poor understanding of illness and care protocols and too few resources have serious effects. Events that culminated in an earlier instance of an informant's rescue from a hypertensive crisis exemplifies how such factors contribute to injudicious decisions. She was prescribed three drugs for hypertensive cardiovascular disease: an antihypertensive agent, a diuretic to prevent fluid buildup, and a potassium supplement, often prescribed with diuretics.

With her Medicaid benefits temporarily suspended, she was told 100 antihypertensive pills cost $57.00. She had half of the prescription filled, then titrated her dose based on the price of the drug and misconceptions about the illness. Rather than taking one pill four times a day, as prescribed, she started at twice a day then cut down to once a day. When the supply was exhausted, she reasoned that because she was on three drugs for the same illness, she would take only the least expensive one. When she collapsed and nearly died, she was taking the potassium pills regularly.

In the absence of an adequate understanding of illness and treatment, informants tend to weigh motivation and resources most heavily in formulating self-care plans, basing decisions on bodily cues, expected outcomes, resources, and costs. Costs—expressed as money, energy, time, freedom, convenience, and relationships—were especially critical. A 76-year-old woman who had been on cortisone for 10 years for a rare muscular disease observes:

> You've got to be willing for one reason or another to pay a certain price for whatever health you can hang on to. That's what it boils down to. The first few years I was so disgusted. It made me so fat. I'd always been slim and I'd go by the mirror and gasp. But at my age it's not beauty that counts.

Assets were scarce and costs high for most informants. But because most of them preferred quality over quantity of life, they tend to carefully balance costs of care with available resources, particularly social supports.

Informal and Formal Supports

Three aspects of social support were evident: the meaning of supports, attributes of informal supports and formal services that are specific to the aged who live alone, and the deleterious health effects of unavailable and inadequate supports.

For all but the very isolated, the ongoing exchange of emotional and instrumental goods and services was an intimate aspect of daily life, ranging from infrequent and casual to regular, focused, and intensive. Despite their own problems, informants' vital contributions to families, friends, and community were astonishing. One woman spent weekday afternoons with her daughter, running errands and babysitting, and another grew vegetables and herbs for regular meals with children and friends. This reciprocity peaked just before Thanksgiving, Hanukkah, and Christmas, when most of them hosted and/or contributed substantial time, energy, and money to family rituals in these festivities.

Informants who had cared for deceased spouses also knew the toil of caregiving firsthand. Reciprocity, acquired skill, and exquisite pain exude from this 83-year-old man's account:

> We were married 51 years. She got sicker and sicker. She had four spinal operations and was in sheer misery those last few years. I had to retire to take care of her full time for 10 years . . . from 1973 to 1983. She was in a full-body cast and I was here at home with her by myself, you know in the middle of the night, and I was pushing 80 myself. I got up all night long to turn her over and clean her and all that. She begged me to let her die but you can't do that. No matter what. No sir . . . . I thought, too, about all she'd done for me. So we'd talk a lot about the good times and we'd pray every day, not together you see, but we'd say separate prayers that God would take her. What a relief when the end finally did come.

Informal supports in late life often repersent invested ties between people who have nurtured a sense of mutuality in their shared lives. Most informants were optimistic about availability and quality of supports and professional assessments corroborated the enthusiasm. Two thirds spoke with friends or relatives at least four times a week, and 71% were confident that their primary helper would continue to help for as long as needed. No one was deemed to have very poor or absent supports; 16 were rated as excellent or very good.

Support needs of older people who live alone differ from those of persons with coresidents in important ways. Interviewees were reluctant to request help because it implied a dependency that was incongruent with actual or desired self-image; they regarded their supports as precious, finite reservoirs not to be squandered indiscriminately. During crises a relative, often an adult child, helped briefly. But informants avoided asking for this help and were even more reticent to approach friends or neighbors, who often helped them day to day. An 80-year-old man explains:

> It's so embarrassing. You never know when you'll really need someone and if you've asked for help all along it would be a lot harder. You ought to wait until you really need something. I stopped seeing a lot of my old buddies because they always had to pick me up.

Several informants had an extraordinary capacity to assess, order, and prioritize proximal and distal needs, to creatively construct supports by filling gaps in care with "passers-by" who would not be taxed by excessive demand. Treated as stop-gap measures to meet emergency or intermittent needs, these included beauticians and barbers, a pharmacist, a paper boy, a supermarket clerk, an Avon representative, and me. Though violating rules that govern social distance in relationships, the strategy was ingenious and effective. A very old man captured it nicely, instructing me:

> As long as you're gonna be comin' to see me, I'd like for you to make yourself at home. At home people usually do things like fix up things that don't work, you know, and do a little cleaning up, and uh, then they might have lunch and watch a little TV. I'd also be grateful if you'd help me make out my will. I've been wanting to get that done. But in the meantime, of course, I need to get some eyeglasses and some new teeth.

Contrary to expectation, informants living in senior housing do not feel less isolated or more supported than those living in private quarters. These facilities are in many ways a microcosm of the heterogeneity in the larger population, comprising diverse cultures, personalities, interests, and capabilities. Three of the most isolated interviewees lived in senior housing but did not interact with other residents. One notes, "I never chose my friends based on geography." A retired physician came to the dining hall for meals but read newspapers and rode public transit trains weekday mornings to converse and socialize with commuters.

A final significant support was the committed friendship that developed between several interviewees and in-home public service workers. For four very isolated individuals, these workers served as close companions and as a vital link to the outside world—a role equally if not more important than the instrumental help. Other formal services used most often, case management and mobile meals, were often provided by informal supports when available. The main criteria for using formal services were a potential for ensuring an adequate level of personal care; a clean, safe home environment; and sufficient contact with the world. The latter objective, which requires a minimal amount of strength, comfort, and sometimes help and transportation, was especially lacking.

As with other strategies for managing illness, the need, availability, and costs of informal and formal supports were strategically assessed and weighted vis-á-vis other needs and resources to arrive at a schedule of caregiving that could provide sufficient coverage yet not outstrip the capacity or jeopardize the good will of supports.

Conclusion

Interviews with these 20 chronically ill, older adults were replete with idiographic comments that provide a rich gestalt for a nomothetic understanding of problems, needs, and strengths. Accounts of integrating disease and illness into ongoing lives were remarkably similar to stories of incorporating other experiences perceived as invariant eventualities of the passage of time. They juxtapose the event of disease and the experience of illness, but they clearly distinquish between the two. Each regards functional decline and attendant loss of independence as the most dreaded aspect of illness and of aging.

The pleasure of reminiscence and its psychologically integrative function are apparent. Discussions of declining health parallel chronicles of loss—of critical people and places that grounded and oriented them through the middle adult years, power over their own minds and bodies, and control over the nature and scope of their social worlds. But bitterness and disappointment are extremely rare, as most worked actively to understand and order their lives to make sense of and justify continually renewed efforts to care for themselves and those they loved.

As participation in the occupational and economic sectors wanes in late life, the context of household organization assumes greater saliency. The choice to live independently for as long as possible becomes central for older adults. To define and respond to the needs of this burgeoning group through clinical practice and public policy, social workers must generate, synthesize, and disseminate relevant knowledge using the entire range of available research methods.

Using grounded theory field methods, I have elucidated some of the social psychological processes that interact to influence the lives of chronically ill elders who live alone. Information gleaned on sociodemographic characteristics, cognitions and ways of managing illness and functional decline, types and roles of social supports, and values about quality of life inform us about how ill, aged persons sustain integrity in the face of disruptive symptoms and diminishing capabilities. This knowledge can further be used to justify sufficient support for the significant others who perform the critical work of helping with activities of daily life. And, in addition to identifying and addressing the problems facing chronically ill older persons who live alone, the research hopefully engenders an appreciation of the astounding strengths of those who persevere in late life despite formidable odds.

Note

1. This chapter reports findings from the second phase of a mixed-method investigation of how older persons who live alone manage chronic illness. The first phase of the study compared sociodemographic factors, medical, cognitive, and functional status, and informal and formal supports of 218 older adults who lived alone after acute hospitalization with those of 322 otherwise similar counterparts who lived with others. Logistic regression modeling showed that being unmarried, female, and poorer, having less cognitive/functional impairment, receiving help from friends, neighbors or paid helpers, and being referred for home nursing and mobile meals were associated with increased odds of living alone. Details are available from the author.

References

Beland, F. (1987). Living arrangement preferences among elderly people. *The Gerontologist,* 27(6), 797-803.

Benjamin, A. E., Feigenbaum, L., Newcomer, R., & Fox, P. J. (1989). *Medicare Post-Hospital Study. Final report to the Commonwealth Fund Commission on Elderly People Living Alone.* San Francisco: University of California, Institute for Health and Aging.

Beresford, J., & Rivlin, A. (1966). Privacy, poverty, and old age. *Demography, 3,* 247-258.
Beyer, G. A. (1980). Living arrangements, attitudes, and preferences of older persons. In C. Tibbitts & W. Donahue (Eds.), *Social and psychological aspects of aging* (Vol. 1, pp. 349-369). New York: Columbia University Press.
Bishop, C. E. (1986). Living arrangement choices of elderly singles: Effects of income and disability. *Health Care Financing Review, 7*(3), 65-73.
Burnette, J. D. (1991). *The management of chronic illness by older people living alone: A multi-method investigation.* Unpublished doctoral dissertation, University of California, Berkeley.
Charmaz, K. (1983). The grounded theory method: An explication and interpretation. In R. Emerson (Ed.), *Contemporary field research* (pp. 109-126). Boston: Little, Brown.
Corbin, J., & Strauss, A. (1985). Managing chronic illness at home: Three lines of work. *Qualitative Sociology, 8,* 224-247.
Gilford, D. M. (1988). Social, economic, and demographic changes among the elderly. In *The aging population in the twenty-first century: Statistics for health policy* (pp. 52-64). Washington, DC: National Academy Press.
Glaser, B. G. (1978). *Theoretical sensitivity: Further advances in the methodology of grounded theory.* San Francisco: Sociology Press.
Glaser, B. G., & Strauss, A. L. (1964). Awareness contexts and social interaction. *American Sociological Review, 29,* 669-679.
Glaser, B. G., & Strauss, A. L. (1967). *The discovery of grounded theory.* Hawthorne, NY: Aldine.
Gruenberg, E. M. (1977). The failures of success. *Milbank Memorial Fund Quarterly, 55*(1), 3-24.
Kasper, J. D. (1988). *Aging alone: Profiles and projections.* Baltimore, MD: Commonwealth Fund Commission on Elderly People Living Alone.
Kirk, J., & Miller, M. L. (1986). *Reliability and validity in qualitative research.* Beverly Hills, CA: Sage.
Kobrin, F. E. (1976). The primary individual and the family: Changes in living arrangements in the United States since 1940. *Journal of Marriage and the Family, 8,* 233-238.
Kovar, M. G. (1986). *Aging in the eighties: Age 65 and older and living alone; contacts with family, friends, and neighbors* (Advance Data from the Vital and Health Statistics, No. 116; DHHS Publication No. PHS 86-1250). Hyattsville, MD: Department of Health and Human Services.
LeCompte, M. D., & Goetz, J. P. (1982). Problems of reliability and validity in ethnographic research. *Review of Educational Research, 52*(1), 31-60.
Michael, R. T., Fuchs, V. R., & Scott, S. R. (1980). Changes in the propensity to live alone: 1950-1976. *Demography, 17,* 39-53.
Mui, A. C., & Burnette, J. (1991). *A comparative profile of frail elderly living alone and those living with others.* Manuscript submitted for publication.
National Center for Health Statistics. (1989). *Aging in the eighties: The prevalence of comorbidity and its association with disability* (Advance Data, No. 170). Washington, DC: U.S. Department of Health and Human Services.
Reinharz, S., & Rowles, G. D. (Eds.) (1988). *Qualitative gerontology.* New York: Springer.
Rice, D. P., & Feldman, J. J. (1983). Living longer in the United States: Demographic changes and health needs of the elderly. *Milbank Memorial Fund Quarterly, 61*(3), 362-395.
Rice, D. P., & LePlante, M. P. (1988). Chronic illness, disability, and increasing longevity. In S. Sullivan & M. E. Lewin (Eds.), *The economics and ethics of long-term care and*

disability (pp. 9-55). Washington, DC: American Enterprise Institute for Public Policy Research.

Schatzman, L., & Strauss, A. L. (1973). *Field research: Strategies for a natural sociology.* Englewood Cliffs, NJ: Prentice Hall.

Schwartz, S., Danziger, S., & Smolensky, E. (1984). The choice of living arrangement by the elderly. *Retirement and economic behavior.* Washington, DC: Brookings Institution.

Strauss, A. L. (1984). *Chronic illness and the quality of life* (2nd ed.). St. Louis: C. V. Mosby.

Strauss, A. L. (1987). *Qualitative analysis for social sciences.* Cambridge, UK: Cambridge University Press.

Strauss, A. L., & Corbin, J. (1988). *Unending work and care.* San Francisco: Jossey-Bass.

Strauss, A. L., & Corbin, J. M. (1990). *Basics of qualitative research: Grounded theory procedures and techniques.* Newbury Park, CA: Sage.

Trost, J. E. (1986). Statistically nonrepresentative stratified sampling: A sampling technique for qualitative studies. *Qualitative Sociology, 9*(1), 54-57.

U.S. Bureau of the Census. (1979). *Population Characteristics: Household and Family Characteristics, March, 1978* (Series P-20, No. 340). Washington, DC: Government Printing Office.

U.S. Bureau of the Census. (1991). *Population Characteristics: Household and Family Characteristics, March, 1990* (Series P-20, No. 450). Washington, DC: Government Printing Office.

Verbrugge, L. M. (1984). Longer life, but worsening health? Trends in health and mortality in middle-aged and older persons. *Milbank Memorial Fund Quarterly, 62*(3), 475-519.

Wall, R. (1989). Leaving home and living alone: An historical perspective. *Population Studies, 43*, 369-390.

2. Examining Social Work/Physician Collaboration: An Application of Grounded Theory Methods

JULIE S. ABRAMSON

TERRY MIZRAHI

Changes in health care are occurring rapidly as the population ages, diseases become chronic, and regulations to control costs are put in place (Caputi & Heiss, 1984; Jansson & Simmons, 1985-1986; Mizrahi, 1988). Shifts to a prospective reimbursement structure based on diagnostic categories and recent developments in managed care have severely curtailed physician autonomy in medical practice. One by-product of regulatory changes is an increased emphasis on timely discharges, resulting in greater dependence by physicians on social workers for discharge planning. Provision of care to larger numbers of elderly and chronically ill patients with complicated social needs requires effective and well-coordinated care among their caregivers. Physician/social worker relationships are affected by changing regulatory, disease, and demographic factors; however, their impact on collaboration remains largely unexplored.

AUTHORS' NOTE: This research project received funding through faculty research awards from the State University of New York at Albany to Julie Abramson, and from the Professional Staff Congress of the City University of New York to Terry Mizrahi, as well as from a grant to Julie Abramson from the Lois and Samuel Silberman Fund.

Our qualitative study (in progress) examines process and outcome in actual collaborations between physicians and social workers. The overall objectives are as follows:

1. Discover patterns of collaborative practice between the two professions
2. Identify the structural and interactional factors that contribute to positive and negative collaborative experiences
3. Compare generalized perspectives on collaboration with specific (self-reported) collaborative behavior
4. Ascertain social worker and physician perceptions of the social work role and function
5. Develop a set of research-based practice principles and models for use in social work and medical education

This chapter applies grounded theory methods to collaboration. We develop categories, concepts, themes, and a preliminary typology. One aspect, perceptions of physicians and social workers of the latters' role, illustrates the process of inquiry and data analytic approach. We selected the social work role because it is central to collaboration and the profession. First, we review initial coding decisions—the open coding strategies used in grounded theory to move from "raw" transcript data to preliminary conceptual categories (Strauss & Corbin, 1990). We then discuss the further conceptual evolution of role-related variables—a process described in grounded theory as *axial coding*. Third, we examine the process of "discovering" our still evolving typology, through selective or theoretical coding (Strauss & Corbin, 1990), which classifies physicians and social workers according to their views of collaboration and collaborative relationships. We illustrate here aspects of the typology that focus on the role of the social worker. Finally, we discuss some methodological limitations and alternative interpretations that have emerged so far.

History of Social Work/Physician Collaboration

Historical strains between the professions of social work and medicine remain, despite the progress in establishing social work as an integral part of the health-care system (Butrym & Horder, 1983; Dana, 1983; Hess, 1985; Lowe & Herranen, 1978, 1981; Schlesinger & Wolock, 1983). Collaboration has been impeded by differing professional socialization processes in relation to values, patient-care goals, the role and rights of patients, teamwork, and the structure, goals, and processes of professional training (Huntington, 1981; Mizrahi & Abramson, 1985; Roberts, 1989; Wilson & Setterlund, 1987;). Remaining power, status, and gender differences have also served to undermine collaborative process (Kerson, 1980; Murdach, 1983).

Changes in patterns of medical practice and the societal view of the physician are additional influences on collaboration. Until the 1980s, physicians had a professional monopoly over the education, organization, and practice of medicine (Freidson, 1970; Starr, 1982). Physician training historically emphasized autonomy and self-reliance (Mizrahi, 1986), hence the reluctance of physicians to trust others and share authority. With little training in collective decisionmaking, physicians have discounted the opinions of other professional groups (Bucher & Stelling, 1977) including nurses (Fagin, 1992) and social workers (Mizrahi & Abramson, 1985).

Recent developments in health-care policy, however, have deeply affected the practice of medicine and physician autonomy (Freidson, 1984). These include the soaring costs of medical care, increases in malpractice suits, greater consumer dissatisfaction, increasing demands for professional autonomy by other health disciplines (nurses, pharmacists, chiropractors, and social workers), and government and corporate involvement in health care.

Concomitant changes have occurred in the role and practice of hospital-based social workers. Traditionally, social workers were involved with patients only at a physician's request; they now independently screen patients. The centrality of the discharge planning role to physicians and the financial well-being of the hospital has enhanced the organizational importance of social work's contribution to patient care (Dinerman, Seaton, & Schlesinger, 1986; Schilling & Schilling, 1987). Yet some social workers denigrate the role of discharge planner, conceptualizing it as a "concrete service" that does not utilize professional skills. Others articulate the clinical complexity of helping patients and families make critical decisions about post-hospital care (Bailis, 1985; Bendor, 1987; Blazyk & Canavan, 1985).

Whether social workers dichotomize or integrate their clinical and concrete roles affects the nature of collaboration. Role ambivalence and role blurring may serve to confuse collaborative interactions (Davidson, 1990). Social workers do have an advantage over physicians, however, in dealing with the impact of regulatory changes on patient care. Social workers historically have been agency-based, rather than private autonomous practitioners, and consequently are accustomed to and more skilled at handling the multiple levels of accountability now facing physicians (Kurzman, 1976). Nevertheless, social workers in health settings also are confronting increased levels of stress, frustration and "burnout" as they try to maintain professional practice standards and deal with regulatory constraints (Siefert, Jayaratne, & Chess, 1991).

Social work/physician collaboration remains largely unaddressed in major medical journals of the last two decades. Occasional relevant pieces appear in nursing and social work journals on nurse-physician (Fagin, 1992; Lamb, 1991; Pike, 1991; Prescott & Bowen, 1984) and nurse-social worker relationships (Kulys & Davis 1987; Mullaney, Fox, & Liston, 1974; Temkin-Greener, 1983).

The social work literature on the topic is largely anecdotal. Prescriptions and exhortations are characterizations rather than grounded observations or analysis of practice. There is a decided absence of data about interaction between social work and the two major medical disciplines— internal medicine and surgery. Available literature focuses on medical specializations that, although important, are somewhat marginal to mainstream American medicine, such as pediatrics, psychiatry, and family practice (Bergman & Fritz, 1981; Pfouts & McDaniel, 1977; Stine, 1976; Tanner & Carmichael, 1970; Toseland, Palmer-Ganeles, & Chapman, 1986). In both numbers and status, internal medicine, surgery, and their subspecializations shape the education and practice of medicine. Our study focuses almost exclusively on these two medical disciplines.

A few scholars have begun to examine physician attitudes and behavior toward social workers, and the broader psychosocial dimensions of medical practice (Gropper, 1987; Pray, 1991). Others report on physician expectations of social workers in comparison to social workers' own role expectations. Findings are consistent: Physicians expect more of social workers in the provision of concrete services and less in the area of professional consultation and counseling, compared to social workers (Carrigan, 1978; Cowles & Lefcowitz, 1992; Lister, 1980; Olsen and Olsen, 1967). There are no studies that compare actual collaborative experiences among the two professions, a gap our research begins to fill.

Our Grounding in the Theory and Practice of Collaboration

The first stage of the project on social work/physician collaboration began in 1985 when we recognized a shared area of interest as well as different, but complementary, experiences and perspectives on the issues. Drawing on a theoretical understanding of the impact of professional socialization processes on collaboration, synthesized with existing literature, and our research and practice experiences, we developed two companion articles—one theoretical and one applied—about collaboration between social workers and physicians. The former analyzes the sources of strain in physician-social worker relationships (Mizrahi & Abramson, 1985). The article compared the two professions in relation to socialization processes, role, and perspectives on patient, teamwork, and knowledge. The second (Abramson & Mizrahi, 1986) proposes that differences in socialization be taken into account in developing collaborative strategies. Given the lack of equality between the two professions, approaches to increasing social work influence on patient care need to include exchange, bargaining, negotiation, and reciprocity (Brager & Holloway, 1978; Jansson & Simmons, 1985-1986; Levine & White, 1974) at the individual/interactional level and department/organizational levels.

Despite extensive interactions between the two disciplines, there has been little research to systematically describe and analyze this activity. It is assumed (but insufficiently documented) that changes in the organization, delivery of health care, and patient populations are affecting all hospital professionals; as a result, professional relationships are likely to be changing. Potential exists at the present time for a better coordinated, cooperative model of patient care, but we need to understand the complexities and dynamic tensions inherent in interdisciplinary work. A study of collaboration between social workers and physicians is long overdue.

Methodological Rationale and Perspective

The debate between a qualitative and quantitative approach to research seems to have lessened as researchers (a) recognize the limitations and validity of each (Allen-Meares & Lane, 1990; Epstein, 1985; Waitzkin, 1990); (b) understand that there are different ways of knowing that yield different types of data (Lofland, 1971; Schatzman & Strauss, 1973; Schwartz & Jacobs, 1979); and (c) appreciate that comprehensive studies use a combination of methods (Waitzkin, 1990).

Given the dearth of systematic and comprehensive research on physician/social work collaboration, our study is exploratory and descriptive. We used the grounded theory approach (Charmaz, 1990; Glaser & Strauss, 1967; Strauss, 1987; Strauss & Corbin, 1990) to construct a model of relationships. We assumed that physicians would not share a common language with social workers about collaboration or role; as a result, it was important to collect data that would capture points of view "in participants' own words." Social workers, we anticipated, would be more familiar with the issues but would be variable in their capacities to conceptualize elements of collaboration.

Qualitative data provide richness, diversity, accuracy, and contextual depth. They can be used to characterize a group or process (in our case, physician/social work collaboration); uncover the analytic ordering of the world being studied (social workers and physicians); develop categories for rendering explicable and coherent the flux of raw reality; and locate structure, order, and patterns as well as variations (in social worker/physician interactions; Lofland, 1971). We chose open-ended interviews with limited use of close-ended items, and compared responses to both kinds of questions.

We tried to achieve balance between being close enough to subjects to understand and evaluate meaning and being distant enough to maintain some independent assessment (Becker, 1970). If too far removed, researchers are divorced from the world of experience; too near and they "go native," losing the outsider's alternative lens. We chose a topic that was familiar to us, but we examined it in unfamiliar settings.

The Settings and the Subjects

In selecting our sample and settings, we attempted to balance breadth and depth. The sample is large enough to allow comparisons within and across groups (MDs and social workers), limited generalizations, and descriptions of typical patterns. At the same time, it is small enough to probe deeply and begin to understand the context and meanings of respondents' experiences.

Interviews were conducted on a nonrandom sample of 51 physicians and 54 social workers in 12 hospitals—4 in the New York City area, 5 in the Albany, NY area, and 3 in western Massachusetts. The hospitals were selected for diverse size and location. They were in urban, suburban, and small-town settings and were divided among medical-school-affiliated teaching hospitals, community-based teaching hospitals, and nonteaching hospitals. Three hospitals were considered large (600+ beds), four were medium (350-600 beds), and five were small (under 350 beds).

To study collaboration within the largest and most influential branches of medicine, the sample includes social workers and physicians in internal medicine, surgery, and related subspecialites. Social workers were selected first; permission was sought from social work department directors to approach staff with inpatient caseloads drawn from designated services. Where social work departments had only a few members on relevant services, all participated in the study, and significant percentages participated in larger departments. The sample includes 54 social workers, most with MSWs; 9 had BA or BSW degrees (all in the latter group were from the Albany area or western Massachusetts hospitals).

The physician sample was obtained by having social workers select an inpatient case that involved extensive collaboration with a physician. We then asked the physician identified in the case to participate in the study. Out of a possible sample of 54 physicians, 3 refused. Therefore, the sample consists of 51 pairs of social worker/physician collaborators.

To achieve a mix of physicians, social workers with more than one appropriate case were asked to select cases of underrepresented physician groups such as housestaff (interns and resident physicians) or surgeons, or from subspecialties where teams are common (e.g., oncology, nephrology, rehabilitation medicine). Participating physicians were diverse in their specialties: 2 in rehabilitation medicine, 2 family practitioners, 10 surgeons, and 31 internists; 6 housestaff participated (5 in internal medicine and 1 in surgery).

We personally interviewed 68 of 104 subjects. The remaining interviews were conducted by four individuals we hired and trained. Interviewers' comments on substance, quality, and process of the interview became an integral part of data collection and analysis.

In summary, we attempted to achieve a balance of breadth and depth in the sample. It was large enough to provide comparisons within and across groups of subjects (MDs and social workers), make some limited generalizations, and suggest typical patterns within those environments. At the same time, the sample was small enough to allow us to probe deeply, achieve some limited level of saturation, and begin to understand the context and meaning of the respondents' reported perceptions and experiences.

The Interview Schedule

We drew on many sources to develop the interview schedule: (a) our already developed conceptual framework (e. g., questions about team and other structured opportunities for interaction, personal relationships with the other discipline); (b) our own experiences (e. g., questions about discussion of psychosocial issues); (c) literature (e. g., social work role); (d) integration of literature and our experiences (e. g., the structure of medical and social work hierarchies, the status of social work in the hospital, responsibility and authority for patient management decision-making); and (e) a combination of all the above (e. g., presumed factors contributing to positive and negative collaboration).

The interviews (taped and transcribed) took from 60 to 90 minutes and were divided into four sections, each with a different focus. The first provided demographic and historic information (subject's background; current and past experiences with collaboration; current and past professional and personal experiences with the other profession; current and past practice settings) and provided context for understanding the patterns of collaboration. The second section examined an actual case shared by a physician and social worker. Using the case as a control, comparisons between collaborative views of respondents were based on a common situation. Perceptions were sought regarding psychosocial aspects of the case and interventions by the social worker. Data about case outcomes were also obtained, including satisfaction with the outcome, collaborator, and comparisons with other cases and collaborators.

Respondents were asked in the third section to discuss their most positive and negative collaborative experience with the other profession, providing information about approximately 200 additional cases. We first asked respondents to briefly describe the case and reasons for the choice, then to select items from a checklist of behaviors that best reflected reasons why the collaborative experience had been so positive or negative. The checklist consisted of predetermined categories we had developed to identify factors that contribute to positive and negative collaborative interactions.[1]

In both the shared case and positive/negative descriptions, we deliberately skewed selection toward atypical cases. Not expected to reflect normative collaborative experiences, we assumed cases involving extensive interaction, complex decision making or strong feelings (for case or collaborator) are highly influential in shaping interprofessional perspectives. Using extreme examples, we could tease out the most salient features and dynamics of collaboration.

The final section of the interview asked subjects to discuss general collaborative strategies and provide hypothetical advice to social workers and physicians about the necessary ingredients for successful collaboration. They compared current and past viewpoints and experiences, compared themselves to others in their profession, and described how they would teach collaboration.

The Process of Discovery:
Phases of the Grounded Approach
to Data Collection and Analysis

Grounded theory assumes data collection and analysis are tightly inter-woven; preliminary analysis directs the amount and type of further sam-pling. We modified the approach but employed three levels of coding: open, axial, and selective (Strauss, 1987; Strauss & Corbin, 1990). Some caveats first: Although coding steps are defined, discussed, and illustrated in sequential order, in reality, each level overlapped the others. Interpre-tation is preliminary because data analysis is in process. Concepts and the typology discussed below did not always fall into distinct and discreet categories.

Open Coding: The Preliminary Phase of Analysis

We needed a strategy to convert the mass of qualitative data into a systematic schema and used the constant comparative method proposed by Glaser and Strauss (1967), augmented by other approaches (Lofland, 1971; Miles & Huberman, 1984; Strauss & Corbin, 1990; Waitzkin, 1990). Initially, we reviewed a sample of 10 transcripts, closely scrutinizing each to produce provisional concepts that fitted the data. In the mode of open coding suggested by Strauss (1987), each response and related responses were compared to those already reviewed until saturation was reached.

As a result of initial coding we (a) added and modified questions, (b) directed our additional sampling to less represented groups, (c) began to record impressions and themes, and (d) improved our own and other inter-viewers' techniques. Preconceived questions became sensitizing concepts that we gave up or modified as necessary (Charmaz, 1990). Clues to refram-ing a question or reinterpreting a response came as we found ourselves commenting on "surprises," that is, unexpected findings that exposed our taken-for-granted assumptions. As social workers, for example, we pre-sumed to know more about their world compared to physicians'. Early on, however, we discovered more variability within disciplines and a greater overlapping of perspectives than anticipated.

Among our surprises, for example, a number of physicians expressed strong interest in psychosocial aspects of patient care and appreciation of the counseling social workers provide. Consequently, we developed ques-tions for both professions regarding the sharing of psychosocial informa-tion and assessments; our coding decisions changed as we saw how physicians acknowledged, assumed, or delegated psychosocial issues. We began to recognize that our assumption that physicians had superficial relationships with patients and families was based on observations of physicians in training. Community-based, private practitioner physicians in the sample often knew patients and families better and longer than social workers. We followed the open coding process to look at questions of the social worker's role. We noted that information regarding role was found in many sections of the interview. We uncovered a more complex characterization than originally anticipated. We made lists of all role-related quotes in the 10 transcripts until they were repetitive of ones already noted (saturation). Both social workers and doctors, for example, refer to the social work responsibility for "moving bodies," "discharge planning," "placement," "disposition," "helping patients make a smooth transition," and "home care"; all seemed to reflect a limited social work discharge planning role. Another group of responses referred to social workers who "provide counseling to patients," "integrate counseling with discharge planning," "do crisis intervention," "help with adjustment to illness," "help patient and family deal with placement," and "assess patients and families." These social work and physician responses seem to address a broader social work counseling function with patients and families regarding adjustment to illness and decisionmaking for discharge. Still other responses contained aspects that related to resource provision ("shuffling paper," "get services for patients," "match patient/family with resources"); advocacy ("go to bat," "advocate for patients," "run interference"); dealing with the medical system ("negotiate the medical system," "help patients with the hospital system"); teamwork ("team member," "consultation for staff," "shared responsibility"); and education of other providers ("get social information," "share psychosocial problems").

We took categories from our analysis of 10 transcripts and applied them to another round of data to see if they fit. We also compared the actual shared case and general social workers' and physicians' descriptions of their most positive and negative collaborative experiences. We found a similar range of social work roles described throughout.

Axial Coding:
Connections Among Categories

Reading additional transcripts, we saw a social work role set that was composed of activities in different areas with the patient, family, hospital system, resource system, and physician. By this point, having moved to axial coding, we were putting the data derived through open coding back together in new ways, making connections between categories. We had evolved from a simple enumeration of tasks (what social workers do) to a grouping of like properties (spheres in which they carry out their roles). We began to understand the complexities of the very concept of role. Table 2.1 (taken directly from the codebook) presents how we dimensionalized the social work role and coded transcripts.

Theoretical Coding:
Evolution of a Paradigm and Conditional Matrix

Consistent with Glaser and Strauss' (1967) process of "discovering" theory, we identified underlying uniformities (from the original set of categories and their properties), and formulated theoretical ideas from a set of concepts. We moved back and forth between inductive and deductive thinking, checking propositions about collaboration against the data. As we immersed ourselves further, patterns of collaborative behavior and attitudes emerged. Collaborators and collaborative relationships could be classified along a continuum that we have ultimately identified as traditional, transitional, and transformational. The dramatic differences among types of physicians became apparent first (we were initially unclear whether the continuum applied to social workers). As we returned to the data, we saw collaborative characteristics of social workers could be classified similarly.

Perspectives on the Social Work Role

Although not every respondent exhibits the full range of attitudes and behaviors, we conceptually classified them predominantly into one of three types in their views of the social work role.

The *traditional* physician sees the social worker as having one function—discharge planning. The role is seen as a necessary evil, to help the physician "dispose of" or discharge patients who need services to leave the hospital. As one attending physician said (speaking of his experiences with social workers when he was a resident physician):

> Social workers were helpful in terms of moving patients along and doing things that none of the house officers had a clue as to how to do.

TABLE 2.1 Coding Social Work Role Activities

With *Patient* regarding:
Patient assessment/screenings
Planning with patient (home, placement, etc.)
Patient counseling (support, adjustment to illness, resolution of conflict, etc.)
Education/information as separate function
Other

With *Family* regarding:
Family assessment/screening
Planning with family (home, placement, etc.)
Family counseling (support, adjustment to illness, resolution of conflict)
Education/information provided to family
Other

With *Resource System* regarding:
Referral to resources (facilitation, paper work, etc.)
Advocacy with resources
Coordination with multiple outside services
Other

With *Hospital System* regarding:
Coordination/planning with other professionals
Consultant to other professionals
Advocacy/mediation with other professionals/hospital system
Education/information as separate function
Other

With *Primary MD* regarding:
Provision of patient/family information to MD
Coordination/joint planning with MD within team or informally
Advocacy for patient with MD
shared advocacy with MD
Provision of information/education (regarding external/internal system/rules,
   regulations, etc.)
Negotiation/education (re professional role definition)
Other

Like others, he views discharge planning as consisting of technical interventions to obtain services for patients and families, "getting ambulances and getting people plugged into visiting nurses" Another housestaff doctor said: "anything that vaguely impinges on a nursing home, I call social workers."

The traditional group of physicians rarely understands or acknowledges obstacles encountered by social workers in obtaining services outside the hospital for patients. The complexity of decision making necessary for discharge planning is not apparent to them, nor do they accept or value counseling—helping patients and families make frequently difficult decisions.

Transitional physicians also see the concrete aspects of discharge planning as paramount. However, these physicians seem less burdened by psychosocial aspects of patient care and are aware of the complexity of the discharge planning process. They also acknowledge dependence on the social worker for assistance, in assessment of patients and obtaining necessary resources for them. As one attending physician noted:

> The social worker is a tremendous asset to the physician in practice . . . when somebody has to be admitted to a nursing home . . . or to find other sources of support at home. The social worker is a key figure and a great help actually. I feel comfortable when I have a social worker in a case.

Another reveals understanding of the supportive aspect of social work:

> The social workers here in this hospital . . . help the family cope with some of the difficulties, spending some time with the patient's wife and children, and sitting with the patient and giving him some personal encouragement and helping him understand the issues involved.

Like traditional physicians, most transitional physicians are primarily interested in what the social worker can accomplish; they don't understand or care much about the process that occurs with patients, families, or the resource system:

> The way I viewed it was that she's been doing this a long time, she knew how to do it and got the job done. What specific skills she used, I don't know—and I wouldn't think about it either—I would just say "Good job . . . next case."

We did not anticipate the view of the social work held by *transformational* physicians. They generally appreciate the process and outcome of social work intervention and use social workers for a broad range of tasks, including helping patients and families make decisions, deal with treatment, adjust to the impact of illness, and obtain resources. They are familiar with the wide variety of social work positions and roles outside of hospitals. They discuss referring patients for therapy to social workers in private practice. They see psychosocial aspects as integral to patient care and work jointly with other professionals to provide it, as represented by one internist:

> I think that the interrelationship here is one of shared responsibility . . . to get families through times of stress. Each of us, the nurse, the physician, and the social worker, will have their own perspective after they evaluate what is going on . . . I think we all bring our perspective to a family situation and discuss how we can help each other to help the families.

Applying our typology to social workers, we labeled social workers as *traditional* if they define their role primarily from the perspective of others (usually physicians and hospital administrators; Berkman & Rehr, 1969). These social workers are preoccupied with responding to regulatory and administrative mandates to discharge patients within administratively defined time frames. Although they sometimes recognize the need to incorporate counseling into the discharge planning process, they do not feel the practice environment permits such "indulgences." Discussing his interventions with family members who objected to a particular discharge plan, for example, one social worker represented the hospital in a family meeting and did not function as a family advocate or mediator:

> I was trying to explain to the family that if she was ready for discharge, that we would want to be able to discharge her wherever there was space available as long as it was within a reasonable distance.

Transitional social workers also stress the discharge planning role; however, they emphasize adjustment to illness for patients (families, too) particularly those social workers assigned to intensive or coronary care units, oncology, and renal services.[2] Despite emphasis on counseling, these social workers often separate counseling and concrete service provision. One veteran social worker compared her discharge planning activities with her role on a renal unit:

> On the renal unit, I do much more counseling than discharge planning . . . with the transplant patients, there's a great deal of work with adjustment to transplant . . . to the hospitalization and . . . to the possibility of having an unsuccessful transplant.

Some transitional social workers prefer to work independently of physicians, partly due to a desire for autonomy, and because they sense physicians don't understand or appreciate their contribution or might even obstruct their plan for the patient:

> I would avoid them unless I needed to speak with them on an issue . . . if I can speak with the nurse, I'll do that. . . . You get from the doctor, I can't talk to you now. . . . It's infuriating and frustrating . . . so I learned other ways of getting information.

Others feel educating the physician about psychosocial issues is part of their role:

> Sometimes I would make it my business to explain the circumstances of Mrs. So and So; this is why she seems cranky.

This worker also explains the systems obstacles she encountered:

> I'd contact the doctors to . . . explain that this is what we are dealing with . . . this is why she can't go home without help . . . and why it is difficult to get home care.

Transitional social workers try to communicate in the physician's language, responding to the physician's concerns without sacrificing their own priorities.

Transformational social workers are similar to transformational physicians in their commitment to collegial responsibility for patient care. They seem to move beyond concerns about autonomous practice; functioning independently is not identified as a goal. They do not dichotomize the counseling and service provision aspects; in fact, counseling permeates most tasks, and discharge planning is seen as a pivotal responsibility. The social work role is broadly defined to include educational, liaison, supportive, and advocacy activities with other professionals and a range of patient-related tasks. One oncology social worker summarized her role:

> Here on the floor, I'm the liaison between the nurses, doctors, and the patients. . . . I'm the instrument to relay things to the patient . . . to help the patient understand the diagnosis and treatment plan . . . to help the patient adjust to the illness, to work with the family, doing a lot of counseling as well as making concrete arrangements.

There is a sense of interdependence, concern with the "team." The same social worker also spoke as a supportive colleague:

> Most physicians I've come in contact with are happy that there is someone who can assist them in coping with their own feelings about illness and what is happening with their patients.

Developing the Typology

During the course of analysis, we also uncovered additional dimensions of collaboration that could be incorporated into the typology. We mention them only briefly here because they are developed elsewhere (Mizrahi & Abramson, in press). They include (a) the degree of importance ascribed to the psychosocial aspects of care; (b) the degree of emphasis on the process versus the outcome of social work intervention; (c) the allocation of control over decision making; (d) the degree of emphasis on teamwork; (e) the limited versus active communication patterns; and (f) the attitudes toward offering and receiving support from the collaborator.

In sum, we have begun to inductively develop a preliminary theoretical framework to understand collaboration between physicians and social workers. We are now in the process of incorporating it into further data analysis, applying the classifications to additional sections of the interview to elaborate and modify them. Respondents may not necessarily fall neatly into a traditional, transitional, or transformational mode on all dimensions or in all situations. Some may be transitional in one area and traditional in others. We will look for patterns and variations expecting that as health care evolves, so do its practitioners.

Addressing Limitations of the Study

Arguments still exist about subjectivity in qualitative research. Do the findings make sense? Do the concepts have explanatory power? (Becker, 1970). Are the findings and interpretations plausible? (Strauss, 1987; Waitzkin, 1990). Are limitations noted? (Schatzman & Strauss, 1973; Zelditch, 1970).

The "truthfulness" of responses can be questioned—especially those of the physicians. Because social workers picked the physicians for the sample (by selecting the case), it is possible there was a selection bias—toward more positively viewed collaborators. Discussions with the social workers point strongly to case complexity rather than quality of collaboration, however. The cases were so memorable that neither busy social workers nor physicians had difficulty recalling details (even without the patient's medical record). Physicians knew we had already received information about them from the social worker, which may have altered responses. Moreover, several cases were presented where collaboration was seen as negative by one or both, and both groups freely discussed negative instances when directly asked.

Because all subjects knew we were social work professors, some may have omitted or minimized negative feelings and interactions. Large numbers of physicians, for example, expressed the view that social workers were equals. Physicians may not have wanted to offend us, and social workers may have wanted to impress us. As a result, both groups may have underplayed negative experiences.

We developed techniques to deal with our evaluations of subjects' responses. Rather than pretend we weren't labeling and judging behavior, we began to self-consciously use evaluative criteria. Our purpose was not to give up judgment about what we viewed as more and less preferred behavior, but to recognize how it entered into the analysis. We discovered, for example, that some social workers avoided physicians. At first, we labeled this phenomenon "social work autonomy"—they did things on their own. Interpreting the behavior further, we wondered where "autonomy" fit in to our typology of collaborative relationships. It was an accommodation as often as it was deliberately chosen. If autonomy was chosen by design, we identified the social worker as transitional; if was chosen by default, we located her in the traditional column.

Through comparisons, we are beginning to identify which factors in collaborating seem to transcend time, structure, and role, and which seem bound by a particular situation or circumstance using static, phase, and cyclic analysis (Lofland, 1971). Collaborative relationships may have certain characteristics that are stable or that vary across different settings and services with different individuals. Future research will explore the issues further.

Conclusion

We have presented the background, the methodology, and some preliminary findings of a study on social work/physician collaboration in hospital settings. Limited to a description of the evolution of our conceptual framework, we specifically focused on perceptions of the social work role, one dimension of our developing typology. It classifies social workers and physicians into three types of collaborators and collaborative relationships—"traditional," "transitional," and "transformational"—how physicians and social workers in each of the classifications view and experience the social work role. As additional data are examined, we will embellish and modify the typology and assess its application to different types of collaborators and settings.

Our preliminary findings underscore the need for a confident and competent social worker who can conceptualize and communicate the complexities of her role to physicians. The analysis should also be helpful to physician educators who are examining ways to improve housestaff training, cope with physician impairment, and strengthen the doctor/patient relationship. Transformational physicians could be used in training programs to demonstrate equalitarian collaborative models.

We anticipate social workers and physicians will benefit from a more empirically based understanding of how the social work role is framed. Ultimately, we expect knowledge about effective social work/physician collaboration to improve the quality of patient care, by strengthening team functioning and interdisciplinary decisionmaking.

Notes

1. Although the study is primarily a qualitative one, there are quantitative aspects to the research as well. Based on the literature and our experiences, we developed a set of precoded, closed-ended questions to follow several of the open-ended responses for purposes of comparison. The section on positive and negative collaboration was primarily quantitative in character. Following brief, open-ended descriptions of positive and negative cases, respondents reviewed a checklist of factors we had identified as contributing to perceptions of collaborative experiences. They checked off those most important in explaining why the collaboration was so negative or positive.

2. Social workers assigned to specialized units (cardiac or intensive care, rehabilitation, dialysis and oncology services) were almost invariably transitional or transformational in their view of collaboration. It is not clear yet whether the setting shapes the social work perspective or if social workers with certain characteristics select these assignments.

References

Abramson, J. S., & Mizrahi, T. (1986). Stragegies for enhancing collaboration between social workers and physicians. *Social Work in Health Care, 12*(1), 1-21.

Allen-Meares, P., & Lane, B. (1990). Social work practice: Integrating qualitative and quantitative data collection techniques. *Social Work, 35*(5), 452-458.

Bailis, S. (1985). A case for generic social work in health settings. *Social Work, 30*(3), 209-214.

Becker, H. (1970). Whose side are we on? In W. Filstead (Ed.), *Qualitative methodology: First-hand involvement with the social world* (pp. 15-26). Chicago: Markham.

Bendor, S. (1987). The clinical challenge of hospital-based social work practice. *Social Work in Health Care, 13*(2), 25-34.

Bergman, A., & Fritz, G. (1981). Psychiatric and social work collaboration in a pediatric chronic illness hospital. *Social Work in Health Care, 7*(1), 45-55.

Berkman, B., & Rehr, H. (1969). Selectivity biases in delivery of hospital social services. *Social Service Review, 43*(1), 35-41.

Blazyk, S., & Canavan, M. (1985). Therapeutic aspects of discharge planning. *Social Work, 30*(6), 489-496.

Brager, G., & Holloway, S. (1978). *Changing human service organizations.* New York: Free Press.

Bucher, R., & Stelling, J. (1977). *Becoming professional.* Beverly Hills, CA: Sage.

Butrym, Z., & Horder, S. (1983). *Health, doctors and social workers.* London: Routledge & Kegan Paul.

Caputi, M., & Heiss, W. (1984). The DRG revolution. *Health & Social Work, 9*(11), 5-12.

Carrigan, Z. (1978). Social workers in medical settings: Who defines us? *Social Work in Health Care, 4*(2), 149-164.

Charmaz, K. (1990). Discovering chronic illness: Using grounded theory. *Social Science & Medicine, 30*(11), 1161-1172.

Cowles, L., & Lefcowitz, M. (1992). Interdisciplinary expectations of the medical social worker in the hospital setting. *Health & Social Work, 17*(1), 58-65.

Dana, B. (1983). The collaborative process. In R. Miller & H. Rehr (Eds.), *Social work issues in health care* (pp. 181-220). Englewood Cliffs, NJ: Prentice Hall.

Davidson, K. (1990). Role blurring and the hospital social worker: A search for a clear domain. *Health & Social Work, 15*(3), 228-234.

Dinerman, M., Seaton, R., & Schlesinger, E. (1986). Surviving DRGs: New Jersey's social work experience with prospective reimbursement. *Social Work in Health Care, 12*(1), 103-113.

Epstein, I. (1985). Quantitative and qualitative methods. In R. Grinnell, Jr. (Ed.), *Social work research* (pp. 263-274). Itasca, IL: F. E. Peacock.

Fagin, C. (1992). Collaboration between nurses and physicians: No longer a choice. *Academic Medicine, 17*(5), 295-303.

Freidson, E. (1970). *Professional dominance: The structure of medical care.* New York: Aldine.

Freidson, E. (1984). The changing nature of professional control. *Annual Review of Sociology, 10*, 1-20.

Glaser, B., & Strauss, A. (1967). *The discovery of grounded theory.* Chicago: Aldine.

Gropper, M. (1987). Family medicine and psychosocial knowledge: How many hats can the family doctor wear? *Social Science & Medicine, 25,* 1249-1255.

Hess, H. (1985). Social work clinical practice in family medicine centers: The need for a practice model. *Journal of Social Work Education, 21*(1), 56-65.

Huntington, J. (1981). *Social work and general medical practice: Collaboration or conflict.* London: George Allen & Unwin.

Jansson, B., & Simmons, J. (1985-1986). The ecology of social work departments: Empirical findings and strategy implications. *Social Work in Health Care, 11*(2), 1-16.

Kerson, T. (1980). *Medical social work: The pre-professional paradox.* New York: Irvington.

Kulys, R., & Davis, M., Sr. (1987). Nurses and social workers: Rivals in the provision of social services? *Health & Social Work, 12*(2), 101-112.

Kurzman, P. (1976). Private practice as a social work function. *Social Work, 21*(5), 363-368.

Lamb, G. (1991). Nurses practice interaction and decision making with physicians. *Research in Nursing Health, 14*(5), 379-386.

Levine, S., & White, P. (1974). Exchange as a conceptual framework for the study of inter-organizational relationships. In Y. Hasenfeld & R. English (Eds.), *Human services organizations* (pp. 545-560). Ann Arbor: University of Michigan Press.

Lister, L. (1980). Role expectations for social workers and other health care professionals. *Health & Social Work, 5*(2), 41-49.

Lofland, J. (1971). *Analyzing social settings.* Belmont, CA: Wadsworth.

Lowe, J., & Herranen, M. (1978). Conflicts in teamwork: Understanding roles and relationships. *Social Work in Health Care, 3*(3), 323-330.

Lowe, J., & Herranen, M. (1981). Understanding teamwork: Another look at concepts. *Social Work in Health Care, 7*(2), 1-11.

Miles, M., & Huberman, A. (1984). *Qualitative data analysis: A sourcebook of new methods.* Beverly Hills, CA: Sage.

Mizrahi, T. (1986). *Getting rid of patients: Contradictions in the socialization of physicians.* New Brunswick, NJ: Rutgers University Press.

Mizrahi, T. (1988). Prospective payment systems and social work. In J. McNeil & S. Weinstein (Eds.), *Innovations in health care practice* (pp. 1-15). Silver Spring, MD: National Association of Social Workers.

Mizrahi, T., & Abramson, J. (1985). Sources of strain between physicians and social workers: Implications for social workers in health care settings. *Social Work in Health Care, 10*(3), 33-51.

Mizrahi, T., & Abramson, J. (in press). Collaboration between social workers and physicians: An emerging typology. In E. Sherman & W. J. Reid (Eds.), *Qualitative methods in social work practice research.* New York: Columbia University Press.

Mullaney, J., Fox, R., & Liston, M. (1974). Clinical nurse specialist and social work: Clarifying the roles. *Nursing Outlook, 22*(11), 712-718.

Murdach, A. (1983). Skills and tactics for hospital practice. *Social Work, 28*(4), 279-284.

Olsen, K., & Olsen, M. (1967). Role expectations and perceptions for social workers in medical settings. *Social Work, 12*, 70-78.

Pfouts, J., & McDaniel, B. (1977). Medical handmaidens or professional colleagues: A survey of social work practice in the pediatrics departments of twenty-eight teaching hospitals. *Social Work in Health Care, 2*(3), 275-283.

Pike, A. W. (1991). Moral outrage and moral discourse in nurse-physician collaboration. *Journal of Professional Nursing, 7*(6), 351-363.

Pray, J. (1991). Responding to psychosocial needs: Physician perspectives of their referral practices for hospitalized patients. *Health & Social Work, 16*(3), 184-192.

Prescott, P., & Bowen, S. (1984). Physician-nurse relationships. *Annals of Internal Medicine, 103*(1), 127-133.

Roberts, C. (1989). Conflicting professional values in social work and medicine. *Health & Social Work, 14*(3), 211-218.

Schatzman, L., & Strauss, A. (1973). *Field research: Strategies for a natural sociology.* Englewood Cliffs, NJ: Prentice Hall.

Schilling, R., & Schilling, R. (1987). Social work and medicine: Shared interests. *Social Work, 13*(3), 231-234.

Schlesinger, E. C., & Wolock, I. (1983). Hospital social work roles and decision-making. *Social Work in Health Care, 8*(1), 59-70.

Schwartz, N., & Jacobs, J. (1979). *Qualitative sociology: A method to the madness.* New York: Free Press.

Siefert, K. G., Jayaratne, S., & Chess, W. (1991). Job satisfaction, burn out and turnover in health care workers. *Health and Social Work, 16*(3), 193-202.

Starr, P. (1982). *The social transformation of American medicine.* New York: Basic Books.

Stine, B. (1976). Social work and liaison psychiatry. *Social Work in Health Care, 1*(4), 483-489.

Strauss, A. (1987). *Qualitative analysis for social scientists.* Cambridge, UK: Cambridge University Press.

Strauss, A., & Corbin, J. (1990). *Basics of qualitative research: Grounded theory procedures and techniques.* Newbury Park, CA: Sage.

Tanner, L., & Carmichael, L. (1970). The role of the social worker in family medicine training. *Journal of Medical Education, 45*, 859-863.

Temkin-Greener, H. (1983). Interpersonal perspectives on team-work in health care: A case study. *MMFQ/Health & Society, 61*(4), 641-658.

Toseland, R., Palmer-Ganeles, J., & Chapman, D. (1986). Teamwork in psychiatric settings. *Social Work, 31*(1), 46-52.

Waitzkin, H. (1990). On studying the discourse of medical encounters: A critique of quantitative and qualitative methods and a proposal for reasonable compromise. *Medical Care, 28*(6), 473-487.

Wilson, J., & Setterlund, D. (1987). Holistic social work practice in general medical settings. *Social Work in Health Care, 12*(2), 1-13.

Zelditch, M., Jr. (1970). Some methodogical problems of field studies. In W. J. Filstead (Ed.), *Qualitative methodology* (pp. 217-234). Chicago: Markham.

3. Explorations of Pregnancy and Choice in a High-Tech Age

ROBIN GREGG

This chapter describes an interpretive, qualitative study conducted from a feminist perspective, meaning that the research was conducted to illuminate issues from the standpoint of women. The research explores women's experiences of pregnancy and choice, using intensive, in-person interviews with 31 women. This chapter describes two key findings of the research and their connection to my methodology.

"I see this pregnancy as an obstacle course," said Sarah Worthington,[1] soon after we began our first interview. We were sitting in the study/music room of her home on a wintry morning. I asked her the opening question I used with all the women: "Tell me the story of your pregnancy." She started speaking, after a few moments of reflection. Her story, like that of most of the other women I interviewed, begins before the pregnancy, with the decision—rooted in other aspects of a life—to become, or try to become, pregnant in the first place. "This pregnancy was a long time in coming, psychologically," Sarah Worthington said. She described her decision to try to become pregnant, her first pregnancy, the birth of her first baby, and the thinking that led to this, her second pregnancy. The first finding—that for women pregnancy does not begin with conception, and its corollary, that it is possible to be "a little bit pregnant"— emerged as I transcribed and analyzed the taped interviews. A second finding, that pregnancy is a risk-laden "obstacle course," also emerged during the analysis. I return to these findings later in the chapter.

The original intent of the study was to explore pregnant women's decisions, their ways of making choices about amniocentesis and other prenatal tests. But due to the open-ended character of the interviews and the method I used to analyse their contents, additional, unexpected insights were generated, and the focus of the study broadened.

Social workers have long suggested that effective practice and policy must be crafted to take into account the perspectives of those most affected, the "target population(s)" for whom policies and programs ostensibly are designed. "Client-centered practice" and empowerment as a practice goal, for example, attest to social work values and reflect the belief that people possess the ability to solve their own problems if given a chance and appropriate resources. Feminist theory and practice are consistent with social work values in their emphasis on personal autonomy (e.g., women's right to choose) and the struggle against oppressive practices and systems (e.g., sexism and patriarchy). I designed and conducted a study to examine the experiences and perceptions of women, in the hope that their stories might be used to improve procreative health-care practice and policies. My approach reflects both social work and feminist values.

Research Method

I used a method derived from grounded theory and feminist standpoint research (Glaser & Strauss, 1967; Harding, 1986; Levesque-Lopman, 1988; Smith, 1987). Feminist critiques of positivism and objectivity have led to efforts to make methods and topics of research consistent with feminist epistemology and values. Feminist critics of mainstream scientific thinking have promoted qualitative research methods and the articulation of a new view of social research (Bowles & Klein, 1983; Nebraska Feminist Sociological Collective, 1984; Reinharz, 1983, 1984, 1992; Roberts, 1981; Stanley & Wise, 1983).

There are numerous "feminist" research methods, just as there are many forms of feminism. The following features, though, capture three important aspects. One aspect entails "bringing the woman back in," giving credence to women's voices and injecting into scholarly and activist discussions the voices, views, insights, and experiences of women. The second involves addressing the impacts of patriarchy and sexism on individual and social behavior: "A feminist mode of inquiry might then begin with women's experiences from women's standpoint and explore how it is shaped in the extended relations of larger social and political realities" (Smith, 1987, p. 11). A third element calls for the development of a new methodological paradigm, posing a challenge to the assumptions of positivism and objectivity. Three important elements of a feminist research paradigm influenced me as I designed and conducted the study: acknowledgment of interaction between my research subjects and myself, inclusion of reflexivity and self-awareness as an integral part of scholarly analysis, and the empowerment of women as a research goal.

Finding Pregnant Women

I found pregnant women through doctors, word of mouth, and a snowball method. Four New Hampshire health providers made my "Dear Friend" recruitment letters available to patients; 15 of the women I interviewed learned of the study through these health providers. Three of the women were friends of mine who participated in pilot interviews. The remaining 13 women learned about my research through the following: other women in the study (5); a notice I placed in a local maternity and baby store (1); and my professional networks, including the New Hampshire NASW Board of Directors (7). I conducted three pilot interviews while preparing the research proposal. By the end of the project 3 years later, I had talked with 31 women and conducted 51 interviews.

The Final Sample

The 31 women in the sample are a relatively privileged group: North American, white, and middle class. All are high school graduates, all but one have taken some courses beyond high school, and 11 have graduate degrees. All have male partners or husbands. They live in small towns and rural communities in New England: 27 of them live in New Hampshire; 1 lives over the state line in Massachusetts; 1 lives over the state line in Vermont; 2 live near Boston. Six of the women are full-time mothers. The others have part-time (home-based or outside the home) or full-time paid employment: 12 in health or human services and 8 in education. Others work in the computer, travel, or publishing industries. The women range in age from 30 to 40 years old; 18 are 35 years old or older.

Eleven women had amniocentesis with the pregnancy, and one woman had chorionic villi sampling for prenatal diagnosis. Of the 31 women, 28 had at least one ultrasound during this pregnancy. Twelve women were expecting their first baby and 16 already had one child. Two were expecting a third child, one her fourth child. Six of the women told me they had terminated earlier pregnancies, and five talked of earlier miscarriages. Two sad events occurred during the study: one woman's baby died during the seventh month of pregnancy, and another woman's baby died 16 days after birth.

Feminism, Social Work, and
the Role of the Researcher

One way to gain understanding about decision processes is to ask people to describe them. Elliot Mishler (1986) points out that interviewing is a method of communication and a common activity, one in which most of us have a lot of experience. But research interviewing is different from the "interviewing" we do in everyday life, and a range of opinions exists about the difference. The survey research literature, for example, suggests that research interviewing is objective, scientific, and controlled by one participant in the interview, the researcher—which is very different from what happens in everyday conversation. Others reject that depiction of research interviewing and acknowledge the essential humanness of the enterprise and its interactive nature. Some embrace the subjective dimension of the interview process (see Oakley, 1981); others advocate an "emancipatory social science" (see Lather, 1988) in which research is designed and conducted with the empowerment of research subjects in mind:

> What distinguishes feminist research is the theoretical framework. . . . It must be predicated on both the theoretical premise and the practical commitment: its purpose being to understand women's oppression in order to change it. Feminism is, therefore, both a mode of understanding and a call to action. (Kelly, 1988, p. 3)

My approach acknowledges the inherently interactive quality of interviewing, and the empowerment of women was an implicit research goal, but I embraced certain research conventions.

During the interviews I focused on the women's experiences and shared very little of my own with them. I responded in a neutral or affirmative fashion ("mhmm," "uhuh," "mmm," "oh, I see") to the women's stories and took pains to keep my opinions and politics to myself. The interviews were semistructured, and each began with the same question: "Tell me the story of your pregnancy." I used probes and follow-up questions to elicit details and introduce other topics.

When women asked me specific questions about myself, I suggested we wait until after the research was over to pursue my feelings or explore a relationship that might be more reciprocal (sharing information about ourselves). It often felt awkward, but I forced myself to stay "in role." I wanted the women to remain the focus of the study, their insights and voices to remain central to my analysis. Continuing to conduct interviews during the analysis and writing phases of the project helped me maintain focus. My respect for the women allowed them to speak freely and openly during the interviews. The nonjudgmental acceptance I offered, so familiar to social work practitioners, created a climate and space for them to tell of intimate feelings and experiences. As they talked about joys, struggles, and fears, I empathized. But I supressed my inclination to provide support or reassurance, and I kept many of my observations silent to maintain my role as researcher, not social worker or clinician.

At times I felt uncomfortable forcing myself to quash emotional responses in the interest of the research endeavor. When I discovered some of the women had radically different political attitudes from my own, there was tension. I struggled to maintain the same neutral acceptance in those instances as when women expressed attitudes more congruent with my beliefs. When women expressed adamantly antichoice/antiabortion attitudes, for example, or supported punishing pregnant women for "prenatal child abuse," I did not express my opposition. It was very difficult, and I felt a sense of self-betrayal. I sometimes felt a tension between accepting what the women said—being sisterly, so to speak—and wanting to hold onto a particular feminist view, a vision of a feminist future as part of a commitment to social change.[2] Struggling with myself about the appropriate role for the researcher was not unfamiliar, given my experience of similar conflicts during social work practice.

I was also aware of varying ideas about the stance of the feminist researcher. During the study I often thought about Ann Oakley's "Interviewing Women" (1981). She claims that traditional interviewing practices (e.g., the treatment of research subjects as passive objects, the depersonalization of both interviewers and interviewees) are in conflict with feminist goals and perspectives. Conventional research interviewing comprises a male paradigm, she suggests. Oakley's approach to interviewing promotes the development of friendships with research subjects.

I approached the women I interviewed differently. During her research on becoming a mother, Oakley befriended a number of the women she interviewed, shared insights with them, offered information, and attended the birth of six babies. I responded to Oakley's approach in two interrelated ways: (a) I worried that my own tendency would be to develop close relationships with the women I interviewed, so I tried to force myself *not*

to (to avoid "over-rapport"); and (b) I worried that if I developed close
relationships I would lose the ability to honor their needs, which might
include a preference for privacy or distance from the interviewer. I concen-
trated on responding to women's cues when deciding how to approach the
relationship. Upon reflection, I realized that I did so on the basis of feminist
and social work values—autonomy and self-determination—which I wanted
for the women and myself. I wanted to avoid exploiting the women by
assuming an intimacy they might wish to avoid.

I found, as Oakley did, that women posed questions during interviews.
When asked for information I usually gave it, but when asked for advice
or personal opinions, I generally demurred. I operated from a feminist research perspective, just as Oakley did, but we developed different kinds
of relationships with the women we interviewed. There is room for many
forms of feminist interviewing, just as there is room for many different
forms of feminist (and social work) research. A feminist research canon
or orthodoxy is a contradiction in terms. (See Reinharz, 1992, for more
on this theme.)

I kept in touch with the women after our initial contact and between
interviews by sending notes, making phone calls to plan follow-up interviews, and sending out mailings to the entire group of women. I told each
woman to feel free to contact me at any time with questions or observations. I mailed or hand-delivered a copy of the transcript of the first
interview to each woman, when I finished typing it. We exchanged holiday
greetings; I received birth announcements and sent congratulatory notes.
I sent each woman a copy of a research report at the end of the study and
said where she could procure the complete document. Sadly, on two
occasions I sent notes of sympathy. I have not seen either of those women
since the death of their babies, but I have communicated with them through
the mail and with one of them by phone, after she sent me a manuscript
she wrote about her pregnancy and the death of her baby. I continue to
hear from some of the women (through announcements of the births of
second or third babies, for example), and I anticipate seeing and talking
with others in the future.

I struggled to balance my understanding of an appropriate research role
with my sense of myself as a person, a feminist, and a social worker. I thought
about the women frequently during the 2 years of interviewing. At times
it felt as if they were my social work "caseload;" at others as if they were
part of a new and developing friendship network. Was I an objective,
nonjudgmental listener, a social worker, a counselor, or a friend? I wondered
how the women were doing, whether their babies had been born yet. Even

as I struggled to maintain my researcher role, I had an ongoing fantasy throughout the study that the women would all be able to meet each other. I imagined having a big picnic, inviting all of them to come; I even mentioned this to some of them, quickly adding that this would not happen because I was committed to preserving their anonymity.

I continued (quite consciously) to refrain from developing friendships with the women during the course of the study, even though this sometimes seemed artificial and contrived. I did not want them to feel that they had to continue with the study or to feel that they were obligated to reveal things to me out of loyalty or friendship. I also did not want them to feel they should withhold information or insights in the interest of our relationship.

When I ran into someone I had interviewed, we would say hello, I would ask her how she was, and we would go on. These encounters were awkward for me, and I found myself holding back to some extent. I did not want the woman to feel she had to engage in conversation, or even to acknowledge my presence if she chose not to. If women initiated a discussion or responded to my greeting by engaging in conversation I would respond, but I tried to ensure that the women maintained control of our relationship.

On one occasion, I had trouble determining the appropriate "research etiquette." I was on a walk with one of the women during a follow-up interview, and another woman in the study drove by and stopped to talk. This was an awkward moment for all. Aware of the confidential character of our relationships, no one quite knew how to act during this inadvertent encounter. I did not know whether to introduce the two women by name (using their actual names) and not explain our relationship, or to refrain from making introductions altogether (thereby preserving anonymity and confidentiality). Meanwhile, they admired each other's babies and made comments that made clear we all were involved in the same research endeavor. I introduced them, using first names only. Feelings of accountability to the women caused the awkwardness of the encounter, but those feelings also had a positive impact on the study. The women perceived the seriousness and respect with which I treated them, and openly shared their stories and feelings.

Analysis and Two Findings

Interviewing, analysis, and writing overlapped for the duration of the study. The use of a broad, open-ended question to begin each interview yielded a flood of material from each woman. Though at times the amount and breadth of the interview data became overwhelming, the approach resulted in new and unexpected ways of looking at pregnancy and choice. I allowed the women to define the starting point and the scope of their reflections. As a result, I learned things that led me to broaden the study's focus.

After interviewing approximately 10 women, I started preliminary data analysis. As I transcribed each interview, I took notes and developed a list of possible themes and categories from the early interviews. I made notes on the interview transcripts and developed a preliminary set of codes. As I read additional transcripts, I refined, collapsed, and expanded categories.

I wrote preliminary "theoretical memos" (Glaser & Strauss, 1967) and did "free writing" (Becker, 1986) to explore ideas derived from the interviews and from my typing and reading of the transcripts. I began to cluster quotes from individual women under the emerging topical categories, using a word processor. Typing additional transcripts, I added topical or conceptual categories and copied new quotes/interview material into the existing categories and memos. I eventually transformed the material into long memos or conceptual free writing pieces. The data were transformed as I worked, but the original transcripts remain intact and contain handwritten marginal notes and codes.

As I completed additional interviews, I read and reread transcripts, checking the new data against the emerging categories and vice versa. I then wrote additional memos based on the "raw data" I had included in each category. I continued to do free writing, spinning out ideas and impressions based on the total picture, then looked through the entire set of transcripts and developed additional categories. I then did more writing, using individual categories, and looked again at the transcripts for examples, corroboration, or contradictions. In this way my early, provisional codes and categories (created while reading and typing the transcripts and explored through writing memos) were refined and transformed in a reiterative process of constant comparison.

I include these details here, because the process of starting from the data led to unexpected findings, as mentioned earlier. In fact, I reconceptualized the entire study after beginning preliminary analysis of early interviews. Instead of focusing only on the decision processes women use to make choices about prenatal diagnosis, I expanded the focus to include additional choices faced by pregnant women, as well as their perceptions of their pregnancies. I discuss here two specific examples of the way in which the approach yielded particular findings—pregnancy does not start with conception: it is possible to be a "little bit" pregnant; and women's perceptions of the risks of pregnancy are far broader than medical definitions. When I started to make notes following the first 8 or 10 interviews, I was struck with the fact that women began their stories by referring to earlier experiences and choices. When they started telling their pregnancy stories, the women did so contextually, describing experiences and thoughts that predated the pregnancy. They talked about planning that ultimately led to the decision to become a mother.[3]

One form of planning concerned a woman's life circumstances. Laura Aston waited "until I was partway into internship to start to try to get pregnant," and Penny Adams scheduled her pregnancy by waiting until she and her husband both had jobs:

> We said . . . we're going to be together . . . we're going to live here . . . we feel steady and secure, we're ready. So, we said . . . now it's time, and . . . went off the pill.

The second reason women gave me for planning their pregnancies at a particular time relates to earlier decisions about having more than one child. Carol McAllister and her husband knew "when we had our first child that we would like to have a sibling for him." Jane Lowe and her husband talked about attempting pregnancy again when their first child was 7 months old:

> Do we want to start using birth control . . . or should we just go for it . . . . We weighed all the pros and cons . . . and decided we wanted to have a baby close in age to her.

Age was another factor that influenced women's decisions to try to become pregnant. Evelyn Michaels decided to attempt pregnancy "because of my age, I'm 35 . . . . I wanted to do it as soon as possible." In Lauren Fagan's case, age and circumstances made the time right:

> The pregnancy started before I became pregnant. We decided to get married last October . . . related to having a child. We decided . . . we'll get married, and settled, and then we'll be in a position to have this child.

As Lauren Fagan noted, women's pregnancies sometimes start before they actually become pregnant. Pregnancy does not start with conception for all women, and not all women who have conceived a pregnancy feel they are pregnant.

Only one woman began her story by referring to the time of conception. Jill Anderson told me about when she became pregnant, "a special, sort of 3 days that we had." As the interview continued, however, she told about her earlier decision to have a child and her plans with her husband to try to become pregnant. The discovery caused me to ask myself some questions: How do women define pregnancy? When does it begin? What makes women feel they are pregnant? Is there a "pregnant identity?" Initially I set those questions aside, but later, after an interview with Louise Frey, I came back to them.

A Little Bit Pregnant

Popular wisdom and an often-heard joke suggest that it is not possible to be "a little bit pregnant." The stories of pregnant women tell us that it is possible to be, or at least feel, that way. Pregnancy tests detect or "diagnose" the biological reality of pregnancy, but other indicators contribute to women's self-identification as pregnant women. Family members' responses, the labels used by health practitioners, women's own feelings and perceptions, and the physical changes that make women's pregnancies obvious to others (i.e., "showing") are some of the markers that women use to know they are pregnant. Women recognize their own pregnancies and identify themselves as pregnant in part because of these external and internal signs.

A variety of factors may influence the timing and degree of a woman's acceptance of the pregnant identity, including feelings about her body and her own and other people's expectations of her. Louise Frey assumed the pregnant identity before actually becoming pregnant. She welcomed pregnancy and took on the identity after she and her husband attempted conception for the first time. Louise Frey was sure she had conceived, and she responded to her bodily changes through the eyes of a pregnant woman:

> I thought . . . I'd like to begin the pregnancy in August, and deliver this baby in May. And so, when my period came in September, I didn't even think it was a real period. . . . I thought that maybe something was wrong . . . I knew I was pregnant. . . . I went through the first 4 weeks . . . from the time I thought I conceived . . . until my period . . . saying, I feel on top of the world, I don't know about this nausea stuff, I'm doing great. I'm invincible! And then this

period came, and I was like, what is this? I'll have to look this up in a pregnancy book. . . . I really stumped myself, 'cause I was so sure that I was in charge. So, that was the beginning.

Louise Frey became a "mother to be" as soon as she and her husband decided to attempt pregnancy. She felt pregnant, and, in her perceptions, she was. She then acknowledged she was not pregnant and relinquished the pregnant identity, then later regained it, slowly, when she actually conceived. Other women also identified themselves quickly as pregnant women. Jane Lowe readily accepted the identity, or as she put it, the "maternal mode": "My body has been in maternal mode a long time now." Lauren Fagan echoed Jane Lowe's enjoyment of the maternal mode. She experienced a heightened and positive sense of self/body-consciousness:

I was real in tune with every little step. . . . I wanted to be pregnant. I was very interested in everything that was going on . . . very clued into the physical feelings.

Not all women stepped into the maternal mode as easily or thoroughly, however. Some accepted the pregnant identity only partially or temporarily, for several reasons—for example, having had a previous miscarriage, having a history of infertility, and waiting for the results from prenatal diagnostic tests.

The use of amniocentesis can influence women's relationships to their pregnancies and developing fetuses, causing the phenomenon Barbara Katz Rothman has called "the tentative pregnancy" (1986). In previous studies, some pregnant women describe a period of suspended animation when they are waiting to learn the amniocentesis results. Unwilling to commit themselves fully to a pregnancy they might terminate in the case of a positive prenatal diagnosis, these women wait to wear maternity clothes, postpone telling other people about the pregnancy, and in some cases ignore fetal movement ("quickening") until after receiving negative test results. (In addition to Rothman, see Beeson, 1984; Kolker & Burke, 1988; Leuzinger & Rambert, 1988; Petchesky, 1987.) Some of the women I interviewed delayed telling people about the pregnancy until they received negative prenatal test results, which corroborates the findings of earlier research.

Pregnancy can be an ambiguous state: A woman may feel pregnant but not feel she is necessarily a "mother to be." Some women "grow into" the pregnancy, gradually assuming a new identity as their bodies change, and

others acknowledge their new role(s). They may experience role or identity ambiguity, confusion, or blurring. They may not experience a sudden,
complete, permanent acceptance or an outright rejection or relinquish-
ment of the pregnant identity. Instead they shift back and forth between
feeling pregnant, with all that pregnancy implies about a woman's changing roles, and not feeling "any different."

Sara Swanson is an example of a woman whose identification with her
pregnancy was blurred, or muted, during the beginning weeks of her
pregnancy. She was delighted when she learned she was pregnant, but she
wanted to assume the pregnant identity in a more pronounced way. She
wanted to feel "different" and yearned for the physical changes and public
recognition of her new status that would help her to do so:

> The only symptom that was really strong was the fatigue. . . . I had had mono
> before, and . . . these symptoms didn't feel unique or special. . . . Until my
> stomach pops out, I'm not going to really feel pregnant. . . . There's some-
> thing about having that external sign, that is confirming and validating. . . . At
> this point . . . you could be faking it, you could just be getting a little chubby
> . . . . There's something about the stomach popping out that makes it more
> definite.

Women who had experienced miscarriages or had trouble becoming pregnant
also experienced a form of "tentative pregnancy."

Unlike the medical depiction of pregnancy—a developmental, physiological process with a clear beginning, middle and end—women's descriptions of their own pregnancies are fluid and multidimensional. It is
possible to be "a little bit pregnant," to move in and out of the pregnant
identity. Women can be physically pregnant but not feel pregnant; con-
versely, they can feel and act pregnant even when they are not biologically
pregnant (e.g., Louise Frey). A woman can shift in and out of the pregnant
identity for months, until she perceives that her pregnancy actually will
result in the birth of a baby. The perception occurs at different moments
for different women. By the latter months of pregnancy, most women's
pregnancies are public, and at that point it is harder to be "somewhat
pregnant" or to lose the pregnant identity.[4]

When I started the research, I had unwittingly accepted the medical
view of pregnancy, a process or bodily state that begins with conception.
When I asked women to tell me the story of their pregnancy, I assumed
they would start by talking about when they became pregnant, or when they
learned they were pregnant. The question I asked (an open-ended one)

allowed women to start at their own beginning. Women perceive pregnancy very differently from the medical model. Another way women's stories differed from medical depictions was in the perceptions of risks associated with pregnancy.

Women's Versus Medical Perceptions of Risk

Medical protocols for prenatal care are derived from a physiological, decontextualized notion of pregnancy; the assumption is that there is a "normal trajectory." Doctors use a statistically derived model of the "normal" pregnancy as the standard against which to measure individual women's pregnancies, to calculate the "progress" of each pregnancy. Choices (e.g., whether or when to use a prenatal test) are made by the doctor, or the pregnant woman in consultation with her doctor, on the basis of the medical model of pregnancy. Pregnancy is a linear, developmental process and decision points occur at different steps along the way; certain tests are appropriate at certain times, just as particular developments in the pregnancy are expected at particular times. Medical norms regarding stages of pregnancy and childbirth are associated with medical protocols that require doctors to intervene when women's pregnancies differ from those norms. Ironically, although the medical approach to pregnancy and childbirth is based on the idea of a normal trajectory, the medical perspective also includes an expectation that women will deviate from that trajectory; variation and risk are expected. Medically, there is no such thing as a no-risk or low-risk pregnancy.[5]

Pregnant women also talk about and consider risks as they make choices about their pregnancies. Getting pregnant, being pregnant, having a baby, and becoming a mother feel risky or dangerous to women, at least to some extent and some of the time. When a woman chooses to attempt to become pregnant, she risks failing in that attempt. Once she becomes pregnant, she faces other risks, such as losing the baby through miscarriage or abortion. Other risks described by the women include negative or judgmental responses by other people—family, friends, coworkers, and strangers—to their choices and the outcomes of those choices; the risk of being the recipient of unsolicited advice; and the risk of "something going wrong," or having a baby with a physical or mental disability.

Conceiving or birthing a baby with a genetically linked disability, a risk associated in the medical and popular literature with "older" motherhood, was my primary focus at the beginning of the study. I was interested in the ways women perceive and deal with genetic risks, and how they make choices about prenatal diagnosis. My initial focus, once again, reflected my subconscious internalization of the medical view of pregnancy and the medical definition of risks during pregnancy. By listening to women, I discovered that their perceptions are much wider than the medical risk definition, which is limited to physiological problems: involuntary abortion (miscarriage), premature labor, problems during labor or birth, and the risk of conceiving a baby with a genetic condition or disability. Women's stories of pregnancy include these medically defined risks, but they also include risks that go well beyond the medical perspective.

Women referred to many kinds of risk in their stories, despite the fact that I did not use the word *risk* in my questions. Had I asked about it directly, I do not know if women would have responded so broadly. It was during data analysis that I saw that much of what women were saying about their worries and fears could be categorized as risks.

Reviewing the interview transcripts, I made notes about women's fears and worries and searched the interview transcripts for words and phrases such as "danger," "just in case," "to be sure," and "to be safe." I found women used the words *risk, risky,* and related phrases to refer to many things: their changing roles, their private and public identities, and the impact of their pregnancies on family lives and work relationships.

Even women who defined themselves as genetically or physically at risk, in the medical or statistical sense, had an expanded notion of risk. After tests such as amniocentesis, used ostensibly to ascertain risks (of having a baby with a neural-tube defect, Downs Syndrome, or other genetically based condition), women still felt uneasy. They continued to worry about potential physiological and social problems associated with their pregnancies.

Sarah Worthington, for example, who told me she felt her pregnancy was an obstacle course, had given birth to her first child when she was 36, 4 years ago. Last time, she had amniocentesis. This time, she chose chorionic villi sampling. Test results were negative, but she still was anxious about the pregnancy, in part because she was older and knew more about the physical and social risks associated with pregnancy and motherhood, and in part because she was experiencing some specific problems:

I know that I shouldn't worry, but I do . . . my obstetrician told me I should bank some of my own blood, because . . . postpartum, I can hemorrhage. So, I'm sitting there thinking, this could really turn into a disaster. . . . I'm not in a home-free zone by any means.

As it turned out, Sarah Worthington's worries during this, the beginning of her second trimester, foreshadowed what she would experience following the birth of her baby.

She had chosen to get as much information as possible during her pregnancy: "Let's put it this way. I'm 40 years old, and without the diagnostic tests that are available I wouldn't have risked a pregnancy." None of the tests she had—chorionic villi sampling, maternal serum alpha-fetoprotein, and ultrasound—indicated that anything was wrong with her baby. However, when he was born, he had numerous birth defects. His physical and neurological problems were so severe that, despite intensive, extensive treatment in a leading children's hospital, her son died after 16 days of life.

The medical response to medically defined risks did not eradicate Sarah Worthington's worries, nor did they predict or prevent her baby's problems or his death. The problems her baby experienced had not been included in her perceptions or her doctor's assessment of potential dangers in her pregnancy. Thus the limited medical model was inadequate even when it came to predicting, ameliorating, or preventing specific medical, physiological problems. But women's definitions go far beyond that type of problem, and the medical model does not begin to address women's concerns, their notions of the risks associated with pregnancy and motherhood.

From women's standpoint(s), risks associated with pregnancy involve all aspects of their lives as women, patients, mothers, wives, workers, and caretakers of children. They talked about the lack of social supports for pregnant women and mothers; they told me about fears of being judged or blamed for problems with the pregnancy and with their babies and children; they felt they would be blamed for decisions to test or not to test, to terminate a pregnancy or carry it to term. These are not medical risks, but they are central concerns to women. Their existence has implications for medical practice and policies.

Conclusion

When initiating the study, I planned to explore how women make choices about genetic information and prenatal diagnosis: Do they use a rational, costs/benefits model of decision-making? Do they use other ways of choosing? My research was able to answer the original question: For the most part the women did not use a rational, costs/benefits approach. But the research also provides additional, unanticipated answers.

The findings about women's perceptions of pregnancy and risk emerged because the study was not limited by preconceived ideas or a desire to test a particular hypothesis. The approach I used, to listen to the women and let their stories determine the process and shape of the research and its findings, caused me to question my initial assumptions and to broaden the study's focus (the opposite of what usually happens in research), thus yielding unexpected findings and new insights.

I transformed women's initial answers to my original research questions into important research questions in their own right. Choices about genetic information, amniocentesis, and other prenatal tests take place in the context of overall definitions and experiences of pregnancy, which take place in the context of women's lives, and their depictions of these contexts became a focus of the research. The "person-in-environment" idea, central to social work theory and practice for years, was illuminated by the study's method, though the original intent of the research was more limited.

My findings were derived from a particular method and a particular group of women. Clearly it is impossible to generalize from the somewhat homogeneous group of 31 women, or to make statements about other women's experiences. But the stories told are worth considering. The findings are suggestive and have implications for health care providers, social workers, and other people interested in the development and provision of health-care services attuned to pregnant women's actual needs and experiences. I offer a few here.

To develop genetic services and reproductive health programs that truly serve women, it is imperative to start with women's own perceptions and definitions of their situations. In the case of pregnancy, we need to look at the choices they feel are important and their ways of making those choices. We need to expand our definitions of risk and continue to develop and maintain nonmedicalized programs and services that address pregnant women's social concerns, as well as their biological needs. We need to remind ourselves and medical colleagues of the contexts in which women's pregnancies occur. We need to remain open to the insights offered by clients, patients, the people we serve, the subjects of our research, and we need to be willing to reconsider our assumptions on the basis of their perceptions and develop new questions from the answers they give us.

Notes

1. This name, like all of the names of the women used in this chapter, is a pseudonym chosen by the woman at my request.

2. Rahel Wasserfal asks, "What are the commitments of the researcher as a feminist to her woman informants who uphold a contrasting belief-system?" (Wasserfal, 1990)

3. I wish to distinguish here between talking about pregnancy by describing experiences that precede pregnancy; and defining oneself as pregnant prior to conception (or, on the other hand, defining oneself as not pregnant, or somewhat pregnant, despite having conceived). I found the women did both: they talked about their pregnancies contextually, and they felt a little bit pregnant. In this chapter, I mention the former and highlight the latter point. For more on both points see Gregg (in press).

4. With the ongoing development of procreative technologies, the biological "fact" of pregnancy also may become unclear. When does pregnancy begin? When sperm and egg are joined together in a petri dish? When implantation occurs? When cell division begins? These are political and scientific questions that go beyond this chapter.

5. Robbie Kahn relates a story from her work in the 1970s as a consultant in a municipal hospital. In a conversation with the hospital's Chief of Obstetrics, she learned that a major advocate of the fetal monitor had said at a colloquium: "there is no such thing as a normal labor and delivery" (Kahn, 1988, p. 160).

References

Becker, H. (1986). *Writing for the social sciences.* Chicago: University of Chicago Press.

Beeson, D. (1984). Technological rhythms in pregnancy: The Case of prenatal diagnosis by amniocentesis. In T. Duster & K. Garrett (Eds.), *Cultural perspectives on biological knowledge* (pp. 145-181). Norwood, NJ: Ablex.

Bowles, G. & Klein, R. D. (Eds.). (1983). *Theories of women's studies.* London: Routledge & Kegan Paul.

Glaser, B. & Strauss, A. (1967). *The discovery of grounded theory.* Chicago: Aldine.

Gregg, R. (in press). *Pregnancy in a high-tech age: Paradoxes of choice.* New York: Paragon.

Harding, S. (1986). *The science question in feminism.* Ithaca, NY: Cornell University Press.

Kahn, R. P. (1988). *The language of birth.* Unpublished doctoral dissertation, Brandeis University, Waltham, MA.

Kelly, L. (1988). *Surviving sexual violence.* Minneapolis: University of Minnesota Press.

Kolker, A., & Burke, B. M. (1988). Amniocentesis and the social construction of pregnancy. In D. Wilkinson & M. B. Sussman (Eds.), *Alternative health maintenance and healing systems for families* (pp. 95-116). New York: Haworth.

Lather, P. (1988). Feminist perspectives on empowering research methodologies. *Women's Studies International Forum, 11,* 569-582.

Leuzinger, M., & Rambert, B. (1988). "I can feel it—My baby is healthy": Women's experiences with prenatal diagnosis in Switzerland. *Reproductive and Genetic Engineering, 1*(3), 239-249.

Levesque-Lopman, L. (1988). *Claiming reality.* Totowa, NJ: Rowman & Littlefield.

Mishler, E. G. (1986). *Research interviewing.* Cambridge, MA: Harvard University Press.

Nebraska Feminist Sociological Collective (Eds.). (1984). Feminist ethics and social science research [special issue]. *Humanity and Society, 8*(4).

Oakley, A. (1981). Interviewing women: A contradiction in terms. In H. Roberts (Ed.), *Doing feminist research* (pp. 30-61). London: Routledge & Kegan Paul.

Petchesky, R. P. (1987). Foetal images: The power of visual culture and the politics of reproduction. In M. Stanworth (Ed.), *Reproductive technologies* (pp. 57-80). Minneapolis: University of Minnesota Press.

Reinharz, S. (1983). Experiential analysis: A contribution to feminist research. In G. Bowles & R. D. Klein (Eds.), *Theories of women's studies* (pp. 62-191). London: Routledge & Kegan Paul.

Reinharz, S. (1984). *On becoming a social scientist.* New Brunswick, NJ: Transaction.

Reinharz, S. (1992). *Feminist methods in social research.* New York: Oxford University Press.

Roberts, H. (1981). *Doing feminist research.* London: Routledge & Kegan Paul.

Rothman, B. K. (1986). *The tentative pregnancy.* New York: Penguin.

Smith, D. E. (1987). *The everyday world as problematic: A feminist sociology.* Boston: Northeastern University Press.

Stanley, L. & Wise, S. (Eds.). (1983). *Breaking out: Feminist consciousness and feminist research.* London: Routledge & Kegan Paul.

Wasserfal, R. (1990, June). *Epistemological choices and ethical conflicts of an Israeli anthropologist working with Moroccan women in Israel.* Paper presented at the International Interdisciplinary Congress on Women, Hunter College, New York City.

PART II

Narrative Approaches
to Trauma

Social researchers have recently discovered narrative, but the form is old, seen in biography, autobiography and, of course, literary studies. Inherently interdisciplinary, narrative approaches extend the interpretive turn in methods (Rabinow and Sullivan, 1979/1987; Riessman, 1993). As realist assumptions from natural science prove limiting for understanding social life, leading American scholars from anthropology, history, and psychology are turning to narrative as the organizing principle for human studies (Bruner, 1986, 1990; Cronon, 1992; Rosaldo, 1989; Sarbin, 1986). The chapters to follow illustrate how several social work investigators are adapting narrative concepts to study first-person accounts of physical and sexual trauma. Some background on narrative theory (which may be less familiar than grounded theory to readers) places the chapters in context.

It is common knowledge that individuals narrate significant events in their lives. Clients typically represent experience in this way to clinicians, who help retell and reconstruct new, more fulfilling narratives (Laird, 1992; Schafer, 1980, 1992; White & Epston, 1990). Despite common occurrence, the precise definition of *personal narrative* remains ambiguous. The term generally refers to a particular kind of text organized around consequential events in the teller's life. She takes a listener into a past-time "world," and recapitulates what happened then to make a point, often a moral one. Stories are the classic genre, although not the only form of narrative (Riessman, 1987, 1990).

Narrating about the past seems to be a universal human activity, one of the first forms of discourse we learn as children (Nelson, 1989), and is used through the life course by people of all social backgrounds in a wide array of settings. "So natural is the impulse to narrative," writes Hayden White (1981), that the form is almost inevitable for any report of how things happened a solution to the problem of how to translate *knowing* into *telling* (p. 1). Interpretation is inevitable in personal narratives because we construct them from a point of view. Human agency and imagination determine what gets included and excluded, how events are plotted and what they mean to the teller. The stories we tell ourselves about the past *become* the past, and through them we claim identities and compose lives.

> How individuals recount their histories—what they emphasize and omit, their stance as protagonists or victims, the relationship the story establishes between teller and audience—all shape what individuals can claim of their own lives. Personal stories are not merely a way of telling someone (or oneself) about one's life; they are the means by which identities may be fashioned. (Rosenwald & Ochberg, 1992a, p. 1)

Individuals become the autobiographical narratives by which they tell about their lives. These private constructions typically mesh with a community of stories about the nature of life itself. (For a review of narrative theory and methods see Riessman, 1993; for applications see Rosenwald & Ochberg, 1992b; Josselson & Lieblich, 1993; Sarbin, 1986.)

The telling of personal narratives is common in research interviews. Respondents (if not interrupted with standardized questions) will hold the floor for lengthy turns and sometimes organize replies into stories. Mainstream methods suppress narrative accounts; they are typically coded as "asides," seen as irrelevant (Mishler, 1986). Qualitative analysts often fracture the texts in the service of interpretation and generalization, by taking bits and pieces, snippets of a response edited out of context. They eliminate the sequential and structural features that characterize narrative accounts.

Narratives are important units of discourse for research because they allow for the construction and expression of meaning, an essential activity of human existence. Probably *the* primary way we make sense of our experience is by casting it in narrative form. This is especially true of traumatic experiences; as Isak Dinesen says, "All sorrows can be borne if we can put them into a story" (Arendt, 1958, p. 175). Precisely because they are essential meaning-making structures, social work investigators must preserve narratives, respect respondents' ways of constructing meaning, and analyze how it is interactionally accomplished.

Culture "speaks itself" through an individual's story. It is possible to examine gender inequalities, oppression and other practices of power that may be taken for granted by individual speaks. Narrators speak in "natural" terms, the only terms imaginable, but we can analyze how culturally and historically contingent these terms are (Rosenwald & Ochberg, 1992a).

The three studies to follow use narrative approaches to study a contemporary social problem—abuse of women and girls. Similar to clinical social work, each investigator lets the stories unfold in semistructured research interviews and bears witness to her informants' detailed descriptions of physical and sexual trauma. Each investigator applies narrative concepts in a distinctive way, interpreting the narratives historically and culturally, for example, and/or examining how they are composed structurally. Together the contributors produce knowledge about the nature of trauma and its consequences for lives.

Robin A. Robinson examines the life stories told in interviews by 30 delinquent girls. The girls make connections between their public actions—delinquent behavior—and their private lives, specifically experiences of sexual abuse, often by family members. Girls, acting to change their troubling situations, run away and break the law which leads the state to place them in foster homes and residential settings, often repeatedly. Robinson locates these public responses in a historical context, and argues that fears about female adolescent sexuality have shaped U.S. social policy. Unfortunately, policy ignores what got the girls into trouble in the first place—the initiation into sex that often occurs in the family. Regarding methods, Robinson examines the content of the girls' narrative accounts, particularly the recurrent theme of sexual abuse as it emerges in her sensitive interviews (which she often presents interactionally, as conversations). Her approach treats language as a transparent medium, a straightforward path to meaning. No distinction is made between the story and prior experience to which it refers; talk directly reflects reality. (See Young [1987] for a discussion of ontology and narrative.)

Margareta Hydèn extends the narrative approach to examine the constructed character of narrative. Her topic is physical violence in marriage, which she studied in 20 Swedish couples where the wife was assaulted by the husband. In repeated interviews over a 2-year period, she studies how each spouse makes sense of the violent episode through narrativization, how language (and thus meaning) differ for husbands and wives, and what happens to the accounts (and the marriages) over time. She observes a typical three-part sequence—verbal fight, violent incident, and aftermath—which husbands and wives construct differently because of their contrasting standpoints. Half the marriages continue and these couples work interpretively to neutralize the violence. Paradoxically, wives' power increases relative to husbands' (he is dependent on her absolution), but the battering is transformed. It becomes unclear in spouses' retellings who did what. The couple survives as a unit, but at what cost to the woman and the institution of marriage? Regarding methods, Hydèn distinguishes the violent events from the narratives about them, analyzes what is said (content), how it is said (form), and what is not told (omissions).

The next chapter presents my work, also on the topic of physical abuse in marriage. Selected from a larger sample of 104 people who were separating and divorcing (Riessman, 1990), here I present a case study of a working-class woman who was raped by her husband. She could have related the terrible events of her marriage in a variety of ways so, I ask, why does she develop the narrative *this* way? I locate the personal narrative in a larger social discourse about power in contemporary marriage to show the instructive potential in single lives: they teach about social structure. As to methods, I adapt a sociolinguistic approach to analyze how the account develops in interaction with a listener/questioner. The line-by-line transcription method, widely used in narrative analysis, may be unfamiliar (we are accustomed to reading "cleaned" speech in qualitative studies), but the level of detail is essential for my question. Language choice—how someone tells her tale—shapes how we can legitimately interpret it. What on the surface appears to be the reason for a separation—marital rape—misses the mark. It was *her* response that proved unacceptable and turned the tide. Viewing the narrative as a cultural product, I argue that American society now permits women to talk about themselves as victims and survivors, but it still censors women's rage.

Taken together, the studies illustrate how social work investigators, in all their diversity, are beginning to recognize and analyze narrative in research interviews. If we are to take personal narratives seriously, they require a different analytic treatment than grounded theory allows, in my view. Some "unpacking" of the text is called for, that is, attention to language and repersentation of experience in the talk of informants (Riessman, 1993). The degree, of course, depends on the research question and the theoretical orientation of the investigator.

References

Arendt, H. (1958). *The human condition.* Chicago: University of Chicago Press.

Bruner, J. (1986). *Actual minds, possible words.* Cambridge, MA: Harvard University Press.

Bruner, J. (1990). *Acts of meaning.* Cambridge, MA: Harvard University Press.

Cronon, W. (1992). A place for stories: Nature, history, and narrative. *Journal of American History, 78*(4), 1347-1376.

Josselson, R., & Lieblich, A. (Eds.). (1993). *The narrative study of lives* (Vol. 1). Newbury Park, CA: Sage.

Laird, J. (1993). Changing women's narratives: Taking back the discourse. In L. Davis (Ed.), *Building on women's strengths: A social work agenda for the 21st century.* New York: Haworth.

Mishler, E. G. (1986). *Research interviewing: Context and narrative.* Cambridge, MA: Harvard University Press.

Nelson, K. (1989). *Narratives from the crib.* Cambridge, MA: Harvard University Press.

Rabinow, P., & Sullivan, W. M. (1979/1987). *Interpretive social science: A second look.* Berkeley: University of California Press.

Riessman, C. K. (1987). When gender is not enough: Women interviewing women. *Gender & Society, 1*(2), 172-207.

Riessman, C. K. (1990). *Divorce talk: Women and men make sense of personal relationships.* New Brunswick, NJ: Rutgers University Press.

Riessman, C. K. (1993). *Narrative analysis.* Newbury Park, CA: Sage.

Rosaldo, R. (1989). *Culture and truth: The remaking of social analysis.* Boston: Beacon Press.

Rosenwald, G. C., & Ochberg, R. (Eds.). (1992a). Introduction: Life stories, cultural politics, and self-understanding. In G. C. Rosenwald & R. L. Ochberg (Eds.), *Storied lives: The cultural politics of self-understanding* (pp. 1-18). New Haven, CT: Yale University Press.

Rosenwald, G. C., & Ochberg, R. (Eds.). (1992b). *Storied lives: The cultural politics of self-understanding.* New Haven, CT: Yale University Press.

Sarbin, T. R. (Ed.). (1986). *Narrative psychology: The storied nature of human conduct.* New York: Praeger.

Schafer, R. (1980). Narration in the psychoanalytic dialogue. *Critical Inquiry, 7*(1), 29-54.

Schafer, R. (1992). *Retelling a life: Narration and dialogue in psychoanalysis.* New York: Basic Books.

White, H. (1981). The value of narrativity in the representation of reality. In W. J. T. Mitchell (Ed.), *On narrative* (pp. 1-23). Chicago: University of Chicago Press.

White, M., & Epston, D. (1990). *Narrative means to therapeutic ends.* New York: Norton.

Young, K. G. (1987). *Taleworlds and storyrealms: The phenomenology of narrative.* Boston: Martinus Nijhoff.

4. Private Pain and Public Behaviors: Sexual Abuse and Delinquent Girls

ROBIN A. ROBINSON

Katharine: The [court petition] got filed because I stopped going to school when I was eleven and a half, twelve . . . quit halfway through sixth grade. . . . I was a straight-A student. . . . I just flew through school. Until my life started cracking down.

Interviewer: What was the first thing that cracked?

Katharine: My brother started sexually abusing me when I was eleven. I just started doing drugs and began drinking and I stopped going to school. I couldn't deal with that. . . . At school it was just too much pressure. I couldn't work on my own problems. I couldn't handle everything.

Katharine was a patient in an acute adolescent psychiatric unit of a state facility when I interviewed her. She came into the room clutching a stuffed animal in her right hand and wearing a diamond engagement ring on her left hand. Katharine, who was committed to juvenile corrections for operating under the influence of alcohol and driving to endanger, began her career with the youth authorities for truancy, as a child in need of services under the jurisdiction of the Massachusetts child welfare agency, following the onset of sexual abuse by her older brother (unknown to the agency). Katharine felt inadequate and blamed herself because she could not cope simultaneously with the trauma of the ongoing abuse and the requirements of school, her alcoholic mother, and stepfather, so her response was to "crack down," lose herself in drugs and alcohol. She ran away from home 6 months later and became a street prostitute to support herself. The prostitution continued for a couple of years, on and off, as she ran between home and the streets. She reported that she spent time in several treatment programs, including secure treatment and five psychiatric inpatient admissions, that focused on numerous suicide attempts (including jumping from the roof of a three-story building), prostitution and other sexual activity, running away, and finally, the sexual abuse. Katharine offered me the following poem as a testament of her ordeals:

Tears of Guilt and Shame

Giving up on life seems so easy to do
'Cause of all the pain and hurt you have put me through.

I used to keep the pain and hurt buried inside
I never knew it was nothing to hide.

None of the tears I cried those nights and days
Helped me feel I wasn't to blame.

I do not feel as confused
Because I am not the only one to be sexually abused.

I turned to drugs and walked the street,
Not knowing help was right at my feet.

But now I know I am not the one to blame,
So now, no more tears of guilt and shame.

Katharine represents, in many ways, girls involved with youth authorities. They are likely to be in their early to mid teens; have a personal as well as a family history of drug and/or alcohol use; be sexually active, usually with multiple partners; have been physically and sexually abused; and sexually revictimized; and have problems in school. Typically, the girls come from households headed by single mothers, in which the girls assume early responsibility for mothering siblings and often their own mothers. Girls faced with such personal and family characteristics as described here may act in ways that hurt mostly themselves, such as sexual acting out, drug and alcohol use, and other potentially self-destructive actions, including suicide attempts, running away, truancy, and lawbreaking. Socially unacceptable behaviors may bring girls to the attention of authorities who are responsible for restoring or guiding them to normative behavior (Hudson, 1989; Koroki & Chesney-Lind, 1985; Peacock, 1981).

Social policy attention is focused on girls' public behaviors, often driven by a mystique about the perceived power of their emerging sexuality.

Policymakers, social workers, other service providers, and social scientists are often both captivated and perplexed by the possible outcomes of that sexuality, including a high level of sexual activity, prostitution and other sex work, and teenage pregnancy and motherhood. In recent years, the mystique has extended to the delinquency of adolescent girls. Some research has focused on female involvement in gang activity (Campbell, 1984), and occasional news stories focus on cases in which adolescent girls are violent perpetrators. But violent events are not the norm among female offenders—most are apprehended for petty property crimes such as shoplifting, other larceny, and motor vehicle offenses (Chesney-Lind, 1989; Chesney-Lind & Shelden, 1991; Robinson, 1990)—and the public behaviors of female delinquents are not well understood (Hudson, 1989; Koroki & Chesney-Lind, 1985; Robinson, 1990).

Little empirical research analyzes the meanings of delinquent behaviors to girls themselves. Concern with public actions, both sexual and delinquent, misses the troubles in the girls' private lives, descriptions of which can enrich understanding and point to policy recommendations (Hudson, 1989). Seldom have the girls' stories been heard in their own voices.

In 1989, I began a study of female delinquents and their needs relative to particular life stories. In the larger study (not reported here), I sought to discern the differences between girls who had been adjudicated delinquent, that is, convicted of criminal offenses by the juvenile courts, and those who had been placed by juvenile courts under the jurisdiction of child welfare agencies to monitor and manage their behavior. I chose Massachusetts as the site for the study, the state that has been touted nationally and internationally for 20 years by juvenile justice practitioners and researchers as the pioneer in juvenile deinstitutionalization and in progressive programs for juvenile offenders. The study included delinquent girls under the jurisdiction of the Department of Youth Services (DYS) and girls designated children in needs of services (CHINS) under the jurisdiction of the Department of Social Services (DSS). I reasoned that to study female juvenile offenders in an agency environment that operated on a progressive philosophy and agenda would protect, to some extent, the findings of such a study from the confounding influence of harsher, more punitive agency protocols that some other jurisdictions may employ.

I began the research with a conviction that female delinquency would be understood best by examining life stories told by delinquent girls, placing delinquent events in the context of those stories. I assumed that the offenses the girls had committed were but moments in the span of their brief but troubled lives (Hagan & Palloni, 1988), but they were socially significant. Girls had gained the offender label based on unlawful actions, effectively relegating to lesser importance other experiences and moments. After gaining approval from both departments to interview 30 girls, review their official records, and speak with their caseworkers, social workers, and program workers, I sought to recreate the contexts in which the momentary offenses had occurred and to build, as the data allowed, a theoretical model describing the elements of the female delinquent's life context (see Robinson, 1990). The analysis here examines the content of narrative accounts by the girls of their experiences. I discuss the dominant theme of the effects of sexual abuse.

Theoretical Framework

Historical Context

Virtually no primary scholarly literature exists prior to the 20th century to describe what were believed to be the causes of female children's delinquency; what remain are religious tracts for children that admonish duty and obligation to parents, God, scripture, and country. From these, we can extrapolate the characteristics and behaviors "naughty" and delinquent children were thought to have. We know, for example, that in the early days of the Massachusetts colony, children's disobedience to parents could be a capital offense. Similarly, the "visionary girls" of Salem witch trial notoriety in the 17th century were initially perceived by parents and community as delinquents, but were later seen as victims of the deviant wiles of the Goodwives charged with witchcraft. Later analysis of the Salem witch period suggests that the girls may have been participants in activities connected with sexuality, religious practice, and healing powers beyond the norms of the community; the girls invented stories to cover their actions and were thereafter perceived as victims. Witchcraft was highly associated with suspected, unacceptable sexuality (Karlsen, 1981).

What also survive are admonitions in the form of pamphlets designed to lure farm children, particularly girls, to burgeoning industrial centers in the early- to mid-1800s to take jobs as much-needed mill and factory workers (Dublin, 1981). The girls came to the towns and cities, as young as age 10, to live in dormitories and work in the mills for 12 to 15 hours per day. The girls' lives were supervised by the women who operated the dormitories; specific codes of behavior that survive suggest what the definitions of delinquency might have been. Most rules relate to respect for elders, obedience, chastity, rules of work, rules of property, and prohibition of alcohol consumption. Sexual indiscretion was a principal prohibition. The history of the female status offender and female delinquent in Massachusetts is chronicled by Brenzel (1983) in *Daughters of the State: A Social Portrait of the First Reform School for Girls in North America, 1856-1905*. The school, located in Lancaster, Massachusetts, was the first of its kind in the country and served as a model; definitions for appropriate candidates for commitment carry through to today, though legislatively the mandates have changed. Brenzel describes the paternalism of the state's social order and political structure that formalized its fear of poor, non-Yankee, immigrant, minority girls from families whose values and capability to support their children did not conform to Yankee (dominant white) cultural norms. Disparities extended beyond the concerns of material support to produce ethnic, religious, and class fears. Brenzel recounts the influences of class, age, and gender biases on policy and programs for the reformation of the potentially wayward. The ideological bases for reform reflected the intellectual history of the 19th century, leading in a direct line to *The Child Savers* (Platt, 1969).

An ideological shift in the study of crime and delinquency occurred from the mid-19th century to the beginning of the 20th century, a move from reformist idealism to biological determinism. Brenzel parallels the shift with Rothman's description (1981) of a parallel move from altruistic institutionalization to controlling or punitive institutionalization. Society feared those who were a visible threat to the social order, and vulnerable, uncontrolled adolescent girls were highly visible in a moral context. Brenzel suggests further that girls' parents cooperated in the social control (perhaps unwittingly) by perceiving the formal bureaucratic moral structure— the residential institution—as a way of protecting their daughters from the squalid life they likely would have entered otherwise. Parents' complicity was motivated by assurances that daughters would have adequate food, shelter, clothing, supervision, job training, and future employment.

Many a girl went to the State Industrial School for Girls in Lancaster as a "stubborn child," which only ceased in 1972 to be a legal foundation for commitment to the Massachusetts Department of Youth Services. The concept "stubborn child" continues to this day as a tacit (if not statutory) basis for commitment. Brenzel's argument—the purpose of the Lancaster school was to mold morally or culturally recalcitrant girls to the normative values and behaviors of the dominant culture—parallels the beliefs of many DYS and DSS practitioners today. Female status offenders and juveniles guilty of criminal offenses are randomly labeled and placed throughout the youth service system, with social control as the tacit goal.

Frameworks for Analysis

Contemporary empirical research on female offenders (for example, Chesney-Lind, 1973, 1978, 1982, 1989; Chesney-Lind & Rodriguez, 1983; Hudson, 1989) finds gender bias against females operates at all levels of the criminal and juvenile justice systems, from initial police contact to corrections. Social service networks may perpetrate a punitive surveillance of adolescent females who behave in ways unacceptable to the norms of the dominant patriarchal culture. As in the past, tacit offenses are often sexual in origin and/or nature (Chesney-Lind & Shelden, 1991).

Using other frameworks, a few studies document the situations of girl offenders. Gisela Konopka lived among a group of institutionalized female delinquents in the early 1960s, and in *The Adolescent Girl in Conflict* (1966) develops a theoretical model of female delinquency driven by the "normal" tasks of adolescent girls (puberty and menarche and the complex identification process). Working in the context of dominant theories of adolescent psychology (based mostly on boys, including the theories of Erikson), Konopka posits a conflict with authority among delinquent girls. Confrontations with authority figures and abusive situations gradually increase the girls' distrust of people and erode the community's acceptance of the girl as her oppositional behavior develops and continues, forming a vicious cycle. Peacock's ethnographic study (1981) places the onus of female delinquency on the mothers of the girls, for inadequate nurture and expectations for precocious responsibility.

Recent research has begun to explore the causal relationship between physical/sexual abuse and delinquent activity among girls (Koroki & Chesney-Lind, 1985). Using DSS case-file data, a study of delinquent youth in Massachusetts found 38% of the girls were sexually abused and 57% physically maltreated. These data were generated by officially reported and substantiated cases of sexual and physical abuse, not on self-reports by the children (Guarino, 1985).

The juvenile court, since its inception, has viewed girls as particularly vulnerable to moral corruption. The courts are slow to commit girls to delinquent status, but once committed, harsh punishments protect them. Girls are as likely as boys to run away from home, but are more often referred to court for the behavior. Shelden, Horvath, and Tracy (1989) report that girls are two to five times less likely to escalate to more serious crime than boys after a status offense, and that "more often than not, girls are being victimized at home and hence require a completely different response by the court." The discretionary nature of the juvenile court relative to the offenses most often committed by girls allows a wide range of sanctions and exhibits the active practice of paternalism and protection. The work of Jean Baker Miller (1976) contributes additional understanding to the problem of sexual abuse in girl offenders. In relationships of temporary inequality, such as the relationship between parent and child, the power differential serves as a tool for the development of the subordinate, and the power equation shifts as the child matures. Permanent inequality, on the other hand, is galvanized by sustained subordination and dominance. Girls may succumb to powerlessness in situations in which they should be building increasing reserves of personal power and resources. Parent-daughter and other adult-girl relationships that should be temporarily unequal may be scarred by sexual abuse or other physical violence. The psychological burdens of a shift from temporary to permanent inequality block the normal course of development of the female adolescent. Carol Gilligan (1982, 1990; Gilligan, Lyons & Hanmer, 1989) and Brown and Gilligan (1992) document the critical period of early adolescence for girls. The passage from childhood to adolescence includes changes in the strength of self and the development of a morality of empathy and affiliation. Girls are likely to emerge from the period with less sense of self-determination but a greater ethic of care for others, often placed before their own self-interests.

I suggest that girls' struggles to maintain affiliation with abusers create crises in the context of inequality with their caretakers. Those who come to the attention of youth authorities do so as they begin to exhibit self-determination; they make decisions to leave abusive homes, attempt to support themselves (albeit through illegal and unacceptable means), and challenge the rules and constraints that have been placed on them as girls. They defy acceptable standards of girl behavior as they seek to remove themselves from abusive and neglectful situations. In their stories, girls describe the ways they are proactive, including using drugs and alcohol as means of self-anesthesia to cope with abusive situations.

My framework builds on others' work and focuses on four principal elements: (a) Sexually abused girls may feel the perpetrator has betrayed trust, as have other adults and persons of authority (Browne & Finkelhor, 1986); (b) girls' self-blame and guilt are part of a process of self-stigmatization; (c) girls *survive* by running away from home, and commit *crimes of survival* to live on the street or to find shelter; and (d) they struggle with powerlessness

(Browne & Finkelhor, 1986). I suggest that powerlessness is of two kinds: *true powerlessness,* including behavioral manifestations over which the girl has no control or ability to change, such as nightmares, phobias, and depression; and *intermediate powerlessness,* which exists in temporary situations that the girl can change once she escapes the abusive situation or makes a decision to act in some way that makes sense to her given her life circumstances, such as running away, truancy, and delinquency.

As W. I. Thomas (1923) argues in *The Unadjusted Girl,* individuals act according to what makes sense given the particulars of the situation:

> If now we examine the plans of action carried out by children and men (sic) with reference to social values, whether they are good or mischievous, we find that the general intellectual pattern of the plan, the quality of ingenuity, is pretty much the same in any case. When, for example, children have escapades, run away, lie, steal, plot, etc., they are following some plan, pursuing some end, solving some problem as a result of their own definition of the situation. (p. 234)

Thomas' work provides an additional theoretical lens for viewing the sense adolescent girls make of the behaviors that bring them to the attention of the agencies.

Research Method

This was a descriptive, qualitative study of the life stories of delinquent girls as told to me in interviews. My goal was to describe life events and characteristics of the girls from their own perspective, including what led to agency jurisdiction. The research was informed by feminist theory, which privileges the voices of the women studied. It was informed also by the research literature and theoretical perspectives presented earlier.

Three research objectives guide the study: (a) to gain from the girls an understanding of the life experiences and events that led them to the unacceptable behaviors for which they were referred for agency services; (b) to determine the prevalence of abuse in this population of girls receiving agency social services; and (c) to explore what differences existed, if any, between delinquent girls and girls receiving services as children in need of services.

I interviewed 30 girls, 15 adjudicated delinquents and 15 children in need of services, located across Massachusetts. The girls were located for the study by random selection of current cases in representative areas of the state. Face-to-face interviews, depending on the skill of the interviewer, provide an opportunity to develop rapport in the course of the interview, thus provoking more candid responses (Bradburn, 1983) and an opportunity to observe and carry through on cues from the respondent (DeLamater, 1982).

The particular offending behaviors for which the girls had been placed under agency jurisdiction were, in large part, responses to life events; the girls had acted in ways that made sense to them, within their ability to choose and act. To understand their actions, the context of life events was explored for possible or likely meanings. Official agency records rarely capture a life history from the perspective of the client when the client is an offender. Although my study was not intended to be a large-scale prevalence study of child sexual abuse, the rate of such abuse was determined for the sample.

Operational definitions of sexual abuse are not consistent in the research literature (Bass & Davis, 1988). The definition for this study was based on the subjective experiences of the girls themselves. I broached the issue with each girl who related a suggestive incident. When I felt there was a cue, I probed the subject. When a girl responded that she thought she had been sexually abused, I asked her to talk about the kind of abuse, how it felt abusive to her, the identity of the abuser(s) (though I didn't ask for names), and whether she had disclosed it to anyone. Any stories about abuse emerged from these questions, with the extent of discussion controlled by the girls. In the analysis of the 30 interviews, I examined recurrent themes about abusers and the responses of others in stories the girls told.

I began each interview with the following, open-ended question: "Tell me about your family? With whom do you live?" For girls in placement, I amended the question to: "With whom did you live before you came here or went to any other placement?" The open nature of the question prompted a wide range of responses. Each of the family members listed provided a relationship that I explored with the girl. I observed facial expressions, body language, words used to describe people and relationships, and her overall affect. Usually, family stories intermingled with information about school, drug and alcohol use, relationships with parents, other authority figures, peers, sexual activity, and other topics, including official delinquent behavior. In some cases, the girls developed accounts of physical and sexual abuse in their response to my initial question. For example, 15-year-old Diana in secure treatment (locked residential) responded:

> Tell you about my family? Well, my father, he's an alcoholic, and my mom, she's very, very nervous. And she always used to go out and get him beer,

and she always used to say . . . "he ain't gonna drink real heavy and nothing can happen" and I couldn't deal with it anymore, and I couldn't deal with my dad drinking and my mom always going out and getting it for him. . . . It didn't hit me 'til I was around ten or eleven, that my father's drinking began to affect me and stuff, because he began to get real violent, and beat me and my mom up.

Katharine responded to the same question at the beginning of the interview:

There was, like, problems with my brother. [What was that?] Sexual abuse. When I was younger. And my mother had an alcohol problem and she just blew me off the wall. [What do you mean?] She never listened. She was never there for me. The only time she wanted something is when she wanted one of us to go to the store or something. She was a real idiot.

I allowed each interview to flow as a conversation, probing as the girls raised issues in different areas of their lives. In some cases, a girl dropped hints that she wanted to tell something, but didn't know how. I drew the girls out slowly, allowed them the opportunity to retreat and proceed as they felt comfortable. Usually the hints centered around one or more abuse incidents that either she didn't know how to articulate or was afraid to disclose.

Sexual victimization was not the only subject demanding empathy and support. The girls' stories described other events and circumstances in their lives that evoked psychological pain and fear: tales of running away, experiences with illicit drugs and alcohol, satanic cults and ritualistic torture, suicide attempts, self-mutilation, relationships of conflict and betrayal with parents, other loved and trusted adults, troubled peer relationships, and reproductive health problems, especially miscarriages and abortions. I prepared for the interview process by reading related studies, and I also read works of fiction and drama that have similar subjects as themes, listening to the dialogue and acclimating to discussion of the painful issues. I wanted to ensure that I would be well-prepared for the interviews, that neither shock, dismay, nor judgment would censor the girls' stories (Finkelhor, 1986, pp. 222-223).

The Private Pain: Meanings of Sexual Abuse

Sexual abuse and other disruptive traumas combined with the usual developmental tasks of growing up. Often, sexually abusive incidents served as points of initiative for the girls to take action, as they moved from silence to subjective knowledge, as described by Belenky, Clinchy, Goldberger, and Tarule (1986). What follows are excerpts from the life stories of some of the girls in the study who represent recurrent themes across the sample. Of the 30 girls, 23 reported that they had been sexually abused, 10 by more than one person. Six spoke of abuse by their fathers as well as by some other individual(s), and 14 by at least one male relative. Eight had been sexually abused by family friends, neighbors, or foster family members. Among the abusers was one female, a cousin. None recounted abuse by strangers. Sexual abuse with a close family member constitutes a breach of trust. The closer the relative is, the greater the sense of betrayal. Girls who reported being sexual abused by their fathers expressed feelings of devastation, not always at the time, but often later as they reconstructed their lives. In several cases, sexual incidents continued well into early adolescence; as the girls grew older, their awareness was heightened that something was dreadfully wrong.

Annie, a 14-year-old committed to the youth services authority for breaking and entering, had been sexually abused by her father and by "so many other people . . . it's hard to separate them all." Annie was very small and childlike, soft-spoken though animated as she became caught up in the story she was relating. She recounted an early memory of abuse by her father:

> I didn't see my dad much growing up. The last time I saw him I was 12 years old . . . and before that I didn't see him since I was, like, five. . . . I was scared of him . . . because when I was younger, I was molested by him, and a lot of things that happened then, it's hard to believe now, but it happened. Do you know what I mean? I was four when that happened . . . it was my weekend home. It was the weekend my sister and I went there together . . . and he lived in a one-bedroom apartment . . . and my sister went outside to play, and my dad started touching me, and he did some pretty horrid things. . . . It scared me, but I know it happened, but I can't remember what exactly did happen because there were so many other people who molested me in my life, too. So, it's hard to separate them all, do you know what I mean? Cause I see all these pictures, and everybody doing it to me, but the faces really don't come clear.

Annie wrote a poem about her father. She recited it to me, from memory, during the interview:

Love Is Blind

When I'm with you, you don't see my love.
When we're together, you don't see my trust.
We both have to accomplish what's there to be.
Like a blind seagull drifting its way to sea,
Not wondering when and if it awakes.
Love is a four-letter word,
But someone somehow got the wrong meaning.

The transcript from Annie's interview recounts a sequence of sexual victimizations, beginning with her father's molestation of her when she was four, continuing with a stepfather, a friend of one of her stepfathers, a male babysitter, the babysitter's brother, and a foster brother. There was physical abuse and neglect from her mother and first stepfather, and she was placed in a series of foster homes, interspersed with trial stays at home that never worked out. Annie spoke little of her feelings about the incidents, directing attention instead to trying to remember details, names, and places. She did recount that the night she was arrested for breaking and entering a neighbor's house (who was on vacation) she was running away from home because her stepfather had been beating her. She hid under the dining room table in the neighbor's house, and waited for the police to find her. She said she wanted the police to come, so they would take her out of her stepfather's house. She reasoned that if she committed a crime, they would take her away permanently.

Angela, a 15-year-old CHINS (for running away), related the story of how her father had been absent from her life until she met him when she was 12 years old. She spoke of feeling abandoned by her birth father, her grief at finding out at the age of 12 that her first stepfather was not her "real" father, and anger and mistrust toward her birth father when, soon after they met, he sexually abused Angela and her sister.

Angela (R): I've had two stepfathers. Well, one really raised me. I call him my real father. . . . F__ was my natural birth father but he was never around for me. He left me when I was 10 months old. So I don't consider him my real father.
Interviewer (Q): Did you ever know him?
R: Yeah, I know him now. . . . I don't know, I like him I guess because he's my father, but I don't really talk to him that much.
Q: When did he come back into your life?
R: When I was 12.
Q: What happened that made him do that?

R: My mother wanted to tell us sooner but she didn't want us to know that my real father was alive. She didn't want us to know. . . . . The father of the three little kids, I lived with him since I was 10 months old and I always thought he was my natural birth father. And when I turned 12, my mother told me he wasn't my real father. . . . And that's when I started having problems. When I was 12 years old.

Q: Do you think it had anything to do with the problems?

R: I think it had to do with all the abuse that was going on, and my mother, and the things that were going on with my stepfather [physical abuse of Angela and her mother as well as his heavy drug use in the home]. . . . I have feelings for my father, but I never trusted him. When he came back, my sister loved him, but I never did, cause he abused me and my sister.

Q: How?

R: Sexually. He molested me and my sister. Because this show he was looking at in his work . . . where fathers were showing their daughters how to have sex and mothers were showing their sons how to have sex. And he said that he wanted me to try it out, and that he won't hurt, that I didn't have to worry about gettting pregnant if I was worried about that. You know, he tried it with me but it wouldn't work. I kept saying, no, I don't want to.

Q: He tried with you physically?

R: Yeah! And I told him over and over, no, I don't want to. And good thing my sister walked back in, cause he stopped. Then, when we spent the night over his house, with his wife, he tried everything with my sister, and my sister didn't know no better and my sister let him cause she loved him. She didn't want to get taken away from him. So she did whatever he told her to. I didn't. Because I knew it was wrong. And I told my mother about that, and my mother called DSS and told them. And they pressed charges against him. But he lied and he said he didn't do it. And that's what got me so mad at him, that's why I never trusted him again . . . and my sister even lied, too. She lied because she loved him. I wouldn't lie about nothing like that. Just to save his behind. Yeah.

Angela had learned from her experience with her second stepfather, who was physically violent with her, her mother, and her sister, to be wary. In the case of her second stepfather, DSS had removed the children from the home when claims of abuse, filed by an adult friend and neighbor of Angela's, were substantiated. Angela had lived in a foster home for a while, then returned to her mother. Around the same time, she was told about and met her "real" father. Her second stepfather, by that time, had been incarcerated for cocaine possession and was out of the home. A year later, he returned home, the beatings resumed, and Angela ran away to live with a boyfriend. She continued to go to school throughout the sequence of events, because "getting schooling is the only way out." She became pregnant, had a miscarriage, and returned home. During the time she was gone, her mother filed a CHINS petition. Angela's social worker from DSS, hearing of the miscarriage, went back to the court that had issued the CHINS petition and requested Angela be sent to a residential group placement. I interviewed Angela at the group home.

The violence Angela experienced confused her. She perceived that she had followed the rules: She did excellent work in school and tried to take care of her mother and younger siblings. Her stepfather beat them regardless. The discovery at the age of 12 that her biological father had abandoned her when she was an infant, the introduction to him, and the subsequent sexually abusive incidents further confused her and challenged the developmental tasks she faced at adolescence, including finding a place for herself as a self-determining individual. Running away from the abusive situation seemed to make the most sense of any alternative she could fathom.

When Annabelle was 3 years old, her mother left her and her older brother at their grandmother's house, and, with no explanation that Annabelle heard, did not return until Annabelle was five years old. Annabelle quickly came to identify grandmother as mother, not knowing who her mother was until she appeared to reclaim her. Annabelle's story revealed not only physical abandonment, but emotional abandonment subsequently when she left her grandmother's home to live with her mother, stepfather, and older brother. Her brother began to sexually abuse her when she was 11 years old. He would come to her room at night; she responded by staying out most of the night, hanging out in the local park. Because she felt betrayed by her mother and had no one else she felt she could trust, she kept the reason for her nighttime absences secret. Annabelle said her mother assumed she was out all night, partying and having sex with boys. Finally, her mother filed a CHINS petition, charging that Annabelle was a runaway.

R: My brother was doing things that I never told about.
Q: To you?
R: Yeah. So I would stay out at night so it wouldn't happen.
Q: What kinds of things?
R: Sex. Rape. Cause our rooms were right next to each other upstairs and our parents' room was downstairs. . . . So I stayed out at nighttime so I wouldn't be near him.

Q: And you never told anybody about that?

R: Not until . . . last year.

Q: So you were involved with CHINS for 4 years and they never knew about the abuse from your brother?

R: No.

Q: You never told your mom or anyone?

R: No . . . I just started staying out late and my mom got really mad about it. . . . And plus when I was home I would go out more often. Because when you're 12 you start doing things with your friends, you know? And my mother didn't like that. She called me a little slut and everything.

The actions Annabelle took to protect herself antagonized her mother to the point that Annabelle became the object of derision in the household for almost everything. Eventually, she did run away, back to her grandmother's house. She told her mother where she was going, but her mother went to court for a warrant anyway. The police apprehended her at her grandmother's house. The subsequent court appearance resulted in the first of 19 placements over the next 4 years, including residential placements, foster homes, inpatient psychiatric units, and detention units.

Over the 4 years of placements, Annabelle stated that she made a conscious decision to divorce herself completely from any relationship with her mother, stepfather, and brother. She attempted suicide several times, lived with a man for several months by whom she became pregnant, was imprisoned by the same man (he stabbed her on two occasions when she tried to leave him), suffered a miscarriage, and finally ran away. She was subsequently arrested (for contempt of court, again, for running away), spent time in yet another detention and inpatient psychiatric unit, and then was placed in yet another foster home. At the time of the interview, she was living in a temporary foster home and claimed to have contact with no family members except her grandmother.

Annabelle expressed frustration with the legal technicalities that retained her mother as legal parent and guardian; the only nurture she had ever experienced was from her grandmother, yet she was thwarted repeatedly from staying with her in a place where she felt safe, wanted, and loved. No child abuse or neglect petitions had ever been filed against the mother. Annabelle believed that her constant running away focused the family problems onto her, and the mother's proactive pursuit of Annabelle kept her in the position of offender. The sexual abuse by her brother had continued over 4 years, every time Annabelle was sent or taken home, and continued up to 5 months before I interviewed her:

R: [In the context of a discussion of her attempted suicides and in response to a question about whether she really wanted to die] I don't know. The world's fucked up. I mean, I don't want to hang around here forever, but, I suppose if the world was great and no one wanted to die there'd be a population problem. But I don't want to hang around forever and I don't want to die today so, take it as you want. . . . Every time I went back to my mother's my brother would do it again. He's been doing it all along up until 5 months ago. Every time I tried to get out, I'd get arrested and sent to some place to "improve" me. Last time, the court order wanted to send me to another assessment. And I hated it. I ran . . . went back, did my time, stayed on the highest level. Got out. And I went to court, they tried to talk this bullshit about residential. It was fucked. I wouldn't go. But, so, I stayed with my mother, which obviously didn't work out . . . my brother was still doing it. So, I'm like . . . What? I talked to my social worker. . . . I didn't have anywhere else I could go.

Q: So you went back to your mom's?

R: Yeah. I called [my social worker], I was having problems. "Well, I don't have anyplace for you." I said, well, can I go stay with my friend [to get away from my brother]? "Yeah, fine," she said, "give me the phone number and the address," she told me. So I went and stayed there. Gave her the phone number, the address, the mother's name, everything. Three days later I find out I have a warrant out for my arrest for runaway. From my mother . . . *and my social worker!*

In addition to a sense of "badness" the girls felt within themselves, they also expressed differentness and separateness from peers, especially, and from adults. They spoke of difficulties they had relating to others, the need to keep troubles within, self-doubts about how others perceived them. Some related stories of a single, close friendship with another girl who had shared similar troubles. Many could reveal their pain to no one.

I interviewed Lisa, a 14-year-old committed to DYS for larceny of a motor vehicle, in a residential placement. Early in the interview, Lisa spoke of her alienation from the group of girls there because of her personal history, and their rejection of her for wanting to talk about it:

I'm not allowed to talk about my sexual abuse in group, not that and not the Satanism. I'm not allowed to talk about anything I don't feel comfortable talking about, or anything the group is uncomfortable talking about. . . . Some girls here had an attitude toward me about the Satanism and I said to them, please don't let my past get in the way of our relationship.

Feeling marginalized, Lisa's story (the content of which was independently documented from other sources) is informative in several ways. She had been sexually abused by male family members; her uncle and brother dominated her stories on the subject. Her earliest recollection of sexual abuse was an incident that happened when she was 5 years old. Several people over the next 6 years sexually abused her, until she was 11. (Revictimization is a common theme in the life stories of the girls and is supported by the literature on sexual abuse [see Herman, 1992; Russell, 1984].)

Nobody cared. . . . I did what I wanted, how I wanted. When I wanted it . . . I wasn't allowed to do anything when I was little. I wasn't allowed to play with my friends, well, I really didn't have any friends. . . . I was, kind of, basically on my . . . by myself. When I tried to have friends, I'd get into a fight or something like that . . . it just wouldn't work out, having friends. So I basically just grew up having one friend. . . . She lived up the street. She was quite a few years older than I was. And she did drugs, and she got pregnant at 16 . . . and I didn't see her for a while.

Lisa became involved with DSS when a child abuse and neglect petition was filed against her mother. Lisa never disclosed the sexual incidents throughout her years of involvement with DSS, though she told me her social workers had asked. She denied because she did not want to be perceived as the deviant she already had labeled herself. She was embarassed that her mother's neglect was known to the agency, and she didn't want to admit to any other abuse. The fears and secrecy she harbored kept her from seeking friendships.

At the age of 12, Lisa ran away from home with a girl she knew after they had met and become involved with a group of Satanic cultists. Lisa said she felt she didn't belong anywhere, and the Satan worshippers were attractive because they seemed to have power, something Lisa lacked in her own life.

R: And when I was 12, I had gotten involved in a little Satanism. I *was involved* with Satanism. . . . And we started hanging around with these people . . . they were in a cult. . . . We basically went there at first just to party. All's I did was coke the first night that I ever met any of them . . . about thirty people . . . only six girls. After hanging around with them for about a week, me and my friend ran away from home. . . . I saw them as people who had a lot of power, cause anything they said was done. The leader, he had power. . . . He had control. I saw that and I wanted it . . . . We had to do some pretty gross things . . . and sex was always expected. Now, I feel gross, and I didn't like it back then.

Q: Why did you do it?

R: For the power. Cause the more that you did with the group, the more power you got.

Q: Did you feel the power? Or did you keep hoping you'd get it? Or what?

R: You feel . . . [long silence]. It's a different feeling. I don't know how to explain it. You could really, actually, pretty much feel the power. You could feel, I don't know, something more than what I had before. I used to do a lot of acid when I was doing this. It was . . . oh . . . it was sick.

Q: What kind of "more" did you feel? More control over yourself? Other people? Smarter? Braver? Sexier? What more was it?

R: Like I could do anything. You know? No one's going to stop me.

Q: And what did you do with the power?

R: I did what I wanted to do, and how I wanted to do it.

Q: And at that time, what was it?

R: Party. Have sex. Fuck off. Oh, God, it was all so sick.

Ironically, living at the margin of family acceptance led Lisa to seek power from a group that would accept her, if she provided sex. Lisa ended up feeling yet another kind of difference, the stigma of being involved in a Satanic cult. But she acted in a way that made sense to her: She felt powerless and joined a group that she perceived as powerful. Lisa summarized her story:

Oh, there's definitely a connection between my mom and her boyfriends beating on me and my brother and my uncle molesting me, and my drinking and the drugs and the cult and all. Get stoned, forget about it all.

CONCLUSION

There is minimal focus on girls in trouble as worthy subjects of social policy (Hudson, 1989), yet research suggests an association between female delinquency and child sexual abuse. As children and as females, female delinquents and status offenders who have been sexually abused are "victims as well as offenders, [whose] backgrounds and current situations require specialized services that overburdened and underfunded social service and correctional systems will be hard pressed to deliver" (Chesney-Lind & Rodriguez, 1983).

The lack of a public voice that women can use to share common experience in a public forum is a troubling deficiency, especially for adolescent female offenders. The secrecy of abuse feeds the effects of the abuse, encouraging self-stigmatization. Known strategies for change—exit and voice (Hirschman, 1970)—were rarely possible for the girls in my study, except in ways that either labeled them as deviant or jeopardized their safety. Heilbrun (1989) decries the lack of a public voice: "male power has made certain stories unthinkable." Living in isolation and fear, lacking the "sight of a possible life," girls could find a common voice, make sense of their experiences, and find personal power by sharing experiences with others (Herman, 1992).

Over the last 2 decades, an agenda has developed for an ongoing feminist discussion of women and crime (see, e.g., Chesney-Lind, 1989; Chesney-Lind & Rodriguez, 1983; Heidensohn, 1985). More recently, the agenda has come to include and highlight juvenile female offending. Research suggests a strong association between abuse, particularly sexual abuse, and the offending behaviors of girls (Chesney-Lind, 1989; Hudson, 1989; Koroki & Chesney-Lind, 1985), which my study also finds. The feminist discussion provides the foundation for studying how girl victims struggle to survive and effect change in their lives. The stories I collected suggest the strength girls find, ultimately within themselves, to challenge dangerous and abusive situations and to leave. The stories also reveal the remnants of volition the girls retain in the face of horrendous experiences. The accounts draw attention to affiliation and care in the development and behavior of girls, and on the loyalty they may feel to others to the detriment of their own well-being. My research questions the widespread belief that adolescent girls are offenders needing to be controlled and reformed. The control of adolescent female sexuality—a tacit goal of the juvenile courts and the agencies that serve girls committed to their care—misses the mark.

The ideal of the sexually innocent adolescent girl, perpetuated over millenia, seems to be incongruous with the lives of adolescent girls in current American society, certainly with those in my sample. Popular media and current events militate against an ideal of sexual innocence; adolescent girls are challenged *not* to absorb the messages of easy sexuality promoted in the popular culture. Childhood and early adolescent experiences of sexual abuse may further exacerbate the confusion of appropriate sexual behavior that girls who experience such abuse may have.

Still, the girls who were the subjects of my study were rulebreakers, by their own admission and by the determination of the juvenile courts. It is difficult to distinguish the meanings society holds of their rulebreaking relative to the meanings the girls convey. An understanding of the meanings the girls give for their behavior may serve to enlighten policymakers and practitioners who work in the agencies that serve girls like these. Understanding the girls' actions, in the context of their experiences with family, may aid service workers.

Because girls constitute a minority of the total population in the juvenile courts and related services, it is difficult, though essential, to organize resources to deal specifically with them. Concern with boys has dominated the theories and research guiding program philosophy and standards, perception of juvenile crime and risk, and assumptions about the needs and characteristics of juvenile offenders. The special life issues and characteristics of girls suggest that they are a special population with special needs, which are addressed ineffectively by traditional programs.

Four major areas of policy reform are suggested by my study:

1. Routine screening and treatment for girls who have experienced sexual abuse by specially trained personnel

2. Universal discussion of and education about sexual abuse in schools and community programs, to target the age groups at greatest risk (primary grades through junior high school)

3. Legislative, juvenile court, and agency reformulation of response to juvenile female offending, particularly in cases of nonviolent and other victimless crimes

4. Development of ongoing, interagency collaboration between decision makers and street-level practitioners to focus on the needs of girls and their families

It is tempting to say that society must change the way it views girls, as objects to be controlled, whether the views are intended to be benevolent, punitive, or abusive. It is tempting to say that no social control is better than harmful or stigmatizing social control. But otherwise how do we provide aid and guidance to children who grow up with inadequate nurture or experience profound violations? How do we honor and support girls' individual talents, will, and volition? Given the findings of my study, perhaps the best course is to focus on policy change in existing agencies that provide services, so that they can more closely respond to needs as voiced by the girls themselves.

References

Bass, E., & Davis, L. (1988). *The courage to heal: A guide for women survivors of sexual abuse.* New York: Harper & Row.

Belenky, M. F., Clinchy, B. M., Goldberger, N. R., & Tarule, J. M. (1986). *Women's ways of knowing: The development of self, voice, and mind.* New York: Basic Books.

Bradburn, N. M. (1983). Response effects. In P. H. Rossi, J. D. Wright, & A. B. Anderson (Eds.), *Handbook of survey research.* New York: Academic Press.

Brenzel, B. M. (1983). *Daughters of the state: A social portrait of the first reform school for girls in North America, 1856-1905.* Cambridge: MIT Press.

Brown, L. M., & Gilligan, C. (1992). *Meeting at the crossroads: Women's psychology and girls' development.* Cambridge, MA: Harvard University Press.

Browne, A., & Finkelhor, D. (1986). Initial and long-term effects: A review of the research. In D. Finkelhor & Associates, *A sourcebook on child sexual abuse* (pp. 143-179). Beverly Hills, CA: Sage.

Campbell, A. (1984). *The girls in the gang.* Oxford, UK: Basil Blackwell.

Chesney-Lind, M. (1973). Judicial enforcement of the female sex role. *Issues in Criminology, 3,* 51-71.

Chesney-Lind, M. (1978). Young women in the arms of the law. In L. H. Bowker (Ed.), *Women, crime, and the criminal justice system.* Lexington, MA: Lexington Books.

Chesney-Lind, M. (1982). Guilty by reason of sex: Young women and the juvenile justice system. In B. R. Price & N. J. Sokoloff (Eds.), *Criminal justice system and women* (pp. 77-104). New York: Clark Boardman.

Chesney-Lind, M. (1989). Girls' crime and women's place: Toward a feminist model of female delinquency. *Crime & Delinquency, 35*(1), 5-29.

Chesney-Lind, M., & Rodriguez, N. (1983). Women under lock and key: A view from the inside. *Prison Journal, 63*(2), 47-65.

Chesney-Lind, M., & Shelden, R. (1991). *Girls, delinquency, and crime.* Pacific Grove, CA: Brooks-Cole.

DeLamater, J. (1982). Response effects of question content. In W. Dijkstra & J. van der Zouwen (Eds.), *Response behavior in the survey-interview.* London: Academic Press.

Dublin, T. (1981). *Women at work: The transformation of work and community in Lowell, Massachusetts, 1826-1860.* New York: Columbia University Press.

Finkelhor, D. & Associates. (1986). *A sourcebook on child sexual abuse.* Beverly Hills, CA: Sage.

Gilligan, C. (1982). *In a different voice: Psychological theory and women's development.* Cambridge, MA: Harvard University Press.

Gilligan, C. (1990). Joining the resistance: Psychology, politics, girls and women. *Michigan Quarterly Review, 29* 501-536.

Gilligan, C., Lyons, N. P. & Hanmer, T. J. (1989). *Making connections: The relational worlds of adolescent girls at Emma Willard School.* Troy, NY: Emma Willard School.

Guarino, S. (1985). *Delinquent abuse and family violence: A study of abuse and neglect in the homes of serious juvenile offenders* (14, 020-200-74-2-86-CR). Boston: Excutive Office of Human Services, Dept. of Youth Services.

Hagan, J., & Palloni, A. (1988). Crimes as social events in the life course: Reconceiving a criminological controversy. *Criminology 26*(1), 87-100.

Heidensohn, F. (1985). *Women and crime: The life of the female offender.* New York: New York University Press.

Heilbrun, C. (1989). *Writing a woman's life.* New York: Norton.

Herman, J. (1992). *Trauma and recovery.* New York: Basic Books.

Hirschman, A. O. (1970). *Exit, voice, and loyalty: Responses to decline in firms, organizations, and states.* Cambridge, MA: Harvard University Press.

Hudson, A. (1989). "Troublesome girls:" Towards alternative definitions and policies. In M. Cain (Ed.), *Growing up good: Policing the behaviour of girls in Europe.* London: Sage.

Karlsen, C. F. (1981). *The devil in the shape of a woman: The Witch in seventeenth century New England.* Unpublished doctoral dissertation, Yale University, New Haven, CT.

Konopka, G. (1966). *The adolescent girl in conflict.* Englewood Cliffs, NJ: Prentice Hall.

Koroki, J., & Chesney-Lind, J. (1985). *"Everything just going down the drain:" Interviews with female delinquents in Hawaii.* (Youth Development and Research Center, Report No. 319) Manoa, HI: University of Hawaii.

Miller, J. B. (1976). *Toward a new psychology of women.* Boston: Beacon Press.

Peacock, C. (1981). *Hand-me-down dreams.* New York: Schocken Books.

Platt, A. (1969). *The child savers.* Chicago: University of Chicago Press.

Robinson, R. (1990). *Violations of girlhood: A qualitative study of female delinquents and children in need of services in Massachusetts.* Unpublished doctoral dissertation, Brandeis University, Waltham, MA.

Rothman, D. (1981). *Conscience and convenience: The asylum and its alternatives in progressive America.* Boston: Little, Brown.

Russell, D. E. H. (1984). *Sexual exploitation.* Beverly Hills, CA: Sage.

Shelden, R. G., Horvath, J. A., & Tracy, S. (1989). Do status offenders get worse? Some clarifications on the question of escalation. *Crime and Delinquency 35,*(2), 202-216.

Thomas, W. I. (1923). *The unadjusted girl.* Boston: Little, Brown.

5. Woman Battering as a Marital Act: Interviewing and Analysis in Context

MARGARETA HYDÈN

In the everyday world, individuals commonly ask, "Why does a woman stay with a man who repeatedly beats her?" The question contains an undertone of skepticism about her: Can a woman who lives with a violent man be entirely normal? Strangely enough, the man's motivations are not so carefully scrutinized. Thoughts lead to personalities. In all likelihood, these are people who cannot make reasonable decisions about their lives.

I too have been concerned with the problem of violence against women in marriage, as both a therapist and researcher in Sweden, but my questions concern marriage. How can repeated violence occur in a relationship predicated on trust? How do a husband and wife make sense of their participation in violent episodes? Searching for answers to these questions, I studied a group of 20 couples who had lived together in marriage where the husband repeatedly beat his wife. Over a 2-year period, in individual and joint interviews, I learned about the two parties' characterizations of the situation—their reflections on what happened, their interpretations of the meaning of the events for their marriage. In an effort to render the violent actions sensible, interpreting violence enabled partners to go on with their lives.

Wives and husbands interpreted "what happened" in contrasting ways. In one respect, however, they were the same. Each considered woman battering to be a morally unacceptable act, something a woman within the Swedish context should not expect. Over the past 50 years, Sweden has developed from a society in which sex segregation was characteristic of the social order, to a society where the integration of the sexes within many spheres is an explicit societal goal.

Due to the feminist movement of the last years in Sweden and elsewhere, women's experience of men's violence has turned from an unspeakable reality to a conceptualized social problem. For scholars, three frameworks have guided analysis. The individual psychology perspective focuses on the personality characteristics of the victim (Gayford, 1983; Snell, Rosenwald, & Robey, 1964) or of the perpetrator (Cullberg, 1984; Faulk, 1974; Gondolf, 1985; Hamberger & Hastings, 1986; Schultz, 1960), in contrast to the sociological (Finkelhor, 1988; Straus & Gelles, 1990) and feminist (Dobash & Dobash, 1979; Schechter, 1982; Walker, 1979; Yllö & Bograd, 1988) perspectives. My work is tied by kinship to the feminist view, and studies the kind of violent actions a woman can be submitted to within marriage, that is, violence against a woman at the hands of her husband. The difference between *wife battering* and *woman battering* is important: A wife is unable to understand being beaten outside of the social context in which it occurred, that is, her marriage. A violent act committed within marriage is a marital act. The marriage constitutes the interpretative framework for understanding it.

I studied how husbands and wives made sense of violent action (Hydèn, 1992) and developed a research approach that allowed me insight into the points of view of the women and men I interviewed. (On feminist research approaches, see Haavind, 1987; Kelly, 1988; Yllö & Bograd, 1988.) Gaining access to narrative accounts about moments of violence, including spouses' explanations for them, I learned that people define and interpret, explain and justify, in light of beliefs about what marriage is supposed to be. Couples create what marriage is by doing it. Before turning to the accounts of violence in marriage, I introduce my research approach, particularly the process of gaining access to violent couples, and how I interviewed them.

Gaining Access and Interviewing

Over the course of 1 year, 141 cases of repeated assault or aggravated assault in which a woman was the victim and her husband the perpetrator were reported in one of Greater Stockholm's police districts. From these cases I located a balanced sample of 20 couples who became my informants. There was a range of experience, from minor violence (being pushed, grabbed, or shoved) to severe violence (being hit with fists or beaten up). Of these, 16 male informants had been reported to the police for beating their wives, and the remaining 4 men were similarly known to the social welfare authorities. In all cases, the battering had continued over a long period, from 1 to 17 years. Of the men, 3 had committed minor violence, 11 semiserious violence, and 6 serious violence: 9 had been sentenced for assault and battery. (*Assault* is used here to indicate acts that are typically included under the legal category of assault and battery. There is no separate category in the Swedish Criminal Code for wife battering, which is defined as assault.)

Battered women have often been described as fragile, sometimes as a consequence of the violence (Walker, 1979) or as a contributing factor (Gayford, 1983). In police and social services records, half of my female informants were similarly described. A "fragile woman" was considered to have severe difficulties dealing with her life, manifested in anxiety, depression, or other psychiatric problems. The other half of the women were described as "strong"; in their contacts with the police or social workers they appeared capable, decisive high achievers. Socially, half of the couples belonged to the working class; the other half were senior salaried or self-employed workers and professionals.

I arranged the first meeting with my informants shortly after the latest violent incident known to the police or social authorities. In an initial telephone call to the woman, I introduced myself and my work. My message was very simple: I wanted to talk to her and her husband because they had experiences that would be valuable for others to know; many people found themselves in similar situations. In general, women sympathized with my work, and accepted the invitation to participate.

> I think it's good you're doing this kind of study. Lots more should be written about woman battering. It's horrible when you think about how many women are in the same situation as I am. (Woman, 34, telephone call)

In the telephone conversation with a woman, I asked how to contact her husband. Obtaining the husband's participation was not always easy. Women said their husbands needed to talk to someone, but were scared to do so. I was instructed either to call, write, or both. In general, husbands also sympathized with the purpose of the study once it was presented to them, although they revealed hesitation.

> I don't think there's much to find here. Anyway, you said that you're doing a study about wife battering. There's none of that going on here. (Man, 33, telephone call)

The majority of the individual interviews with the men were conducted by a male colleague. But as the research project leader, the task of introducing the study and obtaining consent to participate was mine. To overcome the men's hesitation, I had to use all my inventiveness and sensitivity.

I remember one case particularly. After the initial interview with the woman, we agreed she would inform her husband soon about me and the research project. Weeks passed without her telling her husband. Finally, she asked me to come to her home to discuss the matter once more. The following summarizes my field notes:

> When I arrived at the house at the agreed time, her husband opened the door. He was large and stocky, dressed in jeans and a sleeveless T-shirt that revealed considerable arm muscles. I perceived him as threatening, which undoubtedly was reflected in my facial expression. I stepped backwards. In the hall behind the man, I could see the woman who was small and delicate, almost completely hidden behind him. "I haven't told him anything yet; I thought it was better if you did it yourself," she said, a remark that caused her husband to look, if possible, even angrier. I felt very small, and no research method assisted me in that moment. The only guidelines for how to react I had learned from my parents, so I held out my hand, said "Good day." The man took my hand; when I felt how sweaty his hand was I understood how afraid he was. I suddenly felt calm. I told him my name, apologized for disturbing them, and suggested that we go into the hallway for a few minutes so that I could make my request. I was allowed in, fully aware how generous this was of him. A Swedish man's home is his castle; it was I who had invaded the privacy of this home, forced my way in.
>
> I introduced myself briefly. He looked skeptically at me. I told him of meeting several men in similar situations "with a police report hanging over their heads," and they had felt relief to have a chance to talk about these things, as strange as that might sound. I said I wanted to listen to his and his wife's experiences, since they had gone through things that affected many people. He looked curious. I thanked him for letting me present my request, and backed out towards the door. He conferred briefly with his wife and asked me to come in. I replied "a half an hour in that case, since I do not want to disturb you for any longer than that." Before the time was over, he had expressed an interest in my research project.

With few exceptions, the initial and joint interviews with the 20 couples took place in the informants' homes; my male colleague interviewing the men, myself interviewing the women, and both of us conducting the couples' interviews. Over a 2-year period, 143 personal interviews were completed, 30 with men and 59 with women separately, and 54 with the couples together (lasting 45 to 60 minutes and 60 to 90 minutes, respectively). Interviews were conducted within a strict time framework. This turned out to be important especially for the joint interviews, where the emotional atmosphere sometimes rose to such a pitch that violence seemed imminent. We never allowed the emotional temperature to rise above a certain level. Consistently, we interrupted a fight by turning to each of the parties individually and trying to get them to discuss the impending violent situation.

Interviewing as a Discourse Between Speakers

During a telephone conversation prior to our first meeting, one of my male informants said,

> Yeah, of course I'll be part of your study. I have been through a lot, truly I have. If you think someone else can be helped by this, then that's good. But I am not at all convinced that you will get anything out of this. The fact is that *I know* nothing about what happened. (Man, 33, telephone interview)

He had much in common with other informants. He has been "through a lot," but he is still unclear about what happened. The events seemed ripped out of context with no internal relationship. He is a living question mark; he is truthful when he says he "knows nothing." His wife too had a very unclear picture of what happened; the events for her were shrouded in fear and unsuccessful attempts to protect herself. Events of this nature are not easy to reconstruct. Even my unfailing sympathy and their desire to tell were insufficient. Something more was required.

If I had to identify a single factor that allowed me to gain access to the couples' narratives of marital violence, I would identify my growing insight that the process of interviewing is a joint enterprise between interviewer and interviewee. (See Bruner, 1990; Mishler, 1986; Riessman, 1990.) I allowed the interviews to be actively shaped and formed by my informants in a joint process with me. Questions and answers become a circular process, how we tried to make continuing sense of what we were talking about. The method of interviewing differed from standard practice, where a question has a predetermined meaning and serves as a stimulus to elicit a response (Mishler, 1986). By transforming the effort to obtain answers to questions into a conversation between informants and myself, I was able to overcome many difficulties.

I was also guided by a theoretical interest in woman battering as a marital act. In marriage, the partners form a joint marital project. Each contributes

to it from the starting point of an individual biography. As spouses interact, they design a unique structure for their venture. The marriage, however, does not consist only of the joint project, but of two individual projects.
The types of projects constantly interact with one another.

In the example below, taken from the initial individual interview with
a 23-year-old wife, my questions and her answers intertwine, gradually
shaping her view of herself and her life project:

> **Interviewer:** If you were very briefly to describe yourself to me, who had never
> met you before, what would you say?
> **Respondent:** Oh . . . I don't know . . . yeah, I am rather shy. So I am rather unsure
> of myself. I am pretty calm, I am. I don't know what more to say.
> **Interviewer:** In what ways are you unsure of yourself?
> **Respondent:** Well, for example, if I am on the subway . . . and someone starts
> looking at me a little too long . . . I get embarrassed and start thinking, "what
> do I do now?"
> **Interviewer:** Aha.
> **Respondent:** I would do anything I could to change that behavior.

In the subsequent interviews, she would often take the initiative, as in
this example from the third individual interview. The pattern of intertwining questions and answers remains:

> **Respondent:** What I think about most of all is the future. Worrying about this
> trial just starting.
> **Interviewer:** What you're afraid of . . . if you could tell me about that?
> **Respondent:** (sighs deeply)That I won't be able to get through it . . .
> **Interviewer:** What does "get through it" mean?
> **Respondent:** That I won't fall completely apart. . . . Everything is turned upside
> down for me right now . . . you know, it's like watching an old movie. I think
> about everything I've been through these past years . . . just the fact that I
> could have trusted him.

Living with a violent husband meant she had removed herself even further
from the aims of her life project.

I asked my informants' about their understanding of themselves ("if
you were briefly to describe yourself"), their partners ("if you were briefly
to describe your wife"), the partners' understanding of them ("if your wife
was asked to briefly describe you, what would she say"), and the marriage
itself ("How did you meet. . . . What made you cast your eyes on her. . . .
How would you describe your marriage today"). I wanted my informants

to share what happened in connection with and during the violent episode ("How did it begin. . . . Then what happened. . . . Is this the way it usually happens"), and finally to tell me about their lives before the marriage.

Narratives of Violence

By asking questions like "how did it begin" and "then what happened," I invited my informants to transform personal experience into a narrative. A prototypic form of talk we acquire as children, narrativization is used throughout life to make sense of what happens and convey personal experience to others (Riessman, 1990). *Temporality* is usually seen as a defining characteristic of narrative; that is, events are told in the order in which they are believed to have unfolded in actual life. A typical narrative contains a beginning, a middle, and an end (Ong, 1982).

Male and female informants form their narratives somewhat differently. Women concentrate mainly on the middle part, the violent incident itself, and the consequences of violence, especially their feelings of powerlessness, fear, being "mentally broken." The men's narratives are not as focused on the violent incident, but emphasize what provoked it. They narrate the argument that preceded the outbreak of violence. Some also include their fears of the legal process and being condemned by others, which could be triggered if wives decide to report what they had done. Without encouraging the men to elaborate in narratives, filling in what had been omitted, they would not in all likelihood have done so.

Informants construct their narratives as dramas in three parts, beginning with a *prehistory* (typically a verbal fight), progressing through the *violent incident*, and ending with the *aftermath*. Husband and wife, batterer and battered, make sense of what had happened in the context of the marital project. I examine the content of the accounts and their form, including missing parts. In other words, I analyze what they told, how they told it, and what they did not say.

The Prehistory

Most of the narratives (18 of 20) include a verbal fight, an argument, or a quarrel as a precursor to the battering. The first turn in the fight was an utterance about a commonplace issue, constructed by one of the spouses as an opposition. There was a difference in understanding about an "antecedent event," and/or an effort to influence the other's behavior:

He drinks too much. Most of our fights start with me getting impatient with his drinking. His daily rhythm is disrupted when he drinks. He can stay up and party all night, sleep all day, and then party again all night. That makes it impossible for me to relax. And he blows a lot of money this way. Our fights are often about money. His defense is often: "This has nothing to do with you. This is my life." That type of answer saddens me every time. (Woman, 39, individual interview)

The second turn in the sequence of the verbal fight indicates disproval of the first speaker, expressed in a way that makes the first utterance provoking. An exchange of pejorative personal descriptions and insults follows. The spouse who is portrayed (and constituted) through these utterances is a restricted person. One spouse "puts down" the other through a communication of worthlessness.

Another example illustrates the typical sequence when one spouse is charged with a bad trait: A wife got severely upset when her husband doubted her intellectual capacity. In the first turn in the exchange, he said, "As dumb in the head as you are, one would think you would be in a special class." In her turn, she pointed out that "there are so many good-looking guys around" and "lots of them are standing in line for me." She thought her most effective comment was "I don't talk to underaged boys." Her utterances challenged her husband's status and pride. He was 10 years her junior and not pleased with his appearance; he felt fat, inexperienced, and immature.

The Violent Incident

The verbal fight triggers battering. Vivid narratives told in the interviews about the violence have many common features. Well-formed stories, as Burke (1969) points out in his work on *dramatism,*

> are composed of a pentad of act, agent, scene, agency, and purpose. Any complete statement about motive will offer some kind of answer to these five questions: What was done (act), when or where it was done (scene), who did it (agent), how he did it (agency), and why (purpose). (p. xv)

Here is an excerpt from a man's longer narrative about his violence:

> It was just "stop it, stop talking shit." Like, I just didn't want to hear any more. I had heard enough. But I never wanted to hurt her. She means too much to me for that. This hitting stuff is just a warning. Otherwise, I could just as well take a pistol and shoot her. I know I am hard-handed. She says

that too. But I'm not hard on purpose. I am also soft. She admits that. But women are different from men. Women are psychologically stronger, they say. I just react: "Now, damn it. You are going to keep quiet. Don't say another fucking word." I don't say "now you are going to get it so you die." It's not like that. (Man, 25, individual interview)

When I attempted to code the fragment using Burke's structural categories, a core story is apparent (different in emphasis than his wife's):

In the living room of their joint home (scene), the husband (agent) hits (agency) his wife in order to stop (purpose) her from talking (act).

I found concordance in basic structure between the narratives of husbands and wives; that is, all constructed stories out of similar elements. There were many dissimilarities, however, in emphasis. He stresses the *purpose* of his action, she stresses *agency,* how he did the battering, and its *consequences.* Woman spoke of being "spiritually broken." Burke's (1969) story elements were combined in contrasting ways because meanings were so different.

The purpose of battering, husbands suggest, is to change the wife—to prevent her from injuring herself or someone else, to get her to act differently. Wives talk about fear, what husbands had done to them, how they tried to escape. Purpose, according to wives, is to harm.

Contrasting Language

In previous research on woman battering, surprisingly little attention is paid to how husbands perceive the violent event as compared to wives. Most of the literature deals with *battering* as if it has a unitary meaning—not the case in my research.

Of the 20 male informants, 13 had been reported to the police and their acts of violence investigated as assaults. In the remaining cases, the local social service bureau similarly defined the actions, yet only 5 men used the word *assault.* Of the others, 14 labeled it a fight, and one man called it harassment. Here is a typical perception:

Assault, that's the real hitting. But to call pushing assault . . . that's ridiculous. But if the police come then, you go to jail anyway. They don't even need any witnesses, it's enough if the woman says that that's what happened. It's really horrible, that just a shove can be called assault. I think that's what most people would say. If someone said, "He beat me," then I think of real hitting, the worst stuff. No, otherwise you should call it quarreling or fighting. People can get mean, and you may have to defend yourself. It is often enough to draw the line, but you may have to strike out. Hell, the way people carry on, do you have to take that? . . . You'd end up like a bloody puppy-dog by the end! But if you continue swinging away, even after the other one has given up—some do just keep going, even kicking. God damn! Now *that* is real assault, and that is bad! Those types ought to be put away! (Man, 23, individual interview)

For him, the seriousness of the violent attack and the degree of reciprocity between victim and attacker describe assault. His rhetoric distances and depersonalizes the agent from his action. He says, "you may have to" and "you continue swinging away," not referring to himself but to people in general.

Among the 14 men who labeled the act "a fight," suggesting reciprocal activity with no clear division between attacker and victim, is the following account:

We have fights, sure. When she starts nagging, and keeps it up, I get real depressed. First comes that screaming, back and forth, then maybe some flowers go flying . . . but I don't consider that assault or battering, there was no hitting with fists or in the face. . . . It was more like this [simulates slaps and shoves]. . . . It was just a reaction . . . you start shoving . . . react like a human being. Maybe sometimes you spit in her face. (Man, 30, individual interview)

Here is his wife's description of these "fights":

The first time he hit me . . . yeah, it was when I was pregnant. But then he hit me carefully, because he was also real afraid of hurting me while I was pregnant. It was mostly what you'd call smacks. Like shoves and slaps. Then, after the boy was born, it got more serious, but he has never kept on hitting me after I was down on the floor, like you read about. So maybe it's not battering after all. . . . But it is battering if you get hit so much that you are completely broken . . . terrified. (Woman, 27, individual interview)

For most women, the violence constitutes an assault. The man was in a clear position of dominance over her. Where dominance was not obvious, where some form of reciprocity of hitting prevailed, a violent act was an assault if the woman was "broken" by the violence. It is the *effect,* more than what he had done, that is decisive in her understanding. The risk of being spiritually or physically "broken" was greater if the violence was serious than if it was minor, yet for women there is no simple correlation. Even minor violence can have disastrous consequences, as in the following description:

> He has a way of screaming, long and hard. He continues for hours on end. I get so frightened because I don't know what he's going to do. If I raise my voice, I just get more of it. So I lower my voice and slip away, but this doesn't help. He usually says that my way of avoiding fights leads to more fights. This scares and demoralizes me as much as when he hits me. He twists my breast, he hits me in the face so that my glasses fly off and then I can't see anything. But the worst is his contempt as he carries on: "You disgust me, you bitch . . . now you are really going to get it." (Woman, 33, individual interview)

In contrast to men, only one woman used the word *fight* to describe the violent act itself.

Of all actions in a marriage, assault is the most difficult to integrate, that is, to maintain a marital relationship with violence as a component (though without accepting it). The attacker exploits his dominant position to place the victim in an even greater position of inferiority, creating fear, pain, and injury. Assaults challenge the love and care normally associated with marriage. To integrate a fight, by contrast, is much easier. Not nearly as morally reprehensible as an assault, the responsibility for a fight is shared. The majority of the wives described an action that was very difficult to integrate into the marriage, whereas husbands defined one that was a feasible element in marital life. *Assault* assigns responsibility to one of the parties, the offender; *fight* suggests joint action.

The Aftermath

In the aftermath of the violent incident, the man and the woman develop an understanding of what happened, separately or jointly. They reach conclusions about the meaning of the violent incident for their marriage and their individual lives. During this phase wives and husbands decide to continue the marriage or to separate.

I obtained accounts of the previous two phases soon after the violent incident. Several of the initial interviews took place when the spouses were apart, because the man had been arrested or had left home to live temporarily with friends or relatives. In some cases the woman and children had obtained temporary placement through the social authorities; they were living at a women's shelter or with relatives. Accounts of the aftermath, by contrast, were recorded after a period of time had lapsed. In some cases the parties were once again living together. Time since the initial interviews ranged from weeks to months.

The nature of the accounts also differed from the previous phases. The prehistory and violent incident were formed around narratives told in retrospect; that is, I asked my informants to tell me what had already happened. In contrast, the analysis of the aftermath is based on narratives developed prospectively. Interviewing continued over a 2-year period to follow the development of informants' thinking—how they made sense of the violent outburst over time. In the aftermath, a great concern with moral responsibility is revealed.

Lyman and Scott (1968) provide a starting point for analyzing the aftermath accounts. When untoward or unanticipated behavior occurs, a gap arises between action and expectation. The agent accounts for his action in such a way that the gap is spanned, developing excuses and justifications. Extending Lyman and Scott's theorizing, I began my analytical work by classifying the accounts with attention to process. I found them to be constructed in three different ways: (a) *jointly,* by the man and woman in cooperation; (b) *individually* constructed by the man; or (c) *individually* constructed by the woman. Informants' accounts tended to follow one of the following patterns:

- Neutralization of the violent act in a jointly constructed account that encompasses hope for a good life.
- Neutralization of the violent act in a jointly constructed account that alters the meaning of the act.
- Rejection of the violent act in an individually constructed account. This involves dissociation from the other or from oneself.

Both kinds of accounts that neutralize the act are jointly constructed by husband and wife. The man generally initiates the enterprise by dissociating himself from his own violent behavior. When the violence was serious, resulting in severe injuries for the woman, it cannot be easily dissociated. Instead, the act is altered so as to neutralize it. This is done in various ways, including changing the perpetrator. For example, alcohol was responsible for the battering, not the husband. One man alleged that it was his mental constitution that was to blame:

You see, in our heads there is a place with two poles. There has to be a certain distance between them. When you get angry, you get close to one of the poles. In my head, the poles are too close together, so that when I get angry, they crash into each other. I can see on you that you don't believe me, but it is in fact true. A doctor himself told me this. I think it was caused by a motorcycle accident I was in. (Man, 45, joint interview)

Neutralizing accounts releases the man from responsibility for his violent actions. Similar to calling it a fight in the prehistory phase, blame can also fall on the other party. When it came to the aftermath phase, almost half of the male informants made an effort to neutralize their violent acts by altering them. In most cases they succeeded in jointly accomplishing these accounts with wives.

A less dramatic way of neutralizing violence is illustrated here:

I don't like to fight. I've had too much fighting in my life. So I try to avoid fighting with Annika. And that just ends up in a fight. I walk around steaming. If I've been drinking, then I can't keep it inside anymore. But then it usually turns out wrong. . . . It's hard for me to sit down and explain things, to say what I want to say. After these fights, I am completely shattered. I don't want us to keep this up. (Man, 33, joint interview)

The violence in this case was less serious than in earlier examples. Directing attention away from the act toward its undesirable consequences, husband and wife could join together and plan for a brighter future. They agreed to leave the "dark clouds" behind them and concentrate their energies on the time ahead.

Accounts that neutralize a violent action help preserve a marriage. Over 2 years, seven of the couples I followed remained together, and most redefined what had happened.

Ten couples separated. Violence in half the marriages never was neutralized. On the contrary, it was strongly rejected:

I was never hit at home, not as much as a slap from my parents. I think that that's why I react so strongly. The way as I was brought up, you could get angry, but not hit. . . . You know, I have sometimes been able to calm him down. Maybe I just didn't want to this time. . . . When we are in the middle of a situation that turns into a fight, and I can't give in because I think I am right, that's when I don't want to calm him down. It would mean giving in, and that would be the same as admitting that I was wrong . . . so, it is not only to avoid losing the fight; it is also for my self-respect. But it means that I am becoming more afraid; I don't know what he is liable to do. Whatever I do, it really shatters me. . . . All this has made me more and more unsure whether I have strength to live with him. (Woman, 26, individual interview)

This woman is becoming oriented to her own life project. She had believed she could stop her husband from hitting her by assuming the subordinate position in an escalating situation. But she also anticipates the undesirable consequences for her individual project as a result of such behavior ("it is not good for my self-respect"). She forcefully rejects the act and gradually dissociated herself from the man. Such an account does not preserve a marriage, and divorce was the typical outcome by the 2-year point.

Three couples established "half-way marriages"; they arranged for an alternative place for husbands to live during times of disturbance.

If there is any usefulness to the expression "a violent marriage," one of the defining features is an interactional pattern that neutralizes violent actions. Wives and husbands construct it together. There is a tragic contradiction: Survival of the marriage is coupled with minimizing the significance of violence, perhaps setting the stage for more wife battering.

Effects of the Research

The approach to interviewing I adopted emphasizes the joint construction of meaning (Mishler, 1986). A narrative is never concluded, it is always subject to reconstruction and reinterpretation. Participation in a study thus implies change.

I witnessed dramatic unfoldings and reinterpretations during the research. I remember asking a female informant during our first interview to describe her husband and herself; she used negative terms for herself but enthusiastic ones for him. Next time I met her, she was furious:

After you left, I almost threw up. Listening to me talk sweetly about him. That really made me sick. The truth is that I am through with him. People can think whatever they want. I don't give a damn. Do you know what happened? He started drinking again. And of course, lots of people come running to his aid: his doctor, his AA mates, his colleagues. I get sick, truly I do. Everybody is siding with him, nobody, and I mean nobody is siding with me and my son. And I, I am just another idiot in his fan-club, praising him. My God! (Woman, 37, initial interview)

Over the course of 2 years, she arranged an extra place for her husband to live; it became a condition for their continued marriage that he move out during times of trouble. A second, no less dramatic, reconstruction involved a man. During a joint interview I, my male colleague, and the man's wife were talking as he gazed out the window silently. Suddenly he turned toward us:

> I may give you the impression of not being interested. That is not the case. On the contrary, I am listening to every word. You see, I also have answers to the questions you are asking my wife. But I have never had the questions before. Now you are giving me the questions. And these questions . . . I have searched for them through my entire life. (Man, 42, joint interview)

Because the events discussed in my interviews were morally unaccept-able, people usually keep them secret. The experience of violence remains a private memory, purged often from the public life-story. The process of interviewing, the interaction between the informants and myself, put words to hidden memories, gave voice to silence, pushed informants to make sense of marital violence.

Acting as an informant for a study of a social problem is a demanding task, especially a morally unacceptable action like violence. Participation demands never-failing sympathy for the research, a great deal of courage, and continuing assistance from the researcher. The assistance I offered was the opportunity to talk, in the context of an interview, about what had happened. I did not expect the impossible, answers to questions about incidents that informants did "not know anything about," but in the process of our conversations, together we tried to make continuing sense of what we were talking about.

Over a 2-year period, half of my informants' marriages ended in divorce, eight at the initiative of the women and two of the men. Most women who took the lead declared at the start of the study that they were contemplating divorce. Men reached the decision during the course of the research. Another three couples continued to live together, but with two addresses so that the husband could withdraw "at times of trouble." Seven couples continued living together.

Conclusion

The lack of clear definitions of violence, abuse, and battering is a recurring issue in past studies (Gelles & Straus, 1988). In my view, it is less productive to define wife abuse operationally than to determine what constitutes the action for participants. I introduce a research approach here that offers insight into the points of view of women and men involved in marital violence. The pattern of male dominance and female subordination, so often described by feminist scholars, was evident in my research too. Men used illegitimate means to maintain their dominant position. However, patterns over time suggest greater complexity. The usual hierarchical order was reversed in the aftermath phase. He was the one who had committed a morally unacceptable act, she had been the object and endured it. He fell to a subordinate position, and her relative influence increased.

Integration of the violent incident always implies the woman's individual life project is pushed to the background in favor of the joint marital project. Marriage is highly valued and she (and others) assign a low priority to her life project. For a battered woman to participate in neutralizing violence, she gradually devalues her own life project. On this point, my female informants displayed similar patterns to battered women in other research studies around the world (Araldsen & Clasen, 1983; Christensen, 1984; Dobash & Dobash, 1979).

Paradoxically, devaluation of one's own life may also add something to it. Because the integration process means that the spouses start working together to neutralize the violent act, they may experience an intense feeling that the marital project is gaining something, togetherness and commonality. For the man, the circumstances are somewhat more complex than for the woman. In one sense, his life project gains something from his violent behavior, namely, the experience of power, total control, and dominance over the woman he lives with. With the integration of the violent act into the marriage, he receives reassurance that his actions do not lead to the collapse of the marriage. On the contrary, they result in greater togetherness. But there is another meaning for the man: his actions are morally questionable, even unacceptable, not only from the standpoint of the marriage, but also from the perspective of his own life project.

Men who batter continue in a state of crisis. Wives are the only ones who can absolve their actions. Wives who stay typically cooperate in redefining the violence to the point where it is unclear who did what. The act is transformed into a disclaimed action. The man is freed from responsibility. No one but the wife can do this for the husband. Other male acquaintances may provide support, but they cannot join with him in a neutralization strategy to preserve the marriage.

Dependence on wives is thus fundamental to men who batter. Her power is to grant absolution, to restore his self-esteem and value. The ultimate evidence is her willingness to continue in the marriage. A devaluation of his life project occurs also. To plead with his wife for cooperation in neutralization, he is compelled to refrain from criticizing her behavior during the prehistory of the violent incident. Regardless of how much he feels she has hurt him, he cannot tell.

These conclusions offer partial answers to the question I posed at the beginning of the chapter: why men and women remain in marriages where violent episodes repeatedly occur.

References

Araldsen, T., & Clasen, A-C. (1983). *Kvinnemisshandling—om insnevring av handlingsalternativer* [Woman battering—A curtailment of spheres of action]. Oslo, Norway: University of Oslo.

Bruner, J. (1990). *Acts of meaning.* Cambridge, MA: Harvard University Press.

Burke, K. (1969). *A grammar of motives.* Los Angeles: University of California Press.

Christensen, E. (1984). *Vold ties ikke ihjel* [Silence does not kill violence]. Copenhagen, Denmark: Akademisk Forlag.

Cullberg, J. (1984). *Dynamisk psykiatri* [Dynamic psychiatry]. Stockholm, Sweden: Natur och Kultur.

Dobash, E., & Dobash, R. (1979). *Violence against wives: A case against patriarchy.* New York: Free Press.

Faulk, M. (1974). Men who assault their wives. *Medical Science and Law, 14,* 180-183.

Finkelhor, D. (Ed.). (1988). *Stopping family violence.* Newbury Park, CA: Sage.

Gayford, J. J. (1983). Battered wives. In R. J. Gelles & M. B. Scott (Eds.), *International perspectives on family violence* (pp. 123-138). Lexington, MA: Lexington Books.

Gelles, R., & Straus, M. (1988). *Intimate violence.* New York: Simon & Schuster.

Gondolf, E. W. (1985). Fighting for control: A clinical assessment of men who batter. *Social Casework, 66,* 48-54.

Haavind, H. (1987). *Liten og stor* [Small and big]. Oslo, Norway: Pax.

Hamberger, L. K., & Hastings, J. K. (1986). Personality correlates of men who abuse their partners: A cross-validation study. *Journal of Family Violence, 1,* 323-343.

Hydén, M. (1992). *Woman battering as marital act: The construction of a violent marriage.* Unpublished doctoral dissertation, Stockholm University, Stockholm, Sweden.

Kelly, L. (1988). *Surviving sexual violence.* Cambridge, UK: Polity Press.

Lyman, S. M., & Scott, M. B. (1968). Accounts. *American Sociological Review, 46,* 46-62.

Mishler, E. G. (1986). *Research interviewing. Context and narrative.* Cambridge, MA: Harvard University Press.

Ong, W. (1982). *Orality and literacy: The technologizing of the world.* New York: Methuen.

Riessman, C. (1990). *Divorce talk: Women and men make sense of personal relationships.* New Brunswick, NJ: Rutgers University Press.

Schechter, S. (1982). *Women and male violence: The visions and struggles of the battered women's movement.* Boston: South End Press.

Schultz, L. (1960). The wife assaulter. *Journal of Social Therapy, 6,* 103-111.

Snell, J. R., Rosenwald, R. & Robey, A. (1964). The wifebeaters wife: A study of family interaction. *Archives of General Psychiatry, 11,* 107-113.

Straus, M., & Gelles, R. (1990). *Physical violence in American families.* New Brunswick, NJ: Transaction.

Walker, L. (1979). *The battered woman.* New York: Harper & Row.

Yllö, K., & Bograd, M. (Ed.). (1988). *Feminist perspectives on wife abuse.* Newbury Park, CA: Sage.

6. Making Sense of Marital Violence: One Woman's Narrative

CATHERINE KOHLER RIESSMAN

All sorrows can be borne if you can put them in a story . . . tell a story about them.

—Isak Dinesen
(quoted in Arendt, 1958)

How does a woman tell about a life of marital violence, rape, and her decision to divorce? How does she make sense of the experience in a marriage in which, instead of being honored and protected, she was devalued and demeaned? What does her way of telling teach us about the emotions and actions of women who are sexually abused and how they make the transition from victim to survivor?

Marital rape is not legally considered a crime in more than half the states in the United States (Margolick, 1984). The cultural and legal ideology of marriage is that sex is consensual. Further, marriage is viewed as the normal and preferred state for adults, so one cannot walk away from it lightly— especially a woman with young children. As for other decisions that go against the social grain and often bring new hardships in their stead, a divorcing woman must make her motives and emotions believable to others through forms of symbolic expression. Her situation also derives its meaning

AUTHOR'S NOTE: This research was jointly conducted with Naomi Gerstel and supported by a fellowship from the National Institutes of Mental Health (5F32MH09206). I thank Susan Bell, Uta Gerhardt, Ann Hartman, Joan Laird, Elliot Mishler, Richard Ochberg, George Rosenwald, and Dennie Wolf for helpful comments. An earlier version of this chapter appeared in *Smith College Studies in Social Work*, 3(1989), 232-251. Reprinted with permission from G. C. Rosenwald & R. L. Ochberg (Eds.). (1992). *Studied Lives*. New Haven: Yale University Press.

from the framework of interpretation by which listeners judge it (Burke, 1935). In other words, legitimating divorce—especially on the grounds of marital rape—must be accomplished in social interaction, through talking and listening.

Through narration the teller can persuade a listener who was not there that a marriage was seriously troubled and that she was justified in leaving it. As Sacks (1970-1972) notes, stories are ways of packaging experiences, and in them the teller can figure as hero. Tellers draw us into the world of the story through particular narrative structures. They build tension by describing the setting, characters, dialogue, and unfolding plot. Imposing a narrative line on the disparate images of our lives is not limited to biographers or novelists; as Joan Didion says in *The White Album,* "we tell ourselves stories in order to live." Narrative allow us to create who we are and to construct definitions of our situations in everyday interactions.

But narratives are not simply Machiavellian devices to persuade listeners (Riessman, 1990b). Creating a narrative about one's life is an imaginative enterprise, too, in which an individual links disruptive events in a biography to heal discontinuities—what should have been with what was. Stories are a kind of cultural envelope into which we pour our experience and signify its importance to others, and the world of the story requires protagonists, inciting conditions, and culminating events. A near universal form for ordering our worlds, narrative allows us to make connections and thus meaning by linking past and present, self and society. Psychoanalytically oriented investigators (Cohler, 1982; Schafer, 1981; Spence, 1982) and scholars in family therapy (Laird, 1989) articulate how narrative retelling heals in the psychotherapeutic process. By storifying a life we bring order to random happenings, make sense by reconstructing and reinterpreting. (For more on narrative theory see Mitchell, 1981; Polkinghorne, 1988; Sarbin, 1986.)

In this chapter I analyze the narrative of a divorcing woman to show how, in the context of an interview with a supportive listener, she reconstructs and reinterprets her husband's sexual abuse of her. Narrative retelling enables her to transform her consciousness: to name the abuse, to interpret it as oppression, to reexperience her anger, and to make the transition from victim to survivor. The narrative also persuades, for it draws the listener into the teller's point of view. She renders the events in her life meaningful by constructing a storied account; she finds a language for her husband's domination and rejects the definition of the situation that he, as well as others in her social world, offers to rationalize the abuse. I argue that the narrative is both an individual and a social product; she goes into memory to reexperience the violence and to try, once again, to make sense of it. At the same time her consciousness is shaped in important ways by a cultural discourse and the interactional context of the interview itself. She interprets her experience in the specific terms that American culture provides in the 1980s, which are taken for granted between teller and listener. Yet there is a contradiction in this background knowledge that is evident in her talk: contemporary feminism has opened up new possibilities for action by women, but there are continuing limitations on the emotions they may legitimately display. Women are not supposed to express rage, even when raped.

There is much that is generalizable in the woman's narrative, It displays many of the features common to battering situations in general. The family is the most frequent single locus for violence of all types in American society, and most of such violence is directed against women, Nonetheless, practitioners who work with women often overlook the battering (Gelles & Straus, 1988; Stark, Flitcraft, & Frazier, 1979; Walker, 1984). To see how one woman challenges prevailing social definitions, I examine her long reply to a question in a research interview about divorce. The narrative preserves her way of organizing the account, displaying her talk as a text to be interpreted. Narrative analysis is particularly well suited to understanding the process of making sense of difficult experiences because it lays bare the interpretive work narrators do in collaboration with listeners (Mishler, 1986). I attend to the linguistic coding of the text and argue that there is a relation between the *way* the story about abuse is told and personal and cultural meanings.

The detailed method of transcription used here may not be familiar to all readers. This representation of speech facilitates an analysis of the relationship between narrative form, meaning, and social context. To see how a narrator actually constructs her account—the linguistic choices she makes, the structural function of specific clauses, the role of the listener— "cleaned up" speech is not sufficient. The transcripts must be as complete as possible and thus include both lexical and nonlexical utterances (the actual words and other sounds, like "uh-huh") and pauses in the interview interaction (long pauses of more than 3 seconds are noted as P and shorter ones as p). The lines are numbered for easy reference. The narrator's utterances are indicated by N, and the interviewer's by I. There are alternative forms of transcription (Mishler, 1986). This one type preserves features relevant to theory.

A Case Analysis

Tessa is a 23-year-old white woman who has been living apart from her husband for 2½ years. She looks much older than she is. It was her decision to separate; he "was completely against it," she says. Though she lives in a dilapidated housing project, her apartment is clean and colorful. Her son from her marriage, a preschooler, lives with her, and an older child from a previous relationship is in foster care. Tessa has held a variety of unskilled jobs, mostly in the fast-food industry; is on welfare; and has just begun to attend a community college part-time. She has always loved music, and her ambition is to be a music teacher some day.

Here is the full text of the first of three episodes of Tessa's narrative account of why she divorced.

Transcript 1

01 I: Would you state in your own words what were the main causes of your separation, as you see it?
02 N: (P) um the biggest thing in my mind was the fact that I had been raped three times by him (I: mm-hmm)
03 but at that time it didn't, it wasn't *legal* in a probate court (I: mm-hmm)
04 you you couldn't get a divorce on those grounds
05 but that was my biggest (p) (I: uh-huh) complaint (I: uh-huh)
06 total disrespect for me (I: uh-huh) (P) (I: mm-hmm)
07 I: Can you tell me a little bit more about that? I know it's hard to talk about
08 N: (laugh/shudder) Well, um (p) when it was time to go to bed it was really rough cause (p)
09 it was like we had to go together (p) (I: uh-huh)
10 and (p) if I wanted to go to bed while he was watching TV
11 he'd say "No, stay up with me" (I: uh-huh), you know
12 and um sometimes I just wanted to stay up
13 but he would insist that I go in with him (I: mm-hmm)
14 so it was like we had to do it together (p) (I: uh-huh)
15 um when I, you know, when I finally *was* in bed I'd just roll over and I just wanted to go to sleep
16 I mean scrubbing the floor every day is kinda rough, you know, you're pretty tired (laugh) (I: uh-huh)
17 I guess I'm a little sarcastic about it (I: uh-huh)
18 I: Uh-huh, I know what you mean
19 N: He'd just grab my shoulder and roll me over
20 and I knew what he was I knew what it was what it was doing
21 I said, "I just don't want it tonight," you know,

22 "don't you understand, I just don't want anything tonight"
23 "No, you're my wife and in the Bible it says you've got to do this" (I: uh-huh)
24 and ah, I'd say. "I just I just don't want it," you know. (I: uh-huh)
25 And after debating for fifteen or twenty minutes
26 I'm not getting any less tired
27 I'd grab a pillow
28 I'd I'd say, "I'm going to sleep on the couch, you're not going to leave me alone"
29 I'd get the pillow and a blanket (I: uh-huh)
30 and I went and laid on the couch.
31 Two minutes later he was up out of bed
32 (P) and one particular time he had bought me a dozen roses that day (I: mm-hmm)
33 and they were sitting on top of the television which was at the foot of the couch (p)
34 and he, he picked up the vase of roses
35 threw the roses at me
36 poured the water on me (I: mm-hmm)
37 and dragged me by the arm from the couch (I: mm-hmm)
38 to the bedroom
39 and then proceeded to (P)
40 to make love to me. (I: uh-huh) (p)
41 And uh (P) I didn't know what to do (I: mm-hmm)
42 I tried to push him off me
43 and I tried to roll away (I: uh-huh)
44 ah I tried to cross (laugh) my legs (laugh)
45 and it didn't (p) work. (I: uh-huh)
46 He's six foot seven (p) and I'm five eight. (p)
47 And uh (P) I just had I just closed off my head (I: mm-hmm)
48 all I could do was shut off my brain (p)
49 and uh (p) I got very hostile, I— (p)
50 there was no outlet for those feelings. (p)
51 You know that even my neighbors as far as they were concerned
52 you know, they *they* figured that, you know, when people are married
53 that they love each other
54 I think, was the assumption.
55 That wasn't so,

The reason she gives for divorcing is rape; as she puts it, her husband by his actions showed "total disrespect" for her. Yet the point she wishes to make is that she escaped her husband's domination and brutality.

Tessa's account makes explicit the difficulties of leaving a marriage because of sexual abuse ("you couldn't get a divorce on those grounds").

Her recourse to protection from the courts was limited by the law's casual treatment of rape (Estrich, 1988). Until quite recently, in the state in which she resides a husband could not be prosecuted for forcing sexual intercourse upon his wife as long as they lived together. Far from a rare event, sexual abuse of women in marriage remains a closet crime in large part because women are considered the sexual property of their husbands (Gordon & Riger, 1989; Russell, 1982). Yet because of legal reform Tessa is able to name the form of her oppression as rape; sexual abuse is a legally defined reason for divorce in the state in which she filed. Thus an evolving legal discourse shapes her personal discourse and legitimates her experience of sexual abuse.

How does Tessa construct her compelling account and draw the listener into her point of view? If we look at the structure of the narrative, we see that it is saturated with pattern and reveals a woman who is now in control. In the first six lines Tessa gives a plot summary, or abstract, for the three episodes she will subsequently relate (on the structural parts of a story, see Labov, 1982). Here, she also sets forth the key contrast that organizes the narrative—the tension between two realities. At this point, the specific contrast is between her current reality (she was raped) and the reality of prevailing legal doctrine (marital rape isn't a crime). Using verbal emphasis ("it wasn't *legal* in a probate court"), she draws attention to these contrasting points of view. From Tessa's perspective, which the listener is invited to share, she was a victim of both her husband's sexual violence and the legal system. Her opening also introduces the main characters of the drama about to unfold: Tessa, her husband, and, importantly, the social others (in this instance, the legal system) whose definitions of reality Tessa will ultimately overturn. The way she introduces the narrative conveys its overall message—she triumphed over others' definitions of her situation. The narrative she wants to tell is how she made the transition from victim to survivor, how she is now in charge of her life.

Although Tessa controls the flow of talk in her opening statement, the woman listener-interviewer is by no means passive. The narrative is frequently punctuated by her nonlexical utterances ("mm-hmm" "uh-huh"), which signal interest and invite the narrator to say more. Also notice how the listener responds to Tessa's long pause at the end of the abstract. Rather than using this as an opportunity to back off from the highly charged subject of marital rape, she waits and, after a pause, conveys through a question that she expects to hear more. ("Can you tell me a little bit more about that? I know it's hard to talk about.") Without this affiliative comment, Tessa might have stopped after her summary statement. Instead, she goes on to tell a long narrative in which she constructs meaningful totalities out of scattered events (Ricoeur, 1981).

Tessa's account is consistent with the five-stage process of victimization that Trudy Mills describes (1985), though not in sequential order. She analyzes victimization as a gradual process with five stages: (a) women usually enter the relationship at a time when they are feeling particularly vulnerable and are searching for intimacy; (b) women attempt to manage the violence by attaching meanings to it and developing strategies to cope with it (such as placating violent husbands and/or constructing justifications for maintaining the relationship); (c) women experience a loss of self as they withdraw from social interaction in shame—their various social identities are diminished and they lose the observing self; (d) at some point women who leave reevaluate the violent relationship (often a specific event triggers this, jarring the previous definition of the situation); and (e) in time, women restructure the self. An important manifestation of the final step is taking on the identity of a survivor rather than seeing oneself as a victim.

Tessa invites the listener into the narrative world on lines 8-14 by orienting her to time, place, and situation. Substantively, she tells about the general case of the bedtime ritual: her husband's rule was that they go together and he would not allow her to go earlier or to stay up alone. Tessa attempts to manage the sexual violence by placating her husband, acquiescing to his demands—the second stage Mills (1985) describes. Structurally, Tessa communicates the routine and repeated interaction through the habitual narrative genre, indicated here by the conditional past tense ("if I wanted," and "he would insist"). In the habitual narrative genre, events are not unique to a particular moment in time but instead stand for classes of events that happen over and over again. They tell of the general course of events over time rather than what happened at a specific moment in the past (Riessman, 1990a). Tessa continues in the habitual mode by describing in lines 15-31 the usual sequence of events once they were in bed.

Tessa moves in and out of the voices of the characters in the narrative she is building:

20 and I knew what he was I knew what it was what it was doing
21 I said, "I just don't want it tonight," you know,
22 "don't you understand, I just don't want anything tonight"
23 "No, you're my wife and in the Bible it says you've got to do this" (I: uh-huh)
24 and ah, I'd say, "I just don't want it," you know. (I: uh-huh)

Strategically, by embedding a dramatization within a narrative, Tessa draws the listener in and by reenacting the typical argument over sex, mobilizes support for her point of view. She communicates in a vivid way the verbal struggle that preceded the physical struggle—her attempts to resist her husband's unwanted sexual advances with repeated strong statements about her wishes. In line 20 "he" becomes "it"—she merges the man with the act.

In lines 15-31 Tessa also reintroduces the organizing theme—the contrast between two realities. Her juxtaposition of his and her voices achieves this in a powerful way. But the conflict between two realities goes beyond their private conversation, which she suggests here by invoking the Bible. The patriarchal church, as well as the state, colludes with her husband to deny her rights.

Several important interactions take place between the two women, teller and listener, in this section. Tessa makes repeated use of the phrase "you know"—affiliative appeals suggesting that the listener should understand the implications (and thus the truth) of Tessa's reality. Perhaps Tessa is also appealing to the listener's experience with men and marriage, thereby creating an intersubjective world of meaning between them. There is some evidence that she is successful, judging by the interviewer's nonlexical expressions. Even more, the narrator steps out of the role of storyteller in the midst of a highly dramatic episode (which one might think of as uninterruptable) and, as a woman, makes an active alliance with the woman interviewer. The interviewer responds in kind:

15 um when I, you know, when I finally *was* in bed I'd just roll over and I
    just wanted to go to sleep
16 I mean scrubbing the floor every day is kinda rough, you know, you're
    pretty tired (laugh) (I: uh-huh)
17 I guess I'm a little sarcastic about it (I: uh-huh)
18 I: Uh-huh, I know what you mean

Tessa's statements strike a responsive cord in the interviewer; "I know what you mean" suggests a solidarity between the women is developing. They share the understanding that women are vulnerable, do housework that is often grueling, repetitive, and boring, and have to deal with sexually demanding men. (For more on women interviewing women see Riessman, 1987.)

Out of this growing affiliation, perhaps, Tessa goes deeper into memory:

32   (p) and one particular time he had bought me a dozen roses that day (I: mm-hmm)

33   and they were sitting on top of the television which was at the foot of the couch (p)

Tessa moves from recapitulating the general situation of coercive sex in her marriage to a particular and dramatic instance of it—rape. As the content shifts, so must the form of the narrative. Tessa changes genres from a habitual narrative to a story, the first of several she will ultimately tell. (In contrast to habitual narratives, which encode a general state of affairs, "a story can best and most simply be thought of as a specific past-time narrative that makes a point," often a moral one [Polanyi, 1985, p. 189]). She uses the story form in this episode to create a unique past-time world and by reenacting sequential events, tells of a significant change in that world.

She makes the transition to the story in line 32; it emerges in an almost seamless way from the habitual narrative that preceded it. A short pause signals the shift. (Tessa's speech is fluent, and pauses carry meaning. They had been largely absent from the previous twenty lines of text.) She begins the story by providing the listener with the necessary information needed to follow it. Because the roses will figure prominently in the rape, Tessa introduces these props and their exact placement in the living room, just as a skilled novelist might make the reader aware of a particular physical object that will be used in a later scene.

But the roses are more than a prop. They have symbolic meaning, as do the television set and the couch—Tessa's refuge from her husband's sexual demands. The mention of flowers also introduces an ambiguity into the text. Tessa does not explain why her husband "bought her a dozen roses that day," but such gifts are often a way in American society for men to demonstrate romantic love or ask for forgiveness. Because Tessa's husband has a working-class job, the purchase of a dozen roses may have caused financial strain. In other words, there is a gap in Tessa's story, though the value of the gift is suggested by her displaying the roses on the living room television—the centerpiece of the modern American home. Whatever may have "really" happened, Tessa's juxtaposition of the roses and the rape in the narrative makes *her* interpretation evident. The linguistic choice emphasizes the clash between two realities—romantic love in marriage and Tessa's actual experience, as she has come to define it.

The narrator brings the roses and the rape together in the climax of this first story, told in a series of short, terse clauses in the simple past tense:

34   and he, he picked up the vase of roses
35   threw the roses at me
36   poured the water on me (I: mm hmm)
37   and dragged me by the arm from the couch (I: mm hmm)
38   to the bedroom
39   and then proceeded to (p)
40   to make love to me. (I: uh huh) (p)

The story is poignant and effective not only because of its content but also because of its expression, and by its contrast to the earlier (habitual) form of the narrative. There is every evidence that the interviewer gets caught up in the story, judging by the frequency and placement of her nonlexical utterances.

But this episode is more than the factual reporting of events. Tessa distinguishes key events in the story in several ways. When describing the rape (lines 39–40), she uses a loaded phrase ("make love") rich in tenderness, positive connotation, and cultural meaning to describe what she earlier referred to as "rape." As with the roses, there is an ambiguity and a paradox here. Tessa pauses to punctuate and thus mark the significance of these lines. She pauses even longer at two other critical points in the story:

41   and uh (P) 1 didn't know what to do (I: mm-hum)
47   And uh (P) I just had I just closed off my head (I: mm-hum)

Because pauses are not characteristic of her speech, they draw attention. Structurally, they recreate in the listener the state of feeling of the story-world and, in this case perhaps, the futility the narrator experienced in trying to protect herself from her husband's sexual advances. Consistent with the victimization process Mills describes (1985), there is a loss of self. Tessa "closed off" her head and "shut off" her brain—the observing ego in the language of psychoanalysis.

Battered women rarely experience their anger directly. As Elaine Hilberman (1984, p. 225) observes, there is "a constant struggle with the self to contain it and control aggressive impulses." Yet Tessa says in line 49 that she "got very hostile," a statement that, like earlier ones, is ambiguous and invites multiple readings. It may refer to her resistance to the sexual abuse—that she fought back; yet the previous lines suggest otherwise. The line can also be read as a more generalized statement about her emotions—both at the time and as she has reinterpreted them. The abstract, clinical language ("hostile") is noteworthy and suggests control, not rage.

Structurally, the clause also signals a shift in genres; Tessa is gradually moving out of this particular story and into a "way of the world" moral telling. She justifies her lack of effectiveness in resisting the rape in line 46 through reference to men's physical size and associated strength and women's consequent vulnerability to abuse. Feminists have argued that a woman is likely to be sexually victimized not only because she is physically weaker than her opponent but also because she is socially less powerful (Bart & O'Brien, 1985; Gordon & Riger, 1989). Tessa develops her account in the context of these contemporary understandings. She also draws on another aspect of contemporary American culture when she explains both her passivity and her "hostility" by drawing on an explanatory scheme widely available in our psychologically oriented society—strong feelings require expression. ("There was no outlet for those feelings.")

By communicating her moral attitude, Tessa solves the teller's problem (Riessman, 1990a). She convinces the listener (as well as herself, perhaps) that she is a good person, that she behaved correctly, and that she did the best that could be expected under the circumstances.

Tessa concludes the first episode by returning to the theme of two realities. This time she invokes her neighbors' views:

51 You know that even my neighbors as far as they were concerned
52 you know, they *they* figured that, you know, when people are married
53 that they love each other
54 I think, was the assumption.
55 That wasn't so.

The neighbors, like the legal and religious systems earlier, stand for definitions of the situation that differ from Tessa's own. Through these contrasts between public ideology and private experience, she further defends her reality over that of her husband and others. She also says explicitly that she didn't love her husband, a theme to which she later returns.

Structurally, lines 51-55 function to bridge the first episode—about her husband's physical domination—and a second and closely related episode —about her economic inequality. The episodes are linked by the common theme of powerlessness. Tessa continues:

Transcript 2

56 N: I, you know, I married my husband because I wanted to escape
57 but I didn't know that then, I couldn't—

58 I: Escape from what?
59 N: Poverty
60 I had, you know, my first apartment when he proposed to me
61 was two rooms, flea-ridden (p) (I: uh-huh)
62 and (p) it had a leaky roof (p) (I: mm-hmm)
63 it was just *awful*
64 and I I sort of expected higher, you know, better things. (I: mm-hmm)
65 It improved a little bit but (p) there was still very little money and uh (p)
66 he was gone for a couple of weeks at one point
67 with nothing, and there was no food in the house
68 and he couldn't get any money to me cause he was out on a camping thing
    with the army (p)
69 and uh (p) his friends (p) went and got some food for us
70 from the kitchens of the (p) the mess halls, I guess
71 and they brought my son and I a whole great big box of food.
72 You know, it wasn't the best, there wasn't any fresh (I: mm-hmm) vege-
    tables or fruit
73 but it was meat and cake and stuff like that
74 so we ate. (p)
75 But I was totally uh dependent (I: uh-huh) and powerless at the same time
    (I: uh-huh)
76 I was just like I was when I was raped. (I: uh-huh) (p)
77 And those things, you know, those things happen.
78 As far as I'm concerned, I was raped I was raped from the first day (p) (I:
    mm-hmm)
79 but I didn't feel so hostile about it at that point. (p) (I: mm-hmm)
80 I just felt like it was something that you had to go through because you
    were married.

The second episode, which comes immediately after the first, is tightly
structured and, also like the first, begins with a plot summary: Tessa says
she married to escape (lines 56-57). Because of the interviewer's interruption ("Escape from what?"), Tessa elaborates. As in the first episode,
she orients the listener to time, place, and social circumstances—the
flea-ridden apartment with a leaky roof that was all she could afford before
she married. Going back in time and shifting scenes, Tessa seeks to explain
her divorce to her listener by explaining why she married in the first place.
In this flashback she again sets up a contrast: her reason for marriage as
she understands it now, compared with what she thought then. She says
she married her husband to escape her poverty, not because she loved him.
(Listeners may begin to feel some empathy for Tessa's husband at this

point and reinterpret her earlier story about the roses. Was he trying to woo her, to persuade her to love him?)

The content of the second episode is consistent with Mills's (1985) analysis of the first stage of victimization. Tessa entered into the relationship at a time when she was feeling particularly vulnerable. Like other women before and since, Tessa's susceptibility to poverty was, in large part, a consequence of her gender. She had the sole responsibility for care of a child, an inadequate welfare allowance, and limited job possibilities. As a member of American culture, however, she "expected better, you know, higher things." Her solution, consistent with the American dream for white women, was to find a man; she thought the traditional conjugal family would improve her circumstances. Although marriage hardly proved to be a protective haven for her or her child, it did help their economic situation. Yet, she says, "there was still very little money."

In this episode too, Tessa moves into the story form, on line 66, providing an illustration to persuade the listener how difficult things were. She tells of a sequence of events: Her husband could not provide for her financially and his friends did, getting food from army mess halls. Although the story lacks the linguistic elaboration of the first story about the rape, and hence the associated tension and drama, it nevertheless makes its point. If we have any doubt about the causal link that ties the two episodes together, Tessa states it explicitly:

75   But I was totally uh dependent (I: uh-huh) and powerless at the same time (I: uh-huh)
76   I was just like I was when I was raped. (I: uh-huh) (p)
77   And those things, you know, those things happen.
78   As far as I'm concerned, I was raped I was raped from the first day (p) (I: mm-hmm)
79   but I didn't feel so hostile about it at that point. (p) (I: mm-hmm)
80   I just felt like it was something that you had to go through because you were married.

In these lines, Tessa tells the listener directly how to interpret the two stories and, more generally, her episodic narrative. She creates her own private image to give meaning to her past: The metaphor of rape epitomizes her total domination—financial, psychological, and physical. She moves away from the specific events with interpretive meanings, contrasts how she felt about them then and how she feels about them now. Through metaphor, Tessa makes a moral point: Marriage based on women's subordination is not the way marriage ought to be. In creating a narrative to explain her particular separation, she has produced a discourse about inequality in marriage in general.

But there may be another meaning here. In addition to linking powerlessness and rape metaphorically (to refer to women's structural subordination in the institution of marriage), Tessa may be referring more specifically to her experience of sex: "It was something you had to go through because you were married." Again, the ambiguous meaning may lead some listeners to their own interpretations of the roses, and even the rape. Tessa also reintroduces the topic of her anger here, again choosing clinical language that distances ("I didn't feel so hostile about it at that point").

Tessa has not yet mentioned precisely when she left her husband. The listener, sensing a missing piece, pauses and asks about it. ("And then what made the difference so that you wanted to get out of that relationship?") Tessa responds by developing a third narrative episode:

Transcript 3

81 I: (p) And then what made the difference so that you wanted to get out of that relationship?
82 N: (p) Oh, when I found myself, when I realized that I was throwing myself at him be—
83 out of hostility (p) rather than out of self-defense (I: uh-huh)
84 it was a little bit of both.
85 But I was so angry at one point when he was moving his things out (p)
86 he had promised, he had told me
87 as an example, he *told* me he'd give me the TV, okay.
88 At the last minute he decided he wanted it. (p) (I: mm-hmm)
89 And I was so *mad* (p)
90 I threw myself at him
91 I went to punch him (I: mm-hmm)
92 and I passed out (I: mm-hmm)
93 I was so mad. (I: mm-hmm)
94 (laugh/shudder) It's, my God, there's nothing like it
95 I don't ever want to feel that again, never (p) (I: mm-hmm)
96 I'd sooner scream at somebody and (p) and pound
97 I've punched my fists into walls
98 I punched in the front door in that apartment on Main Street (I: uh-huh)
99 and unlocked it.
100 He put my son out on the front porch at one point and I was
101 it made me so violently angry

102   that I I literally punched in the front door
103   and it was just about as thick as the front door here. (I: uh-huh)
104   (p) And uh (p) I, you know, after that incident
105   I lived in Rocky Falls with my mother (I: uh-huh) and my father, my
        stepfather, for three weeks (p)
106   and I tried to get a restraining order
107   and the and the person at the courthouse said it's not worth it. (p)
108   But he did tell me that what I *could* do is go back to him, to my husband
109   and say "if you're not out of here I'll have the police after you." (I:
        mm-hmm) (p)
110   So I did that
111   and he left reluctantly (I: uh-huh) (p)
112   but he did leave. (I: uh-huh)

The third episode returns to the topic of violence, but this time it is hers,
not his. She has hinted at the theme several times earlier. She says that
she went beyond "self defense" and began "throwing" herself at him "out
of hostility."

In this episode, Tessa moves into the story form to recount a specific
instance (lines 85-95) but, unlike her controlled way of telling in the previous
episodes, here her control slips. The emotions of the last days of her marriage
break through as she reenacts the events in the story. She intimates that
the trigger event—the fourth stage in Mills's model—was her own rage,
and she no longer uses clinical language to refer to it ("I was so angry at one
point"). Although the precipitant for her anger is seemingly minor (certainly when compared to the sexual abuse in the earlier story), her husband's
change of mind about the television provokes a violent response, which
she describes in a series of staccato clauses that contrast with the measured
way she told earlier of the rape:

89   And I was so *mad* (p)
90   I threw myself at him
91   I went to punch him (I: mm-hmm)
92   and I passed out (I: mm-hmm)
93   I was so mad. (I: mm-hmm)

Her rage (which perhaps includes her pent-up rage about the rapes) disturbs
her, even in the retelling. She makes her current disturbance clear in the
series of affect-laden evaluative clauses that follow. Unlike her discourse
earlier, here there is a cluster of rhetorical devices, including verbal emphasis,
an explicative, and expressive speech (a shudder).

94   (laugh/shudder) It's, my God, there's nothing like it
95   I don't *ever* want to feel that way again, never (p) (I: mm-hmm)

This moment is the peak of the action in the narrative. We learn later in a series of story fragments that this dynamic—his actions provoking rage and physical violence in her—had occurred through the marriage (lines 97-103). But there is a difference: Previously she had punched walls and doors. This time she went to punch her husband.

Hilberman's (1984) observations of 60 clinical cases of abused wives are relevant here: "The violent encounter with another person's loss of control of aggression precipitates great anxiety about one's own controls. . . . In the life experiences of battered women, there is little perceived or real difference between affect, fantasy, and action. Thus is it not surprising that fear of loss of control was a universal concern [in her sample]. These fears were often expressed in vague, abstract terms but were unmistakably linked to aggression" (p. 225). Social conventions do not allow women to express their rage easily. Tessa does vent hers, and this is the turning point in the narrative. She leaves her husband and goes to her parents for protection (and the court, again unsuccessfully). Tessa can no longer contain her *own* aggression, so she moves out. She has begun to take on the identity of survivor rather than victim—the change that is the final stage in Mills's analysis.

Conclusion

Through her narrative, with its three distinct but related episodes, Tessa has provided a coherent interpretation of the connections between rape and violence, her feelings of powerlessness and ultimately uncontrolled rage, and her decision to separate from her husband. Her point is that she surmounted powerlessness and victimization. Ironically, she took control by losing control and broke out of a violent relationship when she could no longer contain her own violence. She became a survivor and filed for divorce, even though her husband "was completely against it."

Tessa realizes these themes through language and story. She organizes the narrative she tells around her definition of the situation, set against the contrary definitions of others—her husband, the state, the church, her neighbors. She gives shape to her experience and makes it meaningful by talking about power and subordination. She tells a series of linked stories (Bell, 1988) in three episodes that focus on highly memorable intolerable moments set against a backdrop of how intolerable her marriage was in general. The rape story is quintessential, a dramatic incident that illustrates her overall theme of powerlessness. Through narration Tessa not only reconstructs the temporal sequence of the events that led to separation but invests these events with meaning and morality. She constructs a reality and a surviving self that are sealed inside the narrative—a reality that is accomplished as much by the way she structures the account as by what she says.

Why are the episodes of the narrative told in such different ways? Although both the rape episode and the punching episode about the television set use story structure and build to a climax and resolution, there are subtle contrasts between them. The rape story is tightly assembled, told by a controlled narrator who is describing events that, most likely, she has narrated often. From a present vantage point of mastery and freedom from abuse, she tells of a time when she was physically overpowered. The punching episode about the television set, in contrast, presents another dimension of the same protagonist—a "mad" woman who is not in charge nearly to the same extent, either of the narrative or the emotions it relates. Just as her rage toward her husband erupted through the constraints of marriage, so does her recounting the rage disrupt the form of narrative. Terror at the idea of losing control of murderous impulses momentarily breaks the story apart. We sense that though Tessa may have reinterpreted and resolved some of the events, the associated emotions have not been put to rest nearly to the same degree.

But cultural meanings influence the extent to which each can be "privately" resolved. The first episode is about rape—a trauma that has undergone a marked social redefinition because of the contemporary women's movement. The culture is increasingly providing women with a language for talking about and reinterpreting sexual abuse. The punching episode about the television set, by contrast, lacks a normative context. Being "mad" and physically attacking a husband challenge social definitions of women's proper role in marriage. Society provides for women's depressed emotions but not for their rage. Thus, as an individual, Tessa must make sense of emotions and actions that are deviant for her gender. Her difficulty with this cultural problem is revealed in the way she tells the third narrative episode.

Tessa's text is also a cultural product in other ways, situated historically, with assumptions and formulations that could not have been made in another age or by women in many parts of the world today. At numerous points a specifically American cultural discourse shapes her reconstruction of self.

For example, she can be sarcastic about who does housework, she can leave an abusive marriage, and most obviously she can articulate the form of abuse as marital rape. Going beyond a formalist analysis of the text, I suggest that a narrative cannot be fully interpreted without investigating the condition of the person in the society that produces the text (Lennox, 1989). The narrative is contextual in this additional sense because it speaks to the aspects of a survivor's identity with which gender is intimately intertwined, namely race and class. Tessa's narrative does not reflect some essentialist view of women in general (Spelman, 1988) but speaks of the unique experiences of a white, working-class woman who came to define her marital experience as rape. The narrative also was told to a white, middle-class feminist interviewer who "heard" the account in a particular way and shaped the narrative by her questions and nonlexical responses, just as it was told in a cultural context where feminism and personal psychology provided legitimating vocabularies of motive (Mills, 1940). The narrative implies how extensively some psychological concepts and assumptions about women's rights have fed back into popular thought in the United States (Linde, 1986). Tessa's "private" story is embedded in a social discourse in which it is taken for granted that strong feeling requires expression and marital rape should be a crime.

In my analysis of Tessa's narrative, I stayed close to the text as she constructed it and suggested some aspects of the assumptive world that was contained in it and the structural ways she accomplished her communicative aims. To emphasize the performance aspect of language is not to undermine the "truth" of what Tessa said. Although all texts may be interactionally produced, coauthored by listener and teller (Bell, 1985; Paget, 1983), the marital experiences Tessa's text relates certainly are not. Whatever "actually" transpired in the marriage, we must assume that Tessa's selection represents a reality, An interpretive approach need not entail what Paul Ricoeur (1981) calls a hermeneutics of suspicion—a skepticism toward the given, a "distrust of the symbol as a dissimulation of the real" (Thompson in Ricoeur, 1981 p. 6). Yet, at certain points, I noted ambiguities and paradoxes in the text, intimating that there may be a more complex reality than the narrative itself could encompass. Of course, narratives are always edited versions of reality, not impartial descriptions of it, are presentations of the world, not copies of it (Schafer, 1981). Edward Said's (1979) views about issues of representation have bearing for all narrative accounts:

The real issue is whether indeed there can be a true representation of anything, or whether any and all representations, because they are representations, are embedded first in the language and then in the culture, institutions, and political ambience of the representor. If the later alternative is the correct one (and I believe it is), then we must be prepared to accept the fact that a representation is *eo ipso* implicated, intertwined, embedded, interwoven with a great many other things besides the "truth," which is itself a representation (pp. 272-273)

In a word, we don't know all that happened in Tessa's marriage; all we have is her embedded representation of it in the narrative, just as in therapy the client and clinician only have access to narrative truth, not historical truth (Spence, 1982).

Through talking and listening, a woman has rendered the sorrows in a life heroic and meaningful. Her decision to divorce signifies a transformation in this life. This teller has attempted to heal wounds that only narrative can bind.

References

Bart, P. B., & O'Brien, P. H. (1985). *Stopping rape*. Elmsford, MA: Pergamon.

Bell, S. E. (1985, August). *Narratives of health and illness: DES daughters tell stories*. Paper presented at annual meeting of sociologists for Women in Society, Washington, DC.

Bell, S. E. (1988). Becoming a political woman: The reconstruction and interpretation of experience through stories. In A. D. Todd & S. Fisher (Eds.), *Gender and discourse: The power of talk* (pp. 97-123). Norwood, NJ: Ablex.

Burke, K. (1935). Motives. In J. B. Gusfield (Ed.), *Permanence and change*. New York: New Republic.

Cohler, B. (1982). Personal narrative and the life course. In P. B. Baltes & O. G. Brim (Eds.), *Life-span development and behavior* (vol. 4, pp. 205-241). New York: Academic Press.

Dinesen, I., quoted in Arendt, H. (1958). *The human condition* (p. 175). Chicago: University of Chicago Press.

Estrich, S. (1988). *Real rape*. Cambridge, MA: Harvard University Press.

Gelles, R. J., & Straus, M. A. (1988). *Intimate violence*. New York: Simon & Schuster.

Gordon, M. T., & Riger, S. (1989). *The female fear*. New York: Free Press.

Hilberman, E. (1984). Overview: The "wife-beater's wife" reconsidered. In P. P. Rieker & E. H. Carmen (Eds.), *The gender gap in psychotherapy: Social realities and psychological processes* (pp. 213-236). New York: Plenum.

Labov, W. (1982). Speech actions and reactions in personal narrative. In D. Tannen (Ed.), *Analyzing discourse: Text and talk* (pp. 219-247). Washington, DC: Georgetown University Press.

Laird, J. (1989). Women and stories: Restorying women's self-constructions. In M. McGoldrick, F. Walsh, & C. Anderson (Eds.), *Women in families* (pp. 427-450). New York: W. W. Norton.

Lennox, S. (1989). Feminist scholarship and germanistik. *German Quarterly, 62,* 158-170.

Linde, C. (1986). Private stories in public discourse: Narrative analysis in the social sciences. *Poetics, 15,* 183-202.

Margolick, D. (1984, Dec. 21). Top court in New York rules men can be charged with rapes of wives. *The New York Times,* p. 1.

Mills, C. W. (1940). Situated actions and vocabularies of motive. *American Sociological Review, 5,* 904-913.

Mills, T. (1985). The assault on the self: Stages of coping with battering husbands. *Qualitative Sociology, 8,* 103-123.

Mishler, E. G. (1986). *Research interviewing: Context and narrative.* Cambridge, MA: Harvard University Press.

Mitchell, W. J. T. (Ed.). (1981). *On narrative.* Chicago: University of Chicago Press.

Paget, M. A. (1983). Experience and knowledge. *Human Studies, 6,* 67-90.

Polanyi, L. (1985). Conversational storytelling. In T. A. Van Dijk (Ed.), *Handbook of discourse analysis: Discourse and dialogue* (vol. 3, pp. 183-201). London: Academic Press.

Polkinghorne, D. E. (1988). *Narrative knowing and the human sciences.* Albany: State University of New York Press.

Ricoeur, P. (1981). *Hermeneutics and the human sciences.* J. B. Thompson (Ed. and Trans.). New York: Cambridge University Press.

Riessman, C.K. (1987). When gender is not enough: Women interviewing women. *Gender & Society, 1,* 172-207.

Riessman, C. K. (1990a). *Divorce talk: Women and men make sense of personal relationships.* New Brunswick, NJ: Rutgers University Press.

Riessman, C. K. (1990b). Strategic uses of narrative in the presentation of self and illness: A research note. *Social Science and Medicine, 30,* 1195-1200.

Russell, D. (1986). *The secret trauma.* New York: Basic Books.

Russell, D. E. H. (1982). *Rape in marriage.* New York: Macmillan.

Sacks, H. (1970-1972). Unpublished lectures. As quoted in D. Bogen & M. Lynch. (1989). Taking account of the hostile native: Plausible deniability and the production of conventional history in the Iran-Contra hearings. *Social Problems, 36,* 201.

Said, E. W. (1979). *Orientalism.* New York: Vintage.

Sarbin, T. R. (Ed.). (1986). *Narrative psychology: The storied nature of human conduct.* New York: Praeger.

Schafer, R. (1981). Narration in the psychoanalytic dialogue. In W. J. T. Mitchell (Ed.), *On narrative* (pp. 25-49). Chicago: University of Chicago Press.

Spelman, E. V. (1988). *Inessential woman: Problems of exclusion in feminist thought.* Boston: Beacon Press.

Spence, D. P. (1982). *Narrative truth and historical truth: Meaning and interpretation in psychoanalysis.* New York: W. W. Norton.

Stark, E., Flitcraft, A., & Frazier, W. (1979). Medicine and patriarchal violence: The social construction of a private event. *International Journal of Health Services, 9,* 461-493.

Walker, L. E. (1984). *The battered woman syndrome.* New York: Springer Verlag.

PART III

Subjectivity Matters:
The Positioned Investigator

The chapters in this last section do not rely on a single qualitative method but combine them, often in unusual and creative ways. The contributors describe ethnographic interviewing, participant observation, analysis of documents, and even literary narratives. Each author reflects on the process of doing qualitative work, including the problems. Each brings her subjectivity to bear.

Subjectivity has been a dirty word in social research modeled on the physical sciences (but see Keller, 1983; Polanyi, 1958), a source of bias to be controlled in the interest of producing objective, reliable, and valid knowledge. The Doctrine of Immaculate Perception, as Van Mannen calls it (1988, p. 73), is still a rhetorical device. But the old Enlightenment position—the experiencing self is clearly separable from the experienced world—is gradually shifting to a view of subjective experience as part of the world (Polkinghorne, 1988). There is reality outside the self, of course, but "the self organizes it and makes it meaningful" (Stivers, 1993, p. 410). Contemporary feminists in particular are modeling how subjectivity, both informants' and investigators', can enter methodological discussion in social research (see Ellis & Flaherty, 1992; Hollway, 1989; Personal Narratives Group, 1989; Reinharz, 1992).

Even before the recent feminist critique, courageous women social scientists stepped outside the mainstream to explicitly discuss experience as a component in the development of scholarly knowledge (Golde, 1970). For example, Myerhoff (1978), doing fieldwork at a Jewish community center, discovered what it means to be a Jew, for informants and herself. A former social worker with elderly citizens in the same neighborhood she studied later as an anthropologist, she writes of "imaginative identification" (p. 19) and emotion as sources of knowledge. I quote from her work at some length here because it defies summation:

In the beginning phases of my work with the elderly I too suffered severe pangs of guilt. It took many forms and floated about, settling on different issues at different times. At first it focused on questions concerning my competence in the task I was embarking upon. Did I know enough Judaica? Did I know enough Yiddish? Was I too young? Was I too emotionally involved? Should I be working for the old people's welfare instead of studying them? . . . Resolving the question of my right to do the work did not free me from the inner and outer taunts. Many of the Center people continued to "make" me feel guilty. After greeting me warmly, Basha would often ask, "Never mind these other things you all the time ask about. Tell me, who's with your children?" (pp. 25-26)

An involved observer, Myerhoff entered into a relationship with the people she studied and drew on conflictual encounters to enlarge understanding of old people in cultural context.

My presence was a continual reminder of many painful facts: that it should have been their own children there listening to their stories; that I had combined family and a career, opportunities that the women had longed for and never been allowed. And, too, that I knew so little of their background suggested to them that they had failed to transmit to future generations any but fragments of their cherished past. I felt guilty about invading their privacy, for however much I explained my publication intentions, I knew our conversations sometimes crossed the invisible line from informed disclosure to inadvertent confidence. Diffuse and even irrational guilt plagued me until I had to laugh at myself. I had become a tasteless ethnic joke, paralyzed by Jewish guilt: about my relative youth and strength, about having a future where they did not, about my ability to come and go as I chose while they had to await my visits and my convenience, when I relished food that I knew they could not digest, when I slept soundly through the night warmed by my husband's body, knowing the old people were sleeping alone in cold rooms. (In some African tribes, all the elderly are loaned a child for warmth and companionship at night.) (p. 27)

Challenging conventions in anthropology in the 1970s, Myerhoff questioned how much of herself, her words, and her reactions to include in her representation of their lives. Her solution anticipated later developments in social science writing (Behar, 1993; Van Maanen, 1988): The voice and role of the writer is often explicitly present in collecting and rendering data.

> I wanted to focus on the Center, not myself, but it became clear that what was being written was from my eyes, with my personality, biases, history, and sensibility, and it seemed dishonest to exclude that, thereby giving an impression of greater objectivity and authority than I believed in. (p. 30)

A year after *Number Our Days* was published, Reinharz (1979/1991) provided a language for Myerhoff's conflicts, and support for her resolution: experiential analysis and use of the self as an instrument of knowledge. More recently Collins (1991), an African American sociologist, articulates standpoint as a source of insight. Marginality—"the outsider within" —stimulates a distinct angle of vision. Feminist approaches in general encourage investigators to include the self as context in research; the interplay, for example, between our categories of belonging—class, race, religion, gender, age—and those of the people studied.

We are not robots who collect pure information (Gould, 1981), but humans with emotions, values, social biographies, and institutional locations. They shape the problems we choose, the ways we go about studying them, the eyes we bring to observation, and the relationships we have in the field. Locating ourselves in the work, instead of pretending we're not there, helps readers evaluate the situated knowledge we produce.

The message that subjectivity matters is not news to social work practitioners. But reflexivity—reflection about our interpretive practices— strengthens research, as it does clinical work (Scott, 1989). According to post-positivism, it is fruitless to search for unbiased knowledge, free of the researcher's constitutive assumptions. The "new objectivity," according to feminist philosopher-of-science Harding asks the investigator to explicitly declare interests and assumptions (cited in Stivers, 1993, p. 417). Accounts of how research is actually done, including the complex emotions that accompany it (like Myerhoff's, quoted earlier), provide "a corrective to the idealization inherent in methodological instruction" (Reinharz, 1979/ 1991, p. 23). Reflexive accounts are also essential for beginning investigators. Research rarely resembles the orderly presentations in textbooks and journal articles: selection of problem, formulation of hypotheses, analysis of data. Students learn too from investigations that don't go according to plan, where a method is abandoned in favor of one better suited to context.

The contributors to this section bring us backstage, though to varying degrees. They challenge the storybook image of how research is done and the positivist convention that personal reflection does not belong in scientific writing. These are narratives by investigators about the process of doing social work research. It is significant that three of the four contributors write about their doctoral dissertations, transforming what is, for many, an alienating experience.

Rhoda Hurst Rojiani examines the subjective meaning of a social policy. In a meditative first-person account, she contrasts professional discourse about long-term care (seemingly value neutral, objective, and rational) with its meanings for a frail, elderly woman who values personalized, informal caregiving. The multiple realities in a single case come into view. Rojiani locates herself in the research and her position is unusual: she's the woman's home-health social worker, and the ethnographer. She struggles within these roles to enter the life world of her informant, to meet her on her own terms and gain understanding of her point of view. Methods aid the process—participant observation, unstructured interviews (with the client and others in her network of care), examination of medical records—but the investigator's self-awareness and reflexivity are critical components too. They allow her to identify two perspectives on long-term care that speak different languages, have different cultures, values and standpoints. Rojiani argues that professionals construct services and policies on the basis of one perspective only, and marginalize the life-world of care recipients. The subjectivities of the research participants provide important substantive insights about long-term care.

Cate Solomon's chapter describes what happens when welfare workers and homeless applicants interact about benefits. Using participant observation and informant interviewing in a welfare office, she identifies particular hassles, extra burdens workers create for homeless clients. She locates the sources of the behavior in institutions; practice would improve, her findings suggest, if workers' impossible jobs did. Regarding methods, Solomon offers a candid description of how hard it is to do systematic data collection in a busy welfare office. The best-laid plans for sociological interviewing were foiled by the exigencies of the setting, the pressures on clients' and workers' lives. Although a minor voice in the chapter, Solomon monitors her responses and, for example, comes to understand welfare workers' dehumanizing practices from her experience in the center and interactions with clients. Reflection on the experiencing self can become an indicator (Reinharz, 1979/1991).

Cheryl Hyde's tale does not take a conventional form. She writes explicitly about the intersection of personal biography and her research on feminist organizations and the New Right. A community activist, she studied the impact of a decade of conservatism and antifeminism on nine organizations—NOW chapters, health clinics, antiviolence centers—by examining their documents and interviewing past and current members. Here she reflects on the process of doing the research, including relationships with informants (oversimplified as "rapport" in methods textbooks). Feminist commitments both serve the study and create difficulties; she must work to counter her biases and negative responses to certain organizations and participants. More honest than most, Hyde acknowledges doubts, fears, dead ends, how her graduate methods training did not prepare her for the exigencies of the field. Uncertainty, confusion, and tedium are extremely common in quantitative *and* qualitative research, but few acknowledge them in print. Like the messy kitchen that produces the elegant meal, we keep our stumblings invisible, and reconstruct actual experience to create tidy reports. Hyde's personal tale exposes the complex emotions of field work, and some of its ethical dilemmas. She grapples with the goal of "giving voice" to women—a metaphor often used by feminist researchers that Hyde initially embraces but ultimately rejects. She says, instead, that we juggle voices: ours, informants', audiences', and voices from past scholarship.

Suzanne E. England also tells a story—about a study of stories of caregiving. Her "data" are novels, plays, and autobiographies about the experience of living with and caring for someone with Alzheimer's disease. The research goal was to generate concepts and questions from accounts (unfettered by the expectations of service providers and policymakers), but guided by the theory of moral reasoning developed by Carol Gilligan and her group. Like other studies presented here, the research didn't go according to plan. Serendipity and collaboration changed the study. (England designed the project with a humanist and coding was done by a narrative study group.) Achieving consensus about the meaning of a text proved nearly impossible and, based on the experience, England meditates about an alternative vision of research—interpretive and hermeneutic. The reader (coder) is part of the text, she suggests; we cannot step outside ourselves. She warns against decontextualizing and reducing the complexity of a set of responses in the interest of achieving reliability and validity, as traditionally conceived. (For additional ways to think about these topics, see Mishler, 1990; Riessman, 1993.)

England calls, as she ends, for healing the schism between social work practitioners and researchers: "We could begin by returning the human voice to our research, welcoming pluralism in experience, method, and interpretation." I can think of no better statement to close a book on diversity and research methods.

References

Behar, R. (1993). *Translated woman: Crossing the border with Esperanza's story.* Boston: Beacon Press.

Collins, P. H. (1991). *Black feminist thought: Knowledge, consciousness, and the politics of empowerment.* Boston: Routledge & Kegan Paul.

Ellis, C., & Flaherty, M. G. (Eds.). (1992). *Investigating subjectivity: Research on lived experience.* Newbury Park, CA: Sage.

Golde, P. (Ed.). (1970). *Women in the field: Anthropological experiences.* Chicago: Aldine.

Gould, S. (1981). *The mismeasure of man.* New York: Norton.

Hollway, W. (1989). *Subjectivity and method in psychology: Gender, meaning and science.* London: Sage.

Keller, E. F. (1983). *A feeling for the organism: The life and work of Barbara McClintock.* New York: Freeman.

Mishler, E. G. (1990). Validation in inquiry-guided research: The role of exemplars in narrative studies. *Harvard Educational Review, 60*(4), 415-442.

Myerhoff, B. (1978). *Number our days.* New York: Simon & Schuster.

Personal Narratives Group (Eds.). (1989). *Interpreting women's lives: Feminist theory and personal narratives.* Indianapolis: Indiana University Press.

Polanyi, M. (1958). *Personal knowledge: Towards a postcritical philosophy.* Chicago: University of Chicago Press.

Polkinghorne, D. E. (1988). *Narrative knowing and the human sciences.* Albany: SUNY Press.

Reinharz, S. (1979/1991). *On becoming a social scientist.* New Brunswick, NJ: Transaction.

Reinharz, S. (1992). *Feminist methods in social research.* New York: Oxford University Press.

Riessman, C. K. (1993). *Narrative analysis.* Newbury Park, CA: Sage.

Scott, D. (1989). Meaning construction and social work practice. *Social Service Review, 63*(1), 39-51.

Stivers, C. (1993). Reflections on the role of personal narrative in social science. *Signs: Journal of Women in Culture and Society, 18*(2), 408-425.

Van Maanen, J. (1988). *Tales of the field: On writing ethnography.* Chicago: University of Chicago Press.

7. Disparities in the Social Construction of Long-Term Care

RHODA HURST ROJIANI

Long-term care is more a process than a set of services and depends to a larger degree than traditional health care services on notions of community, networks of reciprocal obligations, and competing and changing values among generations.

—Mechanic (1989, p. 253)

The need for long-term care has been well-documented (Howard, 1991), yet need alone does not result in policy. Current fiscal austerity is one factor in delaying the expansion of public and private involvement. Another clue to the stalemate in long-term-care policy development may lie in the subjective meaning it has for people who comprise the long-term-care system (Hennessy & Hennessy, 1990; McAuley, Travis, & Safewright, 1990; Mechanic, 1989).

This chapter compares differences between a client's and professional's perspectives of the long-term-care system. Over an 8-month period I used an ethnographic approach to self-consciously and reflexively examine the development of my relationship as a home-health social worker with a patient, Miss K, who received community based long-term care, services, and planning. Following her routine discharge from a home-health agency, I enlisted Miss K's cooperation in serving as a primary informant for an ethnographic study.

AUTHOR'S NOTE: An earlier version of this chapter was presented at the Annual Meeting of the Gerontological Society of America, November 18-22, 1992.

Here I examine how each of us managed dyadic role transitions—social worker/patient and ethnographer/informant. Not only did the two formal professional roles I occupied affect the quality and content of our rapport and discourse, they also markedly contrast with the informal relationship Miss K clearly prefers and tried to initiate with me. (The "Miss" has not been changed to "Ms." because her never-married status is a central component of Miss K's identity. She "despises" being addressed as either "Mrs." or "Ms.")

The dynamics of the relationship between Miss K and myself, our efforts at constructing her long-term care, occurred in a broader ecological context. Sudden fluctuations in Miss K's health could make care decisions a crisis one day, a receding memory the next week. Social and economic factors restricted how each of us could legitimately perform our roles. Miss K could not afford to retain a part-time private duty aide, for example, which would have enabled her to remain at home safely, and no publicly funded aides were available. Medicare reimbursement structures limited my involvement as her social worker to a maximum of three home visits within a 3-month period.

Social Construction of Long-Term Care

In "providing" long-term-care planning to Miss K, the largest obstacle was that it (like most social services) is not a discrete and measurable service that can be uniformly "dispensed." Long-term-care planning has to be *constructed*, invented and defined, by the people involved. Long-term care is *situated*: it is specific to the context, to the cultural values and beliefs of the particular person in need. In some families, long-term-care planning may occur incrementally over many years. In others, a decision is reached quickly, without assistance. Many factors influence decisions, such as participants' problem-solving styles, history of their social bonds, financial and familial resources, and competing demands on caregivers' time.

Long-term-care planning is most effective if client, family members, and concerned others are full participants in the planning process. The professional, (whether social worker or researcher) must take the time to communicate what long-term care is, in a language and context that enables clients to freely elect, reject, or defer specific choices. People's unique needs, fears, beliefs, and resources can only be ascertained by spending time with them. Allowing information to be revealed, as trust and familiarity increase, means taking time to learn personal history. Social workers have long known this. Only recently have researchers begun to recognize the importance of subjective meanings and context in understanding caregiving (Gubrium & Sankar, 1990).

The long-term-care system can be conceptualized as including an informal support network made up of family members, friends, and neighbors, as well as a formal support network of professional or semiskilled persons who are paid for the services they render (Soldo, Agree, & Wolf, 1989). Although such categories as informal and formal imply a clear dichotomy of services, Gubrium's term *mosaic of care* (1991) is a more apt description of long-term care in the "real world" where formal and informal roles often overlap (Wolfsen, Barker, & Mitteness, 1990). In the "real world" of long-term care, most participants—professional service providers, frail elders, and their caregivers—generally recognize that long-term-care services, particularly those that are community based, are often fragmented (Fortinsky, 1991). Formal long-term care, provided by paid providers, is only a small portion of the care received by dependent elderly. The bulk of care is provided by family members.

The Research Process

I began the research wanting to understand how people construct, understand, and give meaning to long-term care. I modified my goal upon that learning elderly clients often avoid the whole subject. Here I ask instead: What does long-term care mean to Miss K? Does meaning change over time, as she moves in and out of acute and long-term care? What is the significance, to Miss K, of informal care? Does it contrast with the meaning of the formal sector of long-term care in her life?

As I became increasingly aware of incongruencies between my view of the topic and others' views, several additional questions emerged: What does long-term care mean to me, as a professional, a friend of a recipient, a researcher? How does my stake in it differ from Miss K's? To the extent that there is an incongruity of personal meaning between provider and receiver, does it impede the use and delivery of services?

The questions require a qualitative approach (Marshall & Rossman, 1989). I utilized ethnographic methods of participant observation and unstructured in-depth interviews with Miss K and her collaterals: her case manager at New River Valley Area Agency on Aging, her home-health occupational therapist, and her nurse. In the role of her home-health social worker, I consulted her minister; a temporary, 24-hour, paid caregiver; the staff at an assisted-living home; one of her former neighbors; and the boy-friend of one of the many college students who have "adopted" (or have been adopted by) Miss K. I also examined her medical records regarding her state of health and medical history.

In between my two formal roles (home-health social worker and eth-nographer), I occupied an informal one—a concerned community member and potential friend to Miss K. The formal role of caregiver should not be construed as more important than informal caregiving in Miss K's life. Miss K received most of her assistance and had her most meaningful ties in informal, personal relationships, even though she was an only child who had never married and had virtually no kin. My professional standpoint vis-à-vis Miss K is emphasized simply because this is my primary vantage point. The formal relationship I (and other professionals) assumed was inadequate in comparison to the personal ones that Miss K longed for, and into which she tried to entreat me.

In addition to contact with the informal and formal members of Miss K's immediate social network, I participated in several meetings of local- and state-level, long-term-care providers and professionals. I read widely across the long-term-care literature (consumer information, journal articles, and congressional reports). Although a macrolevel analysis of long-term care lies outside the scope of this chapter, the broader discourses provide a foil for Miss K's personal struggle with her long-term care. Collecting data from a multitude of diverse "points" increases confidence in the interpretation of findings (Hammersley & Atkinson, 1991).

Informant Selection

Miss K was not invited to participate in the study because she is repre-sentative of typical elderly women her age. Quite the contrary, she is my chief informant because of her unusual qualities—assertiveness, a pro-pensity for reminiscence, and physical and mental stamina. She is unlike other home-health patients, even others in her cohort, because she never married and never bore children. She was an only child and does not have siblings, nieces, nephews, or even known first cousins. Miss K is a member of two growing minorities, both underrepresented in the literature: (a) never-married women (Allen, 1989) and (b) frail elderly without family caregivers (Barresi & Hunt, 1990). The lack of family caregivers simplified my access and analysis. (Family members would likely not share her perspective about long-term care.)

Miss K's newcomer status to long-term care complemented my own. Instead of viewing our neophyte status as a handicap, I exploited it. The primary goal of ethnography is to use contrast in expectations, reactions, and encounters and to process them reflexively to gain deeper under-standings of process (Hammersley & Atkinson, 1991; Strauss & Corbin, 1990).

Place

In the course of my visits, Miss K gave me a personal tour of her home and its furnishings. She showed me photographs of, and described changes in, the four-block radius surrounding her house (Magilvy, Congdon, Nelson, & Craig, 1992).

Place and location are central organizing components of Miss K's identity. Each piece of furniture, each possession, has a rich history behind it. Although Miss K reliably changed the subject whenever her own need for long-term care was implied, the stories behind her possessions are rich in detail about the aunts and acquaintances who lived at her parents' one-bedroom home, who had been cared for there until death. Miss K herself had left college and the dream of a concert career to return home and be a full-time caregiver to her mother. Her piano still occupies a large portion of her tiny living room. Arthritis has long prevented her from playing it. It stands as a mute reminder of a thwarted dream.

Discourse

In her reminiscence, prompted by artifacts, it was not difficult to decipher Miss K's experience with personalized, informal caregiving, consistently set in a context of naturally occurring, personal relationships. Her expe-rience is distinctly different from the rational, objective model of long-term care that dominates the language of research and practice. If I had used a questionnaire or structured interview or had insisted on using the bureaucratic language of long-term care I would never have captured Miss K's views: She would have simply been coerced into translating her experience into the prevailing research paradigm—giving me what she thought I wanted (Briggs, 1990).

For this reason, the last time I used the term *long-term care* was in the consent form. I knew she did not like the term, because she consistently changed the topic whenever it occurred. Miss K told me she did not like thinking about relying on others for basic needs, especially when she had little discretionary income.

At least twice, this normally cheerful woman, who had an active network of dozens of friends, expressed great pain at the prospect of requesting help: "I just wish people would *know* what I want and need. I can't ask for anything."

She talked about friends who had died or were themselves too frail to be called upon:

> I guess no living soul understands me. Sometimes I feel so . . . I call them "spurts" and I just have to catch myself and *stop* thinking about it. There are some things I do not let myself think about.

Not letting herself think about certain things, especially things she had little control over, is an effective coping skill Miss K consciously uses. I believe it was adaptive with respect to planning long-term care as well. The thought of leaving home seems to be the most painful possibility in Miss K's future. She comfortably alluded to death, though she does not feel ready to die. She cannot bear to contemplate alternative living arrangements, even though she has made tentative and brief inquiries into assisted living.

It was essential that I encourage Miss K to talk in the form and language familiar to her. She sat on the porch in her rocking chair, sharing who she was through her stories, assessing my character through my willingness to listen and my resolve to meet her on her own terms. It also meant that the interview questions Miss K previewed (at her request) were intended to deal more with separation-individuation, coping and problem-solving, and life experiences with the giving and receiving of care, than with the long-term-care system in particular. Most of the questions, as well as much other information, were covered in two interviews, which lasted a total of 5 hours. The interviews were not structured. Instead, Miss K simply used the questions as a reference point, as prompts.

If Miss K dealt with long-term care by changing the subject, professionals (particularly bureaucrats, policy analysts, and politicians) speak of it as measurable, uniform, a single known quantity. Unlike Miss K, they see it as value neutral, something "out there" and objectified. Two male lobbyists I spoke with in the state capital used terms like the long-term-care *industry* as their reference point. For them, the chief "customers" are the legislators who make decisions that in turn affect their respective organizations' earnings and costs. Informants employed by state-level agencies speak in terms of cost-cutting and the presumed interests of taxpayers and politicians. Only the women lobbyists and program administrators, all of whom had worked directly with the elderly and their caregivers, used language that reflected the difficulties inherent in providing a personalized fit to unique conditions. The first approach assumes that the services provided, regardless of their structure, will meet the need. The second recognizes the complexity of fit between institutional structures and human needs.

Data Analysis

In conversation with Miss K and collaterals, I only jotted down cursory notes, with more extensive field notes written as soon as possible. This was usually within 24 hours. Field memos were also written and consisted of my reactions and comments on the observations I had recorded in field notes, as well as some preliminary analysis and hypothesis development. I paid someone to transcribe the 2½ hours of videotape and about 3½ hours of audiotape interviews, and I listened back to these several times to ensure accuracy of transcription and to make corrections. I then read through the transcripts many times and began to note themes, particularly in the stories that Miss K returned to many times. Many themes, such as Miss K's repeated regrets over two lost career opportunities, did not seem to directly relate to long-term care, and so have been excluded from discussion here.

I did not follow any rigid coding scheme, in part because the data were not so prolific as to require it, but also because I wanted to avoid decontextualizing Miss K's words. The themes that emerged from the data came as much from my field notes and memos as from the transcripts.

Analysis was conducted as an ongoing, iterative process with field observations and the writing of field memos. This was facilitated by weekly discussions with Dr. Jan Nespor, an ethnographer at Virginia Polytechnic Institute and State University, and four other doctoral students working on separate ethnographic studies.

Identity, Power, and Standpoint

Identity

Only after observation and analysis were under way did I recognize the saliency of identity management as an organizing feature of behavior. Identity is a multidimensional sense of self, including both self-concept and self-esteem (George, 1990). A person's identity both develops and is constructed through self-talk and stories (McAdams, 1988). Identities are shared and socially created over time through relationships such as between parent and child (Atkinson, 1989), and in the case of this study, between professional and client. *Identity management* is a term I have appropriated from the literature on persons with stigmatized identities (Hubbard, 1992). I use it here to apply more generally to how all persons selectively (whether consciously or not) alter their behavior, in an effort to maximize benefits and minimize costs in a given social interaction (Blumstein, 1991).

Professionals and clients seek to manage their respective identities within the relationship, to minimize shame and maximize opportunities for affirmation. Shame, affirmation, and self-concept are clearly influenced by cultural values, institutional norms, and roles. Within the long-term-care system, the professional occupies a position of higher status, authority, and power relative to the long-term-care recipient. Power differences and the standpoints they produce contribute to the contrasting meanings professionals and users assign to long-term care.

Different Standpoints

For Miss K, and perhaps for other care recipients, the need for long-term care represents a painful reminder of the loss of health, autonomy, and life-style. To the extent that long-term care implies a change in residence and a parting with possessions, it also threatened Miss K's identity and sense of self. Her home is not only the most cogent representation of her personal past, it also connects her to the only family she has, memories of parents and grandparents. Her family had lived in the house for over 150 years. I suspect that many people, particularly highly educated professionals, are unaware of the strength of the bond that develops with a place that has been part of a person's history for so long.

The professional service provider or planner, by contrast, conceptualizes long-term care typically in value-neutral, even positive, terms. Though professionals ideally receive some training about clients' perspectives, the clients do not have an equal voice in the design or evaluation of long-term care (Hennessy & Hennessy, 1990). Professionals (a direct-care provider, planner, policymaker, or researcher) are likely to define long-term care as an array of services and products that is provided to alleviate distress and assist those in need. Well-designed and implemented care justifies the professional's competence and effort. For the provider, long-term care is, to some degree, active and instrumental. For the recipient, it is just the opposite—a reminder of the loss of instrumentality.

Different Power

Neither the client-provider relationship nor the informant-ethnographer relationship are likely to be (or long remain) complementary or egalitarian. In interactions between client and provider, these relationships reciprocally shape the participants' identities. Health professionals' actions affect the client's identity and subsequent behavior, and the client similarly influences the professional.

Health-care professionals are taught values such as objectivity and client self-determination, yet professional identity constitutes a strong component of the sense of self. By virtue of the time, effort, and expense they have invested, professionals are emotionally committed to their professional identities, no less so than the long-term-care patient is invested in maintaining her preferred identity (e.g., dependent or independent old lady). Clients or patients who spurn professionals' offerings of programs and services are often labeled "resistant," "noncompliant," and "incompetent" (Fineman, 1991), not for objective reasons but because the patient's behavior fails to validate the professional, thus threatening the professional's identity and sense of worth.

Society vests professionals with varying degrees of authority to define and label specific people and situations. Researchers (or funding sources) determine what questions are asked (Kimmel & Moody, 1990). The social worker has more latitude than the client in defining the problem and accessing the resources. Professional authority is enhanced (at least implicitly) by the agencies with which professionals associate. Individuals, particularly in the client population, are unlikely to enjoy a similar level of power unless they too have retained organizational connections or are particularly wealthy (Fay, 1987; Rose, 1987).

Power and Standpoint for Miss K

At the outset of the study, I did not think of power differences in the everyday world compared to the professionally constructed world. I assumed my worldview was much the same as Miss K's. But when I committed myself to listening and watching, imposing myself as little as possible, I began to realize that she and I were not one unit. As tactful and grateful to me as she was, there were vast differences in perspective between us.

As I moved through the roles of social worker, friend, and researcher, I gradually became aware that each of these offered a different view of

Miss K and her world. Each role foreclosed other views. She and I altered ourselves in attempting to adapt to these changes. Our changing relationship became a primary source of knowledge for the study.

In retrospect, Miss K grew more guarded as I moved from friend and social worker to the role of ethnographer. When I first visited her as a home-health social worker, for example, she seemed to be trying to place me as a friend. She voluntarily handed me her carefully kept financial records when I inquired about her income. She stated she normally did not let anyone see them but she felt very trusting of me. Yet several months later, after what I believe was a very successful relationship as social worker and client, Miss K refused to sign the written consent form for the study, even though she agreed to give a taped oral consent.

Perhaps it was simply difficult for her to understand all the explanations—how she was being "protected" from harm when she hadn't anticipated any harm. Other researchers are reporting that it is difficult to get older respondents to sign written consent forms (Gibson & Aitkenhead, 1983; Strain & Chappell, 1982). But I think her hesitancy to give written consent to the research was because she knew my agenda was becoming distinct from hers.

As I rose to go at the conclusion of our last "official" meeting in my role as ethnographer, after I had listened to countless fascinating stories that I thought were totally unrelated to our supposed topic of long-term care, Miss K initiated a comment on the topic for the first time. In a wistful voice she said "The 'Aging people' have helped me so much . . . more than anybody else and I do appreciate it. But I sometimes think they want to help me more than I want to be helped." She smiled and gave a sad chuckle. I asked, "Who are the 'Aging people'?" "You . . . and the other lady," she said (referring to her case manager from the Area Agency on Aging).

Miss K went on to say that at times she felt we had wanted her to move out of her home and that *we could never understand how she felt*. She did not sound angry, just resigned. She said she wanted to stay in her home until she had no choice. Surprised by her candor, taken aback by her conception of me as "other" (i.e., one of the "Aging people") I realized her choice was *not* to choose. In holding on no matter what, in deciding to ignore her infirmities as long as possible, she was not simply resisting choice, she had already made her choice. Ironically, from her perspective it was me who had "resisted" her choice.

I was hurt and discomfited by the confirmation of what I only suspected: She had known, long before I, how different we were, what different goals we had. Instead of me waiting patiently to bring her around to the decisions facing her, perhaps she had been waiting tactfully to bring me around to her way of thinking.

No matter how much I as a social worker emphasize the client's right to self-determination, how much I think of myself as an advocate and an empowerer, my professional presence in the life of a client indicates that some funding source of society deems her needy and inadequate in some way. The same dilemma occurs in other professional roles (e.g., gerontological researcher and planner).

There was a stark contrast between the last official visit and the end of our first visit. At the first meeting, I was in my social work role but Miss K was trying to entreat me to be her friend, a role more compatible with her experience. She squeezed my hand for a long time and told me that she felt she could trust me, I was like a long-lost friend. I told her I felt a deep bond with her too, but I warned her that both Medicare reimbursement schedules and the demands of my graduate education and family deeply limited the time I could spend with friends or clients. Clearly though, from the many comments Miss K made about people to whom she felt close, it was in the informal and personal realm that she found the most meaning in relationships. She had grown up at a time and place when there were no professional or agency workers:

> If you needed help, you just stuck your head out the window and called to your neighbor to come give you a hand. None of us were kin but we were like one big family in that way.

Another time, Miss K expressed disgust with the mayor for not seeing that her home was repaired after a town truck crashed into it. She was disdainful of his "by the book" explanation of why the town was exempt from responsibility. She told him times sure had changed if he would use such excuses to get out of doing what he knew was "right." To Miss K, explanations of rules and regulations sounded more like excuses and prevented her from extending her trust. This she seemed to reserve for people who met her on the informal level, where personal character and commitment were the criteria for extending trust. The value formed a continuous thread throughout her stories of the different time periods in her life.

Conclusion

To whom are long-term-care professionals accountable? A close look casts doubt on the idea that we are primarily accountable to our clients. Professionals (researchers, administrators, planners, lobbyists) tend to answer to one another vis-à-vis professional societies, funding sources, and lines of authority within the workplace. If professionals are defined by their expertise in a specific domain of knowledge, are there limits to how egalitarian we can be with clients and still maintain professional identities? This is one reason why the formal care provided by professionals cannot substitute for informal care provided by friends and family. The two systems operate in different cultures, with different values that shape expectations of the actors.

Recipients of long-term care have much to tell us about their needs, yet their voices are all but inaudible in the professional discourse on aging (Dittmann-Kohli, 1990; Gubrium & Wallace, 1990). After an era marked by the recognition of the importance of giving minorities and other marginalized persons a voice in the services and research aimed at them, surely it is reasonable to ensure the aged a voice in shaping the kind of care we offer them. This is particularly important because they are the most heterogeneous of age groups; generalizations about them are apt to be incorrect.

Professionals occasionally call for a client's perspective; perhaps we legitimately fear it. If given a voice, the clients that we love to think we serve might challenge our illusions, our assumptions about the appropriateness and effectiveness of our work. This happened to social workers in the 1960s when welfare rights groups formed and vented their anger over the "help" (and social control) they received. Similarly, African Americans have taken to task (white) researchers' depictions of their family lives, and feminists have challenged male assumptions in mainstream research and policy (Collins, 1991). Neither paternalistic good intentions nor benign neglect substitute for having a voice in determining the form and content of our lives. The frail elderly are capable of telling us many things. We need to listen.

References

Allen, K. R. (1989). *Single women/family ties: Life histories of older women.* Newbury Park, CA: Sage.

Atkinson, M. P. (1989). Conceptualizations of the parent-child relationship: Solidarity, attachment, crescive bonds, and identity salience. In J. A. Mancini (Ed.), *Aging parents and adult children* (pp. 81-93). Lexington, MA: Lexington Books.

Barresi, C. M., & Hunt, K. (1990). The unmarried elderly: Age, sex, and ethnicity. In T. H. Brubaker (Ed.), *Family relationships in later life* (2nd ed.; pp. 169-193). Newbury Park, CA: Sage.

Blumstein, P. (1991). The production of selves in personal relationships. In J. A. Howard & P. L. Callero (Eds.), *The self-society dynamic: Cognition, emotion, and action* (pp. 305-322). Cambridge, UK: Cambridge University Press.

Briggs, C. L. (1990). *Learning how to ask: A sociolinguistic appraisal of the role of the interview in social science research.* Cambridge, UK: Cambridge University Press.

Collins, P. H. (1991). Learning from the outsider within: The sociological significance of black feminist thought. In M. M. Fonow & J. A Cook (Eds.), *Beyond methodology: Feminist research as lived research* (pp. 35-59). Bloomington: Indiana University Press.

Dittmann-Kohli, F. (1990). The construction of meaning in old age: Possibilities and constraints. *Aging and Society, 10,* 279-294.

Fay, B. (1987). *Critical social science: Liberation and its limits.* Ithaca, NY: Cornell University Press.

Fineman, N. (1991). The social construction of noncompliance: A study of health care and social service providers in everyday practice. *Sociology of Health and Illness, 13*(3), 354-374.

Fortinsky, R. H. (1991). Coordinated comprehensive community care and the Older Americans Act. *Generations* (Summer/Fall), 31-34.

George, L. (1990). Social structure, social processes, and social-psychological states. In R. H. Binstock & L. K. George (Eds.), *Handbook of the social sciences* (3rd ed; pp. 186-200). San Diego, CA: Academic Press.

Gibson, D. M., & Aitkenhead, W. (1983). The elderly respondent: Experiences from a large scale survey of the aged. *Research on Aging, 5*(2), 283-296.

Gubrium, J. F. (1991). *The mosaic of care: Frail elderly and their families in the real world.* New York: Springer.

Gubrium, J. F., & Sankar, A. (Eds.). (1990). *The home care experience: Ethnography and policy.* Newbury Park, CA: Sage.

Gubrium, J. F., & Wallace, J. B. (1990). Who theorizes aging? *Aging and Society, 10,* 131-149.

Hammersley, M., & Atkinson, P. (1991). *Ethnography: Principles in practice.* Boston: Routledge & Kegan Paul.

Hennessy, C. H., & Hennessy M. (1990). Community based long-term care for the elderly: Evaluation practice reconsidered. *Medical Care Review, 47*(2), 221-258.

Howard, E. F. (1991). Long-term care: On the comeback trail? *Generations* (Summer/Fall), 31-34.

Hubbard, W. (1992, March). *Identity management in aging Appalachian gay men: Results of a qualitative pilot study.* Paper presented at the meeting of the Southern Gerontological Society, Nashville, TN.

Kimmel, D. C., & Moody, H. R. (1990). Ethical issues in gerontological research and services. In J. E. Birren & K. W. Schaie (Eds.), *Handbook of the psychology of aging,* (3rd ed.; pp. 489-501). San Diego, CA: Academic Press.

Magilvy, J. K., Congdon, J.G., Nelson, J. P., & Craig, C. (1992). Visions of rural aging: Use of photographic method in gerontological research. *The Gerontologist, 32*(2), 253-257.

152 SUBJECTIVITY MATTERS

Marshall C., & Rossman, G. B. (1989). *Designing qualitative research.* Newbury Park, CA: Sage.

McAdams, D. P. (1988). *Power intimacy and the life story: Personological inquiries into the lifestory.* New York: Guilford.

McAuley, W. J., Travis, S., & Safewright, M. (1990). The relationship between formal and informal health care services for the elderly. In S. M. Stahl (Ed.), *The legacy of longevity: Health and health care in later life* (pp. 201-216). Newbury Park, CA: Sage.

Mechanic, D. (1989). Epilogue: Future challenges in health care for an aging population. In M. G. Ory & K. Bond (Eds.), *Aging and health care: Social science and policy perspectives* (pp. 244-255). London: Routledge & Kegan Paul.

Rose, D. (1987). *Black American street life.* Philadelphia: University of Pennsylvania Press.

Soldo, B. J., Agree, E. M., & Wolf, D. A. (1989). The balance between formal and informal care. In M. G. Ory & K. Bond (Eds.), *Aging and health care: Social science and policy perspectives* (pp. 193-216). London: Routledge & Kegan Paul.

Strain, L. A., & Chappell, N. L. (1982). Problems and strategies: Ethical concerns in survey research with the elderly. *The Gerontologist, 22,* 526-531.

Strauss, A., & Corbin, J. (1990). *Basics of qualitative research: Grounded theory procedures and techniques.* Newbury Park, CA: Sage.

Wolfsen, C. R., Barker, J. C., & Mitteness, L. S. (1990). Personalization of formal social relationships by the elderly. *Research on Aging, 12,*(1), 94-112.

8. Welfare Workers' Response to Homeless Welfare Applicants

CATE SOLOMON

This chapter summarizes research on the difficulties single adult homeless people encounter when they apply for welfare benefits. Legal advocates and shelter workers view homeless people as particularly vulnerable to the psychological effects of welfare worker/claimant interaction. Research on homelessness and benefit attainment documents homeless people's need for welfare support (Rossi, 1989), but statistical analyses of survey data (the predominant approach to homeless benefit obtainment), does not address the experiential component of the welfare application process. My study adopts qualitative methods, including the interviewing of workers and claimants and the observation of the application process at a major homeless welfare office in Boston, Massachusetts. I analyze dynamic patterns of interaction, between welfare workers and homeless clients.

Theoretical Contexts

I have extrapolated five dominant perspectives from previous work; each suggests a different explanation for claimants' difficulties in negotiating the welfare system. The theories (which I've titled for the sake of clarity) may be characterized as follows:

1. The "role of welfare in support of capitalism" theory
2. The "incompetent client" theory
3. The "few resources versus many obstacles" theory
4. The "client/worker cultural mismatch" theory
5. The "street-level bureaucracy" theory

The fourth and fifth theories in particular inform my study, so they are presented in greater depth than the first three.

The role of welfare in support of capitalism theory looks at the economic and political structures served by the provision of welfare benefits. Frances Piven and Richard Cloward (1972) developed this macroanalytic and radical perspective. The American welfare system, they contend, reinforces the status quo in a capitalist society and is charged with three social functions: (a) Welfare ensures that some support is provided to those who, by merit of disability, cannot participate in the labor market. (b) Those who have been displaced by business cycles are placated by the provision of benefits to ensure that social insurrection does not occur. (c) The provision of benefits must be kept at a minimum to encourage all who can work to work. This theory explains how exclusionary criteria coupled with an overall derogatory attitude toward welfare recipients reinforce the work ethic.

The incompetent client theory emphasizes applicants' pathology as the primary cause for difficulties in negotiating the welfare system. For example, Wright and Weber (1987) state that some application efforts for the homeless are futile because "some who are eligible for benefits will be too intoxicated, disordered or debilitated to make enrollment efforts worthwhile" (p. 140). This theory is sometimes evoked in discussions about the homeless substance abuser (Schutt, 1986-1987), but it is more consistently applied to work on mentally ill homeless people. Mentally ill clients are often portrayed in a sympathetic light; symptoms of psychiatric illness hinder a person's ability to negotiate the benefit system. Symptoms include anger, fear, paranoia, apathy, low frustration tolerance, lack of trust, low self-esteem, ambivalence, general confusion, difficulty in making decisions, and a fear of closeness with workers who sometimes threaten clients' need for interpersonal distance. The literature emphasizes the role advocates can play in aiding the population (Report of the Federal Task Force on Homelessness and Severe Mental Illness, 1992).

The few resources versus many obstacles theory is descriptive. It focuses on features of the welfare bureaucracy that frustrate even the most competent people. The literature is filled with stories of people who are given erroneous information, who are shuffled from one bureaucratic office to the next, and whose benefit checks are repeatedly lost by the system. Features of the bureaucracy that frustrate claimants include long lines, slow response rates, burdensome paperwork requirements, and eligibility criteria that require applicants to go to numerous other government offices to secure verifications. The perspective highlights the impersonal nature of the applicant's experience, and the enormous time and energy claimants must expend to prove eligibility (Hope & Young, 1986; Redburn & Buss, 1986).

The client/worker cultural mismatch theory posits that differences in values and expectations distinguish public service workers from recipients, which cause hostilities to develop and impede benefit obtainment when they interact. Examples of cultural mismatch between professional workers (e.g., policemen, detox workers, and welfare workers) and "skid row dwellers" are provided by Jacqueline Wiseman in *Stations of the Lost* (1979). Workers approach their jobs as "an act of giving"; in the normative middle-class culture, with which most workers identify, workers see themselves as motivated by compassion. The natural response from the recipients should be gratitude and resultant change. From the workers' viewpoint, the exchange should evoke a degree of mutual trust between workers and clients. Workers become frustrated when they repeatedly see the same clients, their helping efforts producing neither gratitude nor beneficial results. The disappointed workers find it difficult to maintain a level of compassion for clients and redefine them as exploitative.

Clients, on the other hand, feel they owe the workers nothing; the workers are employees who are paid to provide a service. In response to workers who appear unsympathetic, clients view most workers as exploiting them. As Wiseman (1979) states, "it takes little imagination to visualize the spiraling hostilities that have emerged" between client and worker (p. 257).

The street-level bureaucracy theory, derived from Michael Lipsky (1980), focuses on the influence of workplace structure on public service workers' behavior. Public services tend to leave workers feeling alienated due to lack of control over work pace and work outcomes. Alienation causes job dissatisfaction and is "acted out" in the worker's decreased commitment to both clients and agency. Overwhelmed by the demand for services coupled with inadequate resources, public service workers use informal discretionary mechanisms to make decisions about who will and will not receive benefits and services. A high ratio of clients to workers causes workers to limit the time they expend on individual clients. A cycle of mediocrity develops: The demand for service is ever-increasing, but there is no concurrent increase in workers. By diminishing the quality of service provided, workers may discourage clients from seeking help.

Psychological stressors impair workers' personal effectiveness. Role strain originates from goals that are confusing, complicated, and conflictual. The goal of promoting the general well-being of clients, for example, often conflicts with the social goal of eliminating welfare dependency.

Discretionary worker behaviors contribute to a cumbersome application process. For my purpose I have labeled these behaviors "hassles." A worker elicits disqualifying information that renders clients ineligible. For example, a worker may ask clients many questions about employment status before telling the clients that employment disqualifies them from receiving benefits. Workers may also discourage clients from fulfilling benefit requirements and returning for further appointments by the imposition of costs. These include concrete costs of time and effort, such as long waits or forcing the client to go to another office for an extra verification form. There are also emotional costs, such as showing a lack of respect for clients or presenting information so quickly or in such a confusing manner that it is difficult to comprehend. Finally, workers can manipulate information; clients may not be told, for example, about the existence of certain programs and/or methods to expedite the verification process.

The street-level bureaucracy theory differs in important ways from the cultural mismatch theory. In the latter, differing cultural perspectives are seen as the salient reason for conflict between workers and clients; in the former, workers hassle clients as a psychological means of survival for employees in a structure that provides for little personal efficacy. It is workers' adaptation to their jobs that diminishes the quality of client service.

Methods

I used six methods to gather data on homeless welfare applicants: (a) discussions with 8 key informants, (b) observation of a welfare office, (c) observation of 47 application interviews involving benefit applicants and intake welfare workers, (d) observation of 25 interviews between welfare recipients and their caseworkers, (e) individual interviews with 4 welfare application intake workers, and (f) individual interviews with 15 homeless applicants. Data collection began in May of 1989 and ended in August of 1990.

I began the research by talking with a range of key informants—professionals and activists involved in the provision of welfare to homeless single adults. The informants included a legal service lawyer for the homeless, a shelter employment counselor, a day-shelter worker, the head of social services at a city shelter, a homeless-alcoholism researcher, the director of the Department of Mental Health Homeless Services, a staff member of the Coalition for the Homeless, and an assistant director of the Homeless Welfare Office.

I gathered background information about the Massachusetts Homeless "General Relief" welfare program from manuals and program descriptions. The literature describes the program's operation, goals, rules, and regulations. It provided an initial understanding of eligibility requirements and a means for determining how workers should "officially" act, compared to how they actually act.

I gathered most of the observation data during approximately 100 hours at a welfare office, watching exchanges between and among workers and applicants. Impressions of the workplace were noted, including the physical facilities such as the lobby waiting area (often referred to by the workers as "the bullring"). Conversations between workers were noted, with occasional quotes recorded. Included in my daily field notes were handwritten verbatim accounts of interactions between clients and staff, including the 47 application interviews and 25 ongoing interviews. I also recorded my impressions of two staff meetings and two in-service training sessions. In addition, I used the time between application interviews to speak with workers about their jobs, and what had happened in their encounters with the clients whose application interviews I had observed. Field notes consisted of 260 double-spaced pages. Transcriptions of taped interviews of workers and claimants constituted an additional 50 pages.

The success of the study depended on the cooperation of the workers. When the welfare-department management introduced me and asked the workers to be helpful, I sensed animosity between workers and management and suspected that workers were not going to cooperate. To build relationships, I spent two mornings each week for 6 weeks "hanging-out" and talking with staff. I told both workers and management that I was interested in learning about their jobs. During this time I met individually with workers to learn how they did their jobs and how I might be able to observe their work.

Toward the end of the study I conducted taped interviews with four of the five intake workers. Three individual interviews took place over lunch in a restaurant. They lasted between 45 and 90 minutes. The fourth interview was a brief discussion that took place in a back office with a worker who declined to grant me an extensive interview. Interviews focused on the structure of their work and on experiences with clients.

The interviews were guided by a sociological research interviewing technique that, according to Robert Weiss (personal communication, 1990), "aims to learn what the individual has witnessed and experienced in the area of importance." The subject is encouraged to provide real examples of behavior (or the concrete details of events as the subject remembers them) as opposed to rationalizations, generalizations, or philosophy about behavior. The aim is to capture the interviewee's memory of both the external experience (what the interviewee did, what others did, what was said) as well as the interviewee's internal viewpoint (thoughts, feelings, concerns, and beliefs) at the time of the experience. The sociological interviewer is encouraged "to put boundaries on the information" by asking questions such as, "Think about last week. When did you feel this way? Was there an incident that triggered this feeling? What was it? What happened? Who was there? What did you say or do? What did they say or do? What went through your head when that happened?"

Several issues arose when I tried to employ the interviewing technique. I needed to acquire information of importance, in this case information about the application process. Although I tried to discourage interviewees from generalizing about their feelings and opinions, they tended to give short, vague answers to questions. For example, in answer to my question, "What went through your head?" workers often replied, "Nothing much" or "It was okay." I found that my expression of curiosity about the worker's opinion was helpful in eliciting fuller answers. After I listened to the opinion, I requested an illustration of the point the worker was trying to make.

I started interviews by stating, "I want to talk with you about your experience working in the homeless GR unit. I'm interested in hearing what the experience has been like for you." Workers were free to choose the area of discussion, but each sought further guidance, asking me what I wanted to know. Before I began the interviewing process I developed a guide of questions to ask. The first set was designed to get a sense of the worker's original job expectations and self-image. The second set of questions was designed to elicit the worker's job responsibilities. The third provided information about how job structure did or did not support the worker, and the fourth and final set of questions explored the worker's evaluation of the workplace. I found that having a set of guiding questions was both a help and a hindrance. It helped focus the interviews, but at times it hindered my ability to explore what workers were saying in more depth. After a question was answered, I too often relied on the guide by jumping to the next formal question instead of following up on some aspect of what had just been said.

To gain a sense of the application experience from the client's perspective, 15 homeless applicants were interviewed over a 6-day period. Interviews ranged from 3 to 30 minutes; most lasted approximately 8 minutes. Originally, I had planned to conduct a series of two interviews with each applicant. The first part was to take place as clients waited in the lobby prior to being called for an application screening; the second was to occur directly after the screening interview. The plan proved unfeasible due to changes in the application procedure and client reluctance. Much of the data that helped me understand the clients' viewpoint came from discussions that occurred when I was observing the 47 application interviews. When workers left the application interview, I often spoke with claimants for several minutes, asking them questions about their situations and their thoughts about the application process.

I encountered difficulties in attempts to interview clients, for many reasons: absence of a relationship with them, their preoccupation with other aspects of their lives, lack of interest in my subject matter, and the absence of a clear incentive for clients. I approached clients in the lobby before the application interview. I stated that I was a student doing research on the welfare system and wanted to learn from them about their experiences. I explained that their agreement or refusal to speak with me would not affect their benefit application. Clients generally commented, "I don't mind talking while I'm waiting." Only 1 client out of 15 declined to speak with me. I again used a guide of interview questions, and asked clients how they had learned about welfare benefits and why they had decided to apply. At the end of the interview most clients politely agreed to my request that they be interviewed following their application screening. This actually happened in only one case. Initially my effort to reinterview clients failed because I was busy interviewing a new person when clients completed their benefit application interview, or they had quickly departed. After the first few times I missed clients, I made an effort to catch them as they departed but was refused by clients who said they were in a rush to leave. I now see the need for financial incentives to ensure client cooperation in research of this kind.

Clients tended to relate to me as a potential resource. During individual interviews and observation clients tried to elicit information to aid them in their pursuit of welfare benefits. Provision of information to clients posed an ethical and research dilemma for me, as I wanted to be helpful to the client but did not wish to bias the applicant's experience of the application process. In some cases, particularly when I felt sympathy for a client whom I believed was being denied necessary information, I provided the information, such as tips on more expeditious ways to get verifications. In response to clients' direct questions I always answered with whatever information I knew. My actions were in large part determined by the social work position I occupy and value. Not to respond, I believe, would have been unethical. My experience illustrates one way in which the roles of social worker and researcher may conflict.

Clients were even less specific in their answers than workers were. A client, for example, said that people on the street had told him about benefits, but he could not remember what exactly was said or what his thoughts had been when he heard the information. Discussions with clients helped me obtain a superficial view of their current life circumstances and a general immediate history pertaining to the benefit application. Interviews did not provide an in-depth understanding of the applicant's experience of the welfare system.

In sum, I found "sociological interviewing" difficult to conduct successfully. I did discover that the way interviewees interacted with me was as important as the interview content. My experience with clients helped me understand workers' experience, as I too was faced with choices about when (and when not) to provide information to clients. I came to see (or, more accurately, to feel) that both the denial and provision of information is one of the only ways to obtain a sense of efficacy—to have an impact. This insight explained why, in many instances, workers helped even those clients toward whom they expressed antagonism.

Findings

Although workers accept most clients' applications, they do so in a disrespectful and unsympathetic manner. They place burdens on clients that are not consistent with official policy—what could be called "hassling." There are several ways in which workers hassle clients, and several explanations for it.

First, workers challenge clients, questioning their ability to work and their honesty about being homeless. Second, workers belittle clients, making remarks implying that clients are making false claims and are "welfare cheats." Third, workers require that additional verification forms be obtained, such as a letter from another agency to verify some aspect of the client's story. Hassling entails behaviors and requests by workers not in accordance with welfare rules and procedures.

The following excerpt taken from an application interview illustrates various forms of hassling. The client is a casually dressed, 35-year-old black male:

Client: I got no place to stay and no job.

Worker: Homelessness and unemployment does not make you eligible for welfare. You have to have a DPW [Department of Welfare] physical filled out. If a doctor puts on it that you can work . . .

Client: Meanwhile what am I supposed to do? I got no job and no place to stay.

Worker: Doesn't matter. Homelessness doesn't make you eligible. Unemployment doesn't make you eligible. Have to have a medical. If you can work . . . Why, what's wrong with you?

Client: I'm a diabetic.

Worker: Diabetics can work.

Client: But not 'til I get regulated.

Worker: You receive nothing else [the worker waves the application form in front of the client's face] . . . Registered at the unemployment office?

Client: Last week.

Worker: Regular occupation.

Client: Cook.

Worker: When is the last time you worked?

Client: Three months ago.

Worker: Full or part time?

Client: Full time.

Worker: How much did you make?

Client: Five dollars an hour.

Worker: Work at all the last 8 weeks?

Client: No.

Worker: When working, where were you working?

Client: At the University of Carolina.

Worker: File for unemployment?

Client: No, not eligible.

Worker: Great job! Where are you staying?

Client: At a friend's house.

Worker: All my clients are homeless—in a shelter or in the street.... I can request
proof of residence. I can have you go to a shelter. You're not homeless.
Client: If you tell me I can stay at your house a few days, it's not my home.
Worker: Why don't you stay at a shelter? You need help with your diabetes.
They can help you. Your friends can't help you.... What I need is a letter from
unemployment and a medical report.

In this example, the worker hassles the client by imposing emotional
concrete costs. When the applicant begins the interview by stating he is
"unemployed and homeless," the worker tells the client that he must be
medically disabled to qualify for benefits. When the applicant states he has
diabetes, the worker counters that his condition is not severe enough to
preclude working. A disrespectful attitude is demonstrated when the worker
waves the application form in the client's face and warns him, "That's all
you get." As a knowledgeable insider, I understood that the worker was
saying that the client would get an initial food-stamp payment, but without
a medical form completed he could not receive welfare cash benefits or
future food-stamp allocations. I assume the worker's implicit statement
was not understood by the client.

When the client describes his previous employment, a denigrating
attitude is reinforced by the worker's sarcastic remark. As the interview
continues, despite the client's original contention that he was homeless,
the worker asks where the client is staying. To the client's answer, the
worker replies that staying with a friend does not constitute being homeless. The worker warns the client that she can make him get verification
forms to prove residence in a shelter. The worker again conveys that she
does not believe he is disabled; the shelter could help him with his medical
condition more than his friends. The worker concludes the interview by
telling the client that he must obtain a medical form (official verification)
and a letter from unemployment (unofficial verification). The request for
a letter from unemployment exemplifies how workers use illegal discretionary verifications to concretely hassle clients.

There are several explanations for worker negative behavior toward
applicants. Four are relevant here.

Poorly Defined Eligibility Criteria

The homeless welfare program's stated objective is to provide benefits
to single adults who are both "homeless" and "temporarily disabled." It
is difficult to prove these criteria; each is based on a negative state of
being. In the case of homelessness, although one can prove an address, it

is difficult to prove one does not have one. A client might be able to secure a letter from a shelter, but someone residing in the street has no way to verify that she or he is without a home. The lack of specificity in rules reflects difficulties inherent in the verification of homelessness. Although the rules state that clients should be homeless to receive homeless welfare, proof of homelessness is not required.

Clients define homelessness as the lack of a permanent place to reside. One can be homeless while living with family and/or friends. Application for benefits is sometimes motivated by others, who request or insist that clients pay them in exchange for staying with them. One client, a young black man, explained:

> One of my friends' mothers told me. She said to come down [to welfare] 'cause I don't work and I been sleeping over at her house.

Another client, a middle-aged black man, said:

> It's tough, you know, really, especially when if you're gonna be living with different people every day, they gonna expect you to come up with something, you know? They're not gonna feed you and do all this for you.

In most cases, workers allow clients to self-define homelessness. One worker (a lawyer waiting to pass the bar exam before he sought other work) identified with the applicant's viewpoint when he referred to applicants who live with family or friends on a temporary basis as "pseudo-homeless." He describes these clients as "living somewhere without the right to." Other workers indicate that they view such clients as cheating the system. Remember the application interview quoted earlier, in which the worker said to the applicant, "All my clients are homeless—in a shelter or on the street. . . . You're not homeless." Yet, the worker accepted the claimant's application.

Like homelessness, "temporary disability" criterion is also based on a negative condition. A person can prove they can work, by working, but it is difficult to prove one cannot work. It becomes even more nebulous when asked to show that the condition is temporary.

Despite the program's official temporary disability qualification, clients are fairly open about job seeking. Many applicants stated that they had recently been employed and, if the right employment opportunity were presented, said they would be capable of working and more than willing to do so. During the 47 application interviews I observed, approximately one third of the clients said they were able to work but were currently unemployed. Another third of the applicants made no comments about employability; the remaining third claimed disability.

Clients see the interconnection of homelessness with unemployment. Most indicate that disability is not at the base of their homelessness; rather, the loss of work and the inability to replace work keep them in a cycle of homelessness. Clients explain that once a job is lost, the home is soon to follow. Once homeless, a job, which is difficult to secure in the first place, becomes even more unattainable. A 35-year-old, white male explained:

> I've never been homeless before. Without an address people won't hire you. You have nowhere to clean yourself up and employers have nowhere to contact you should they decide they want you.

Others explain how $99 dollars a month obtained through homeless welfare (an average of $3 a day) could help in their employment search to buy a toothbrush, toothpaste, and a comb to look presentable at job interviews. Clients look through want ads, use dimes to make phone calls to prospective employers, buy subway tokens to make job interviews, and buy sandwiches and cups of coffee on job searching days.

Clients frequently tell workers they are interested in finding work, which sometimes elicits a mixed response from workers, who give them an application but hassle them. When I asked a worker what she thought about a particular applicant who said he was searching for work, she said, "Well at least he was honest." The vagueness of the rules allows all clients, even those who admittedly do not fit criteria, to apply for benefits. One worker expressed his frustration:

> The clients bring you in what you need to establish a case. You cannot say no because you think the person's abusing the system. It's not up to you. You're the last person that can say anything. Even if the person says he can work, technically you're supposed to give him a medical and a checklist to get the information you need. Like everything else, I just can't come right out and say [the client can't apply]. They still have the right to apply.

Poorly defined eligibility criteria lead workers to feel ineffectual. They cannot discriminate between who is and who is not eligible for benefits. Rules provide all clients with a means of obtaining benefits, even those clients whose stories do not match eligibility criteria.

Rule/Reality Mismatch

Applying a rule that fails to recognize the reality of many applicant's lives leads workers to view clients as cheating the system. They accept applications from those they believe are not truly homeless or are employable, and in some cases who are actually employed. Workers I interviewed made many statements to indicate they did not believe clients. One said, "About 10% are sick; 90% can work." Another expressed disdain for applicants whom he viewed as able-bodied: "Most of the time they can work. . . . There are more than a few that don't want to work." Another worker echoed this: "They have nothing basically wrong with them, . . . they're just procrastinators." When I noted that there were a disproportionate number of Hispanic men and ex-offenders waiting to be seen in the early morning, another worker commented, "They are probably heading off for work after their appointment." That clients are manipulating the system is highlighted in workers' jokes about clients' crutches and slings as "props."

Client behavior shapes workers' perceptions of clients as "welfare cheats." They sometimes change their stories to fit criteria. A client initially said he could work; the worker replied that he would then be ineligible for welfare, and the client retracted his statement: "I *do* have a back problem." Frequent interactions with clients, who try to portray themselves as fitting criteria that do not reflect lives and needs, obscure inherent problems in the rule base and lead to perceptions that clients are cheating the system.

Lack of Worker Control Over Outcomes

When workers have little control over final outcomes, they assert control in inappropriate ways, as the street-level bureaucracy theory predicts. Workers in the sample experienced alienation when they feel that others make eligibility determinations and that their decisions are incorrect. They voiced resentment that they had little or no role in the benefit determination process.

Medical experts, charged with filling out medical verification forms, determine whether claimants receive benefits. Worker viewpoints are reflected in comments: "You make no decisions." "The doctors make the decisions." "The biggest problem we have is the doctors." One worker resented how physicians enable ineligible clients to get welfare:

I asked [the client] what was wrong with him. He said "Nothing." Asked him if he was able to work. He said "Yeah." I said if you're able to work, you're not eligible for welfare. I go into the screening process, you know, ask him for ID's and whatnot. I says you still got the right to apply, but that doesn't mean you'll get benefits." He got a medical, 'cause he's homeless. He got it filled out today.

Doctors, aware of the rules, manipulate diagnoses to certify all clients for benefits, according to workers. Following an application interview with a 46-year-old white male who slurred his words and belittled the worker, the worker told me the client was a chronic alcoholic. She explained that in the Massachusetts General Relief welfare program, a diagnosis of alcoholism is not an acceptable disability criterion. The worker read the following diagnoses, each written on separate previous medical verification forms in the client's case record: arthritis, left knee; rheumatic heart; irritable bowel syndrome; eye injury; anxiety; and depression. The worker concluded, "Every time it's a different thing." She argued that doctors fabricate diagnoses to help clients, in this case an alcoholic person, fit the eligibility criteria.

In addition to medical experts, other professionals who advocate for the homeless are similarly resented by workers. Clients accompanied by advocates (a shelter or veterans' counselor) are treated with noticeably more respect; workers fear that other professionals will bring complaints against them if they scrutinize clients. Clients who simply mention that someone or some service had referred them for benefits are frequently hassled. One worker explains the penchant to give applicants a difficult time if they invoke the name of an advocate:

[The shelter] is under the impression that everybody is eligible for General Relief. . . . They think they should be, but they're not. . . . There are a lot of times they hurt themselves by doing that, especially with me, 'cause they piss me off. . . . I make 'em get a letter from the shelter. . . . I've made them get every single verification even though I've had them in an old case record . . . . It's kinda funny 'cause [at the shelter] I'm hated. . . . They send [the client] up and I send him back saying he's not eligible. It's funny, I kind of enjoy it though.

Workers feel they have no meaningful role in the application determination process. Workers sense that other professionals falsify verification information, erroneously conveying to clients that they are qualified for benefits. Experiencing little control over work outcomes, they exert control in the only way they can, by hassling claimants.

Worker/Claimant Mismatch

Workers hear clients' pleas for help as exaggerations and evidence of fraud, whereas clients tell stories of urgency in an effort to compel workers to aid them. This mismatch often begins following applicants' initial statements. They often explain the need for benefits by stating, "I'm homeless and unemployed." To workers, clients' statements of need indicate a presumptuous attitude, interpreted as the client attempting, as one worker put it, "to get the upper hand."

Clients seem to assume that the more desperate they appear, the more sympathy and help they will garner. They use the word "emergency" and allude to "death" as an end result, should they not get help quickly. A 38-year-old black male, who appeared agitated, said:

I hope it goes quickly 'cause this is an emergency. . . . I don't expect anything today, but an emergency would be a few hours from now, a few days from now, maybe 2 to 3 days. But 2 to 3 weeks, a person can freeze to death in just about 3 weeks.

Clients appear to believe that urgency encourages workers to be sympathetic and helpful, but in reality, the more urgent a client appears, the less credence the worker seems to accord the client's story. The client who advocates for himself unknowingly risks alienating the worker.

Conclusion

My analysis suggests some of the forces that shape the negative behavior of Massachusetts welfare workers toward homeless clients in 1989 and 1990. Behaviors include challenging applicants, belittling them, and requiring that they obtain unnecessary verification forms. Several explanations for hassling are offered. Eligibility criteria based on negative conditions are ineffective and create conflicts for workers. Outside advocates and experts who play a greater role in benefit determination than the workers themselves are viewed by workers as interferences, even adversaries. Criteria do not reflect claimants' actual needs; as workers apply rules that do not match clients' real needs, they come to perceive clients as cheaters and manipulators. Clients and workers misinterpret one another's behavior and motivations. The conflicts generated by these problems are expressed in workers' hassling of clients.

Qualitative studies offer a way to examine the effects of systems on participants. Homeless people constitute a disenfranchised group with little to no influence in the formation of policy meant to serve them. Studies like this one provide a means for the experiences of clients and public service workers who interact with them to be heard. Research that incorporates an experiential component can inform administrators, policymakers, and the public about how to design programs to better meet recipients' needs in a humane fashion. Better designed programs can decrease worker animosity and the consequent hassling of clients. Rule consistency that acknowledges the reality of many homeless people's lives can convey to clients and workers alike that society is willing to aid the unemployed in returning to work, and the episodically homeless in finding permanent homes.

References

Hope, M., & Young, J. (1986). *The faces of the homeless*. Lexington, MA: Lexington Books.
Lipsky, M. (1980). *Street level bureaucracy*. New York: Russell Sage.
Piven, F. F., & Cloward, R. A. (1972). *Regulating the poor: The function of public welfare*. New York: Vintage.
Redburn, F. S., & Buss, T. F. (1986). *Responding to America's homeless: Public policy alternatives*. New York: Praeger.
Report of the Federal Task Force on Homelessness and Severe Mental Illness. (1992). *Outcasts on Main Street*. Washington, DC: Department of Health & Human Services in cooperation with the Interagency Council on Homelessness and the Task Force on Homelessness and Severe Mental Illness.
Rossi, P. (1989). *Without shelter: Homeless in the 1980s*. New York: Priority Press.
Schutt, R. K. (1986-1987). *Boston's homeless, 1986-87: Change and continuity* (report to the Long Island Shelter). Boston: University of Massachusetts.
Wiseman, J. (1979). *Stations of the lost*. Chicago: University of Chicago Press.
Wright, J. D., & Weber, E. (1987). *Homelessness and health*. New York: McGraw-Hill.

9. Reflections on a Journey: A Research Story

CHERYL HYDE

It is good to have an end to journey towards, but it is the journey that matters in the end.

—Ursula LeGuin,
The Left Hand of Darkness

Many methodological accounts that appear in scholarly works convey nuts and bolts of the research process—how the sample was drawn, data were coded and interpreted, and problems of reliability and validity were addressed. Although dilemmas may be implied, a reader gets the overall impression that the researcher knows her craft and the process runs relatively smoothly. Less common are accounts that indicate the messiness and false starts in the research, the learning about self. This chapter's goal is to convey these aspects by examining my recollections of the process of engaging in organizational research.

My study was a comparative analysis of transformation in nine feminist social movement organizations (Hyde, 1991).[1] The initial and core question was whether encounters with the New Right movement during the 1980s resulted in organizational radicalization. I employed qualitative methodological strategies. Sociological theories of social movement development and a feminist approach to research informed the study.

AUTHOR'S NOTE: I thank Catherine K. Riessman and Patricia Yancey Martin for assistance and suggestions, and Tom Gerschick for his support.

This chapter is not a step-by-step, "how-to" account of the research (see Hyde, 1991) or of organizational research in general (see Martin & Turner, 1986; Morgan, 1983; Rothschild & Whitt, 1986; Van Maanen, 1983). Composed from the advantageous position of hindsight, my story dovetails with discussions of "becoming a social scientist" by Reinharz (1979) or dilemmas in ethnographic representation by Van Maanen (1988). Reinharz emphasizes the meaning of the research process for the individual—acquisition of skills, significance of self-reflection, socialization to academic norms. Both assert that research is a flawed enterprise, and that we learn much about our intended topic and ourselves from the mistakes we make.

Such considerations are important here because the study was my dissertation. A dissertation is bound not only by student hopes and anxieties, but by the protocols of academe as well. As much as I would like to claim that the thesis was written for me, it was not. I was attuned to a specific audience (my committee), resources (assistantships and fellowships), and future prospects (the job market); each constrained the admission of unanticipated findings, unexpected themes, and outright failures.

The intent of the chapter, however, is to move beyond confessions of the dissertation's problems and errors, personal dilemmas, and growth. I learned the craft of research by both doing and reflecting on the dissertation. My hope is that other investigators, as they struggle with myriad decisions involved in research, gain insights into the research enterprise and assurances from revelations of an imperfect process.

The Research Project

The decision to study feminist social movement organizations (FSMOs) stemmed from my involvement in feminist organizing during the late 1970s and early 1980s. During that time, I watched rightwing activists undermine or dismantle many feminist policies and programs. Through research, I hoped to document some of the ways feminists fought for the survival of their organizations given overwhelming political, economic, and social threats. Linking a personal investment with scholarly questions on social movement development, I undertook a comparative study of nine FSMOs to determine what effect the New Right had on organizational change and survival.

All nine organizations (three National Organization of Women [NOW] chapters, three health clinics, three antiviolence centers) were nonprofit; oriented to service, advocacy, and education for the public; and viewed as feminist by members. The sample of organizations varied in size, type of staffing, region of the country, governance structure, age (all were founded by 1977), and degree of service emphasis. All experienced New Right opposition, though the type and intensity of the oppostion differed during the study's time period (1977 to 1987).

The primary data, collected during 7- to 10-day visits, consisted of organizational documents and interviews with past and current members. The documents (approximately 4,000) constituted the skeleton for organizational analysis and included grant proposals, minutes, annual reports, budgets, pamphlets, and correspondence. Interviews with 40 women provided "flesh and blood" for the organizational stories. I kept a log in which I recorded observations of current organizational life. Over time, the log evolved into an analytic journal in which I set forth commentary and assessments as to what I saw occurring in the FSMOs. The analysis was supplemented by existing case studies of other women's organizations and publicity literature from various feminist and New Right groups.

Although public attention typically focused on mass protests, considerable New Right fiscal and policy damage went unnoticed. The research revealed the all-encompassing, insidious means through which New Right activists eroded feminist projects. FSMO participants often mobilized short-term counteractions, yet could not sustain these efforts against rightwing opponents over an extended period of time. This was particularly true when damage involved resource withdrawal, as it constrained or eliminated program options for feminists. Yet even with prolonged New Right assaults, FSMO participants preserved some version of their organizations' feminist visions.

Guiding Frameworks

Three types of literature guided the formulation and initial data gathering—social movement analysis, grounded theory methods, and feminist research perspectives. The role of organizations in the emergence and continuance of collective change efforts is a dominant focus in the sociological analysis of social movements. Movement organizations, such as FSMOs, are arenas in which resources are mobilized, participants are educated, constituents are served, networks are developed, and culture and history are transmitted. Movement development is traced through change patterns in relevant organizations. Organizational innovations suggest movement expansion and success, whereas maintenance or downsizing indicates stagnation or loss of a movement's social change agenda (Klandermans, 1989; McCarthy & Zald, 1977; Staggenborg, 1989; Zald & Ash, 1973). My challenge was to analyze longitudinal change across a sample of feminist social movement organizations, and based on this analysis, to assess the health of the feminist movement in a staunchly antifeminist time period. I am surprised to recall that originally I intended to survey approximately 100 FSMOs. While attempting to design a suitable survey, I realized that this approach would impede needed flexibility in data gathering. Activists and advisors suggested that a survey would be impractical and unwieldy. For these reasons, I abandoned the survey and turned to qualitative research approaches.

As a graduate student, I was introduced to the grounded theory method (Glaser & Strauss, 1967) and at the dissertation proposal stage decided to employ it. As I understood this inductive approach, the researcher simultaneously gathers, codes, and analyzes the data. She then determines what additional information needs to be collected, and from what source. Analysis proceeds with each new case compared to previously analyzed cases. Interpretations are refined, and theoretical formulations emerge.

Theoretical sampling, where cases are selected for theoretical relevance and maximization of differences, would be the means of selecting the FSMOs. In vivo coding, in which descriptive and analytic codes are generated often line by line (Charmaz, 1983), would be the primary coding method. These codes would be the foundation for developing analytical themes, which would eventuate into robust explanations.

Later I explain why I abandoned grounded theory during data gathering and analysis. At the proposal stage, compromises with the approach already had been made. I designated specific organizational properties (e.g., goals, activities, authority structures, and outputs) for analysis and delineated a priori propositions concerning organizational change—steps I believed violated the primarily inductive process of grounded theory. Theoretical sampling was limited because the FSMOs had to have experienced New Right attacks, be one of three types of organizations, and be founded by 1980.[2] One-shot, short-term visits to each FSMO meant I could not go "back and forth" between data collection and analysis.

At the time I was not able to anticipate what these developments might mean for the research process, the result of a surprising lack of attention that I gave to the study's methodology. Unlike my consideration of relevant sociological theory, I did not examine fully the various ways in which qualitative organizational research was done or the particular techniques that worked well in organizational settings. For reasons I do not recall, I assumed I would gather data on specified organizational properties (allowing for some unanticipated findings), plot changes over time, contrast changes among the organizations, determine the extent to which my propositions were supported, then offer a new explanation for organizational transformation based on feminist cases. It seemed a straightforward process.

This lack of attention to methodological planning relates, in part, to my decision to use a feminist approach to research. Three principles captured my initial understanding of it: (a) knowledge is grounded in the experiences of women, (b) research benefits women, and (c) the researcher immerses her or himself in or exhibits empathy for the world being studied (Harding, 1987, pp. 7-9). The voice of the "subject" is actively heard; the subject interacts with and influences the nature of the research project. The knowledge produced is accessible to those studied, informs an understanding of oppression, and suggests liberatory strategies. One objective of my study was to convey or "give voice to" the stories of survival of FSMO activists; another was to suggest strategies for continued movement work.

I believed the approach would allow me to combine my commitment as a movement activist with a scholarly critique of social movement theory from the vantage point of a feminist methodology. Yet I did not move beyond the belief to fully consider how I would accomplish the agenda. An overreliance on a feminist perspective during the initial stages of the study deterred me from adequately addressing questions of method.

Armed with my sociological imagination, my feminist lens, and my (meager) qualitative toolkit, I proceeded over the course of 7 months to visit nine FSMOs in the continental United States. I had little idea what to expect; my desire to start overshadowed my naivete about fieldwork. Challenges and changes occurred instantly. Upon arrival at my first site (South NOW chapter), I quickly realized how unprepared I was to summarize data, negotiate interviews, and even find my way around town. There was the initial culture clash—an overeager northerner in a laid-back southern community. And then there were the data. Out of the NOW chapter president's front hall closet came four very large, beaten-up boxes crammed with materials—no order, no explanations, no logical point of entry. I began to suspect that recording the organization's information on neat forms would not work. For the rest of my fieldwork, analysis, and writing, I struggled with what would work. These struggles, and lessons learned from them, are my focus here.

Reflections

Three themes capture much of my research experience: making order out of chaos, managing emotions, and juggling voices. Each theme suggests the consequences of planning and preparation, the tensions involved in undertaking this kind of research, and how the effort to do the study contributed to new understandings of the process of doing research and myself as an investigator.

Making Order out of Chaos

Fieldwork reaped extensive and rich data. I often felt overwhelmed during data collection, yet it was not until I completed the field visits that I confronted the prodigious task of creating order out of 4,000 documents and almost 100 hours of interviews. How could I manage and eventually analyze all these data without becoming lost? How could I accomplish the project when constrained by resources, time, and skills?

Initially, I wanted to construct a retrieval index that would allow me to locate desired information (e. g., descriptions of goals and activities) across the nine FSMOs. I then would attempt a systematic analysis that addressed my initial research propositions and allowed for the identification of emergent themes. At this point, I engaged in considerable trial and error with data sorting and categorizing, and uncomfortably realized that my understanding of how to operationalize grounded theory did not mesh well with the tasks. I had yet to fully grasp that grounded theory might be inappropriate for so large a data set or for the combined inductive-deductive approach necessary for my study.

During this time, I quite literally stumbled across the process of analytical induction. This approach is premised on systematic data analysis in which a priori propositions and emergent themes are compared and contrasted. There is continuous movement between data and competing theories as the researcher engages in an analytical dance that is both deductive and inductive. She develops explanations that account for the sequencing of and relationships between events and processes (Denzin, 1989; Katz, 1983), an approach well suited to the longitudinal and comparative nature of my study.

Analytical induction provided a logic for using my research propositions without being wedded to them. I began to understand that propositions serve as initial guides to analysis; they need to be challenged, not "tested." One form of challenge was through inductively generated themes.

Because the research propositions suggested relationships between the environment and specific organizational properties (e.g., goals, governance structures), I used the properties as initial guides in organizing the data. My index was designed so I could retrieve information on FSMO properties, related characteristics, and environmental factors. If a document discussed changes in an organization's mission, for example, the index noted the document contained information about ideology, goals, and activities. I composed year-end summaries for each FSMO in which specific attention was paid to organizational change and the presence of the New Right. As I saw connections between organizations, I wrote memos (such as the one here) to indicate the need for further exploration, the possibility of a fruitful line of analysis:

> Marcy at the SHC told me that they would not hire three people who didn't want to learn how to give self-help exams. . . . Marcy also stated that patients and clients no longer wanted groups of self-help services. . . . CHP members also noted this dilemma. They have retained group education sessions during some, not all, of the abortion clinics. . . . Both groups seem to be weighing how to strike a balance between what the client wants, versus fulfilling a feminist educational or social change mission.

In memos I experimented with the clustering of themes and the placement of clusters into tentatively designated chapters. Moving from indexing to summaries, theme identification, and clustering, then chapter designations, I developed a sequenced analysis that goes from the particular to the general, from single subjects to a comparative framework.

Had I limited inquiry to tracking change in prespecified organizational properties, I would have experienced less confusion and, no doubt, finished sooner. Yet the desire not to pigeonhole data, and the "discovery" that I could challenge propositions through inductive analysis, led me to pursue interesting emergent themes. The pursuit resulted in a richer study, though the immersion process generated confusion and eventual renegotiation of the study's content. A memo to my committee suggests the "start and restart" process:

> I am trying to finish a chapter entitled "The Transformation of Organizational Identities." This chapter originally was going to focus on organizational culture, but earlier analysis and write-up proved dissatisfying. After a number of tries on this chapter, I feel that this attack [focus on identity] is the most profitable. . . . This chapter has proven to be both elusive and frustrating, and I feel that once I finish the draft of it I will have overcome a major

hurdle. . . . What I would like to do is take the chapter entitled "A House Divided" (which is on the conflicts and schisms concerning race, gender, class, sexual preference, professionals, board vs. staff) and weave the key points through the other three data chapters.

As it turned out, the ideas for reorganization did not work.

Although analytic induction was extremely helpful, I was ill-prepared to deal with the complexities of inductive analysis. It is one thing to believe in the importance of emergent themes, quite another to understand which themes are truly significant. Everything seemed important, and I worried that I would emphasize the trivial and overlook the essential. In hindsight, I still do not fully understand how or why I made the decisions to discuss certain aspects of organizational life and not others (e.g., I gave superficial treatment to leadership). At the time, I chose to examine what represented the "best fit" between the initial research propositions, the stories of organizational survival conveyed by FSMO members, the sociological literature, and what made sense to me based on my activist experiences. Attempts to make order out of chaos, however, contributed to a growing sense of emotional turmoil.

Managing Emotions

Subjectivity and reflexivity are discussed frequently in qualitative research, including recognition that various emotions arise over the course of a study. Acknowledging an emotional terrain contradicts positivist approaches, where the investigator is a disembodied, dispassionate, objective recorder of "truth." Many feminist scholars articulate how positive and negative emotions are present in, and affect, the research, researcher, and "researched" (Acker, Barry, & Esseveld, 1983; Daniels, 1983; Fonow & Cook, 1991; Krieger, 1985; Taylor & Rupp, 1991). In my study, emotions shaped the connections between FSMO members and myself, interpretations of data, and my evolving view about the overall worthiness of the project.

At virtually every site, I felt a level of warmth and trust from organizational participants. My letter of introduction, in which I conveyed experiences that would resonate with FSMO members, laid the foundation:

> When President Reagan began his term in 1981, I was a feminist organizer in Connecticut. I lost my job because of cutbacks by his administration. Many sister activists also lost their jobs, suffered from burnout, or witnessed

their programs die. When I moved to Michigan, similar events troubled me. And by 1982, a series of articles suggested that the feminist movement was dead. Yet as I studied feminist organizations and activists, I found that the feminist movement was dismissed too quickly. What I hope to tell is the story of how some feminist organizations remained active, including their gains and losses, during this time period.

To gain access I identified my movement "credentials" and shared painful events that perhaps paralleled members' own. To forge connections with FSMO members in the field, I was an inquiring student they could "teach," a conveyor of their stories, as well as a feminist activist.

There were different levels of engagement with and affinity for groups and individuals. As a socialist-feminist, I felt more comfortable with the more ideologically militant, collectivist, and explicitly social-change-oriented organizations. I felt more "at home" in organizations with feminist and socialist posters on the walls and secondhand furniture than I did in more modern, "chromed," offices. I thoroughly enjoyed sitting with and interviewing members who had activist experiences similar to mine. I experienced dissonance with members who held alternative analyses of women's oppressions, who viewed their positions as careers rather than as a means of movement commitment, who used power in traditional, bureaucratic ways.

Disliking organizations and informants was unanticipated. I now understand negative responses occur even toward subjects we want to admire (Fonow & Cook, 1991; Taylor & Rupp, 1991). I did not expect to deal with individuals with whom I disagreed, yet the problem occurred early and often in the research. At the conclusion of my second site visit, I returned home feeling disenchanted and frustrated. My first trip had gone quite well, which added to the confusion. Had I done something wrong during my last trip? I discussed this unease with one of my committee members. After listening to my various theories about what might be going on, he said: "The problem is that you have met some feminists you don't like." I grudgingly admitted he was correct.

I did not care for this revelation, even resisted it for some time. It proved a harsh lesson that "gender is not enough" in feminist research (Riessman, 1987). Different statuses, ideological visions, and problem analyses, for example, altered my ability to find common ground with all members, underscoring my position as "outsider." I wondered how I could pass judgment when I did not have to contend with the daily realities my informants did. I became increasingly uncomfortable with the privileged role of researcher. As the discomfort increased, so too did my fear that I did not know what I was doing.

Although it was unclear how to handle this emotional dissonance, I did understand I had to identify and examine my feelings and attitudes to determine how (not if) the analysis was affected. I used my analysis log and theme memos as places to question how I was interpreting the sites, to track my emotional disposition toward them. For those organizations or individuals toward whom I was positively disposed, the danger was romanticizing or ignoring problems. I was quite fond, for example, of the Community Health Center, an organization that remained committed to a socialist-feminist agenda. Only after several iterations was I able to see the level of intimacy and connection conveyed by documents and participants was not as uniformly positive as I initially believed. I pushed myself to go beyond favorable emotional impressions and began to question in a memo the supposed benefits of strong personal ties among the members:

> In looking at CHC documents of the late 1970s, I am struck by the amount of emotional investment. *Yet it doesn't get fully channeled in terms of doing something.* Emotional investment, particularly trust, serves as the basis for pursing plans and activities. *The group assumes things will work out because they want them to.* Therefore, few decisions relative to the issues get made. Alot of discussion but, in the end, it gets tabled, lost in other conversations, in statements like "It's been a treat to get to know you. I feel confident we can work out this job process to meet people's needs." Except, they don't.

For the organizations or individuals I disliked, I used the analysis log to remind myself to "be fair" and to vent antipathy:

> Be sure not to sell them [MW NOW] short. They have done some things. Yet they still have declined and much of their activity seems to be funding-oriented.

> DVP started staff training seminars "to increase staff awareness of counselling resources and different techniques. Recently a member of the WGC facilitated a beneficial discussion of fee collection methods." Process note: I hate some of this shit.

Rather than denying the emotional connections I felt with members and organizations, I developed ways to record and analyze them, and disciplined myself to be open to contrary evidence, even when it took several passes through the data.

Emotional responses in the field shaped my identification and development of analytical themes. Often an awareness of the plight of the FSMOs was triggered visually: photographs of a firebombed clinic, protesters harassing a young woman, a door smeared with egg and red paint (to simulate blood). Impassioned, provocative words of participants also drew my attention, particularly when they resonated with my ideals and experiences. When emotional responses serve as vehicles for theme identification, however, more mundane aspects of organizational life can get ignored. I recorded and used my reactions as indicators of an organizational property or process that probably characterized all the FSMOs, more salient in some than others.

Illustrations may help clarify. The following letter is a rallying cry to socialist feminism, a cause in which I believe. It captures the zeal of FSMO members during the early years, when revolution seemed possible:

> We of the CHC, as socialist feminists, want to join with the rest of the anti-imperialist movement in the United States in expressing our great joy at your victory and our solidarity and support for your continued struggle against imperialism, sexism, racism and for the building of socialism. . . . The CHC fosters socialist ideas by offering medical care for women, meeting one of the basic needs common to all people. . . . In all of our work we show women that there are basic contradictions under capitalism, which can never be rectified until we have a socialist revolution. (1975 letter to the Viet Cong)

Data such as these prompted me to examine the founding ideologies of the organizations and search for such data in atypical sources (e. g., letters rather than brochures).

An interview with Molly triggered memories of past feminist projects. From the following, one easily imagines her depth of commitment to the health center: "We worked at the collective; we played, we ate, we practically made love to the collective. It took all our time." The interview helped me understand the kind of investment participants had in FSMOs, and how it varied depending on governance structure (e. g., collective versus bureaucratic). When members of the more bureaucratic FSMOs talked about commitment, it was not with the same language of intimacy.

Often a respondent's language better captured a theme than I had. At the time of my interview with Pam, for example, I already was aware that FSMO veterans were concerned about declining membership. Yet numbers alone failed to convey the emotional intensity of the problem. Pam's words—"if we don't get new blood"—reframed the analysis for me. It wasn't just numbers, veterans worried that their visions were not embraced by a new generation:

> It would be a shame if after all of the battles with the New Right we failed
> to survive because no one cared. You see, we have not succumbed to the
> Right and all of its horrible tricks and attacks. But we cannot continue if we
> don't get new blood into the movement. That, and not the New Right, is our
> biggest threat.

Each example suggests how my emotional response to the data resulted in further inquiry and reinterpretation.

I felt emotionally attached to the organizational stories; however, I became increasingly alienated from other aspects of the study. The initial enthusiasm for fieldwork gave way to grinding tedium and exhaustion during data management, analysis, and writing. My journal during the time contains many entries that suggest my boredom and frustration:

> Work has been up and down. The coding is tedious. I finally finished and
> printed SHC's index. Now I'm working on SACC's, which is discouraging
> given its politics. I don't seem to have a sense of a purpose or focus, which
> I need. Part of it might be because I am ready to do a draft and am avoiding
> it; and the bulk of the work is coding which isn't very exciting.

I now suspect that this "unglamorous" side of qualitative methods is one of the most closely guarded research secrets. In hindsight, negative feelings were not surprising given the sheer quantity of my data and the lack of preparation. I felt overwhelmed and confused, which I typically respond to by disengaging. I attempted to maintain enthusiasm by mixing coding with writing drafts, reading relevant theoretical works and movement accounts, and consuming books by Marge Piercy and Armistead Maupin. Yet I could not shake the notion that I was doing something wrong, because I disliked the process so much.

Research is a solitary enterprise. I often felt uncertain and alone. Though I met interesting people and had productive and meaningful conversations with colleagues, my project could not be completed in collaboration with others. For some, the solitary aspect of scholarship is a benefit; for me it was and is not (see Van Maanen, 1988). Feelings of discomfort, being adrift, remained until the end of writing. The following journal excerpt, composed less than a month before my defense, conveys my detachment and apprehension:

It is awful to have to do something for which you have little drive or desire. And to do it alone. This solitary life with the dissertation is slowly coming to a close. Stress and anxiety are high.

Yet I completed the project and engaged in subsequent work on the findings (see Hyde, 1992, in press). I managed to remain engaged by embracing the commitment (perhaps in an overly zealous manner) to tell survival stories, to give voice to those "in the trenches." The decision created a host of other analytical problems, however.

Juggling Voices

As analysis and writing progressed, I increasingly was concerned and confused about whose voice was at the center of the study—mine, the FSMO participants, my committee, or other theorists. Beneath the quandary were my insecurities over needed skills, my understanding of feminist research, and my reticence toward the academy. These factors led to my assertion that the FSMO participants controlled or "owned" the study; that I, as storyteller, would "allow" them to speak for themselves. I went so far as to state in my methods chapter the following criteria:

> Ultimately, if I have provided the reader with a sense of "life in the trenches," and if I have suggested future courses of actions informed by and for the benefit of the participants, then I will consider this study a success. (Hyde, 1991, p. 31)

It was an admirable goal, perhaps, but not an honest one. In claiming a primarily inductive, "for the people" framework, I diminished my learning needs, analytical insights, and previous theoretical preparation—in other words, my voice.

I was aware of, but could not articulate, the tension between conveying (as opposed to analyzing) the stories. I reconciled the tension by asserting that the FSMO participants' voices took precedence. This was, I thought, the "feminist way." It also was a strategy for staying engaged in the research. I could do the study for the sake of the movement; my development as a scholar was not as important. In the dissertation defense, I tenaciously clung to the inductive, "telling the stories" approach. I rationalized it as politically necessary and also as how I kept from being mired in the data.

The justification was cut short, however, when a committee member stated (something like): "You are not coming completely clean on the role of deductive reasoning in the study. I think that is what kept you from going under." He was, I now understand, correct. At that time, I was not prepared to discuss the point.

By composing this chapter, I return to the multiplicity of voices in the study. Juggling voices requires consideration of thorny problems, such as understanding respondents' vested interests, completeness, and variations between their stories, the integration of theoretical explanations, and the use of one's insights. Insisting that the participants' collective voice was the "true voice" served as a smokescreen for what really happened. By not attending to the study's many voices, critical methodological decisions and problems went unacknowledged.

Some stories conveyed through interviews and documents were deceptive. Respondents had particular interests and obscured or withheld information to protect themselves. Others shared information with me to "save face." Still others spoke because of grievances with the organization, and some uncritically praised their feminist projects, perhaps mistrusting my motives. Organizational histories were built, in part, with deceptive accounts by members.

For example, members in one FSMO indicated in interviews that there was no prior knowledge of a massive funding withdrawal occurring 7 years earlier. The information was conveyed with a sense of pride, because the organization fought back and recovered. However, documents from the time of the budget crisis, though vague, suggest that members knew well in advance. My analytical problem was how to reconcile contradictory information. There were few members left from the time of the funding crisis and I had made the discovery well after I had left the field. My solution was to bypass the difference and give preference to current members' renditions. To some extent, the decision was compatible with the way I was analyzing all the FSMOs. I looked for broad themes that cut across the nine cases, rather than focusing on the particular contexts involved in each case. In doing so, however, I did not explore *why* this revisionist story was so important to current members.

I also implied full representation of all FSMO voices. Yet a review of who I interviewed indicates this was not the case. The initial, usually most important, organizational contact was the director or coordinator. Organizational elites, or gatekeepers, were key to my entrance. In two settings, they gave me immediate permission to study the organizations. In other cases, some negotiation was required. Generally I found that the longer the process, the more democratically oriented the FSMO. The contact person always was interviewed and was instrumental in identifying other key respondents, particularly long-term members.

What I failed to realize at the time was how reliance on organizational elites biased my interview sample. The pool was skewed toward white, middle-class women; they were most likely to have been with the organization the longest and to have achieved director or board member status. Entry-level and part-time staff, positions disproportionately held by women of color, were underrepresented in my sample. Although a good indication of diversity problems in FSMOs, it also meant the experiences of particular groups were excluded, not woven into my case studies.

To some extent, I included the voices of nonelite women by incorporating information found in organizational documents. Information varied widely; not all organizations included members at all levels in events reported in documents. Nonetheless, I got access to women's opinions and actions that otherwise would have gone unnoticed. I also confronted an unanticipated ethical issue regarding consent. Most of the women who appeared in documents had left the organizations. It was not possible to gain their consent as I had from the women I interviewed. Occasionally, documents revealed sensitive or personal information, often in a fragmented manner, about former members. I tried my best to shield the identity of individuals, to reconstruct events from a variety of sources. I was not comfortable with the solution, however, and I raise the issue here because I found no guidance in the research literature.

Variation and completeness of record keeping fragmented the organizational cases. Unless there was a regular pattern to what was filed (rare among the nine FSMOs), it was impossible to know what was missing. This necessitated a "gather everything in sight" strategy, often at the expense of a systematic review of data while on location. Occasionally, gaps in written material were obvious immediately and led to unanticipated findings. In one health center, for example, the board minutes for 1980 and 1981 were missing. No one had any copies, a marked deviation from organizational procedures. In asking the director what happened, I learned this was a major crisis period for the center. Many people felt betrayed and took things when they left. The gap spoke volumes about the dynamics of the health center during the period in question. Most of the time, I was not so fortunate to have an informant and had to piece together what happened like a jigsaw puzzle. Triangulation, the use of multiple sources to explain an event (see Denzin, 1989), is often used in organizational research. I could not convey, however, that these were my, not the respondents', explanations.

These dilemmas beg the question: Why could I not be articulate about what was happening during the course of the project? As alluded to earlier, I did not adequately prepare for the process of *doing* qualitative analysis. Tentativeness regarding my analytical and methodological capabilities constrained me from acknowledging my voice. Many problems in coding, analysis, and writing had not been anticipated and, other than to downplay my voice, I simply did not know what to do.

A related issue was my developing position or status within the academy. As the research progressed, I became more doubtful and disillusioned with academics in general and sociology in particular (my field in addition to social work). The following journal entry, written while in the midst of coding, conveys my alienation and identity crisis:

> I think I'm getting tired of meaningless sociology. While some of it is intellectually interesting, it doesn't seem to solve much. I want to do something that will make a difference and I don't think most sociology jobs will let me do that. I am an organizer at the core.

What is interesting about the entry is my assumption that intellectual inquiry is antithetical to activism. My objective—"giving voice"—perpetuated this dichotomy. I presumed it was more important and more accessible than intellectual inquiry. Separation of intellectualism from activism, however, is neither valid nor desirable. Moreover, in my case the dichotomy did not really exist; I clearly incorporated relevant theory, from the project's inception to final writing. Limiting the research agenda to only "giving voice" was an abdication of responsibility to link data from informants with broader theoretical frameworks to advance social change (see Fonow & Cook, 1991; Gorelick, 1991; Taylor & Rupp, 1991). Failure to make connections reifies and isolates subjects' voices, denying them and ourselves essential integration of knowledge from a variety of sources.

Ignoring my presence also grew out of genuine concern as to how to portray the organizations. I truly admired the work accomplished through the FSMOs, often under harsh political and economic circumstances. I feared that being too analytical or critical would make the organizations appear vulnerable, poorly governed, or not feminist enough. In an era of antifeminist backlash, such images are dangerous. By asserting that members' stories were primary, I thought I sidestepped the issues of passing judgment and possibly betraying the respondents. In actuality, I largely avoided the responsibility of providing constructive feedback to the organizations and explicitly owning my interpretations.

The most salient reason for denying my voice revolved around my understanding of feminist research principles, specifically reciprocity and egalitarianism. Considerable emphasis is placed on "giving voice" to subjects. The stance is a way researchers give something back to informants, convey women-centered worlds to outsiders, and minimize inequities with the researched. I did not employ usual measures to cultivate close (thus supposedly equal) relationships with respondents. I did not, for example, develop longstanding relationships with informants, act as a participant in organizational life, engage in action strategies with FSMO members, or involve participants in a review of the manuscript.[3] I thought my capability as a feminist researcher hinged on the "front and center" placement of members' voices.

Feminists now question the very idea of "giving voice." It denies the unequal power in the research relationship, ignores differences such as race and class, fails to connect stories with relevant theoretical frameworks (Acker, Barry, & Essereld, 1983; Fonow & Cook, 1991; Gorelick, 991; Krieger, 1985; Riessman, 1987, 1993; Stacey, 1988; Taylor & Rupp, 1991). Germane to my case, all too often investigators engage in self-denial to "give voice," rather than claiming the research product as their own, influenced to be sure by respondents (see Daniels, 1983; Stacey, 1988).

I now understand that multiple voices flowed through the study. The final product was not solely the members' stories. My rendering was shaped by a complex mix: insights from relevant literature, advice from my committee, evaluation of the original research propositions, and my interpretations and experiences. It is ironic that the initial reason for the study, the desire to blend my developing abilities as a social scientist with my experiences as a feminist activist, went largely unacknowledged during the process.

Conclusion

A good tale conveys a moral. Mine was told for two basic reasons. First, I wanted to examine and reflect upon a research project that was the center of my life for 5 years. Second, I wanted to identify the techniques, struggles, "things I wished I had known," for the benefit of other researchers. I needed to confront the isolation that the project engendered and the myth that research is an unblemished process.

Those predisposed against the researcher's purpose or method can use aspects of the confession to promote a general attack on the person or process. I composed this chapter with some trepidation. It is not easy to admit naiveté, errors in judgment, or imperfections in planning and execution. On this, I take some comfort from Van Maanen (1988):

> Accident and happenstance shapes fieldworkers' studies as much as planning or foresight; numbing routine as much as living theatre; impulse as much as rational choice; mistaken judgments as much as accurate ones. This may not be the way fieldwork is reported, but it is the way it is done. (p. 2)

Within social work, I encountered considerable antipathy toward qualitative methods, which surprised me because both demand ownership of our experiences, biases, and values. The qualitative research paradigm humanizes the researcher (Reinharz, 1979), a process that parallels social work praxis.

The product, I think, speaks for itself. Despite, or perhaps because of, the unpredicted steps in the research process, I produced a robust, comparative study of nine feminist movement organizations. In subsequent work, I have more finely honed my analysis and delved deeper into contradictions that exist within the data (Hyde, 1992, in press). I believe that I offer a more holistic and dynamic interpretation of organizational life than conventional organizational or evaluation research does.

Nonetheless, I wished I had been warned about (or prepared better for) various aspects of the project. Perhaps their mention here will help other researchers. Although not all problems can be anticipated, more forethought to methodology always helps. Regarding research training, I needed to understand how grounded theory, and later analytic induction, worked throughout the course of a research project. Though prepared (somewhat) to gather data, I needed greater exposure to the steps of data management, interpretation, analysis. Analytic induction proved highly worthwhile, but I was aware of no guide that suggested how to manage so large a data set and maintain aspects of the inductive approach. In the course of the research, I learned to value my analytical journal in which I recorded observations, developed themes, and reflected upon my emotions.

I substantially underestimated the time needed for completion of the research. In my case, learning while doing no doubt extended the project (often forgotten during dissertation research). The pursuit of unanticipated themes resulted in missed deadlines, yet made the project much more worthwhile. The emotional struggles involved in doing a dissertation (generally) and immersing oneself in the data (particularly) necessitated more time. Researchers need to build time into their projects to attend to opportunities and demands.

I would have liked to have extended my field visits or returned to the sites. The overall flow of the project precluded moving back and forth between data gathering and analysis. Some of the dilemmas conveyed in this chapter, such as what to do with incomplete or contradictory data, might have been resolved with more time in the field. Time and resource constraints prevented this. Feeling overwhelmed, coupled with not wanting to further burden FSMO members, limited follow-up activities. In hindsight, I wish I had maintained contact with my informants.

I would have appreciated a warning about the multiplicity of voices involved in such a project and guidance as to negotiating the conflicting demands of different ones. I needed assistance in the process of telling the stories; how to construct and interpret narratives (see Riessman, 1993). At times, I thought I needed only to please my committee, other times I worried that activists' would invalidate my work, and most of the time I felt too insecure with my analytical skills to explicitly allow my voice center stage. I think this is common for students at the dissertation stage (some might say it is part of the rite of passage) and may be endemic to research in general. Increased attention to the juggling of voices would enrich scholarship. Successful research involves the skillful integration of many voices.

In the end, during the oral defense postmortum, several friends who had attended the hearing thanked me for demonstrating that one could stay true to her agenda. This surprised, even pleased, me, for at that moment I was filled with thoughts about things I wished I had done differently. Friends spoke of the strength of my convictions and ability to articulate arguments, which gave them hope for their own research. I then understood that through the journey, I had found my voice.

Notes

1. For information on social movement organizations, feminist organizations, and feminist social movement organizations, see Zald and Ash (1973), Martin (1990), and Riger (1984), respectively.

2. Originally the study's time period was 1980 to 1984. Once sample selection was completed, I noticed that all FSMOs had been founded by 1977. Once in the field, I was interested in knowing more about the organizations after 1984. Thus, I expanded the study's time period from 1977 to 1987.

3. As of this writing, I am sending copies of the dissertation to the nine organizations for review and feedback.

References

Acker, J., Barry, K., & Esseveld, J. (1983). Objectivity and truth: Problems in doing feminist research. *Women's Studies International Forum, 6*, 423-435.

Charmaz, K. (1983). The grounded theory method: An explication and interpretation. In R. M. Emerson (Ed.), *Contemporary field research: A collection of readings* (pp. 109-126). Boston: Little, Brown.

Daniels, A. (1983). Self-deception and self-discovery in fieldwork. *Qualitative Sociology, 6*, 195-214.

Denzin, N. K. (1989). *The research act: A theoretical introduction to sociological methods.* Englewood Cliffs, NJ: Prentice Hall.

Fonow, M. M., & Cook, J. A. (1991). Back to the future: A look at the second wave of feminist epistemology and methodology. In M. M. Fonow & J. A. Cook (Eds.), *Beyond methodology: Feminist scholarship as lived research* (pp. 1-15). Bloomington: Indiana University Press.

Glaser, B. G., & Strauss, A. L. (1967). *The discovery of grounded theory: Strategies for qualitative research.* Chicago: Aldine.

Gorelick, S. (1991). Contradictions of feminist methodology. *Gender & Society, 5*, 459-477.

Harding, S. (1987). Introduction: Is there a feminist method? In S. Harding (Ed.), *Feminism and methodology* (pp. 1-14). Bloomington: Indiana University Press.

Hyde, C. (1991). *Did the new right radicalize the women's movement?: A study of change in feminist social movement organizations, 1977-1987.* Unpublished doctoral disseration, University of Michigan, Ann Arbor.

Hyde, C. (1992). The ideational system of social movement agencies: An examination of feminist health centers. In Y. Hasenfeld (Ed.), *Human services as complex organizations* (pp. 121-144). Newbury Park: Sage.

Hyde, C. (in press). Commitment to social change: Voices from the feminist movement. *The Journal of Community Practice, 1*(2).

Katz, J. (1983). A theory of qualitative methodology: The social system of analytical fieldwork. In R. M. Emerson (Ed.), *Contemporary field research: A collection of readings* (pp. 127-148). Boston: Little, Brown.

Klandermans, B. (1989). Introduction: Social movement organizations and the study of social movements. In B. Klandermans (Ed.), *Organizing for change: Social movement organizations in Europe and the United States* (pp. 1-17). Greenwich, CT: JAI Press.

Krieger, S. (1985). Beyond "subjectivity": The use of the self in social science. *Qualitative Sociology, 8*, 309-324.

LeGuin, U. (1969). *The left hand of darkness.* New York: Ace Books.

Martin, P. Y. (1990). Rethinking feminist organizations. *Gender & Society, 4*, 182-206.

Martin, P. Y., & Turner, B. A. (1986). Grounded theory and organizational research. *Journal of Applied Behavioral Science, 22,* 141-157.

McCarthy, J., & Zald, M. (1977). Resource mobilization and social movements: A partial theory. *American Journal of Sociology, 82,* 1212-1241.

Morgan, G. (Ed.). (1983). *Beyond method.* Beverly Hills, CA: Sage.

Reinharz, S. (1979). *On becoming a social scientist.* San Francisco: Jossey-Bass.

Riessman, C. K. (1987). When gender is not enough: Women interviewing women. *Gender & Society, 1,* 172-207.

Riessman, C. K. (1993). *Narrative analysis.* Newbury Park, CA: Sage.

Riger, S. (1984). Vehicles for empowerment: The case for feminist movement organizations. *Prevention in Human Services, 3,* 99-117.

Rothschild, J., & Whitt, J. A. (1986). *The cooperative workplace: Potentials and dilemmas of organizational democracy and participation.* Cambridge, NY: Cambridge University Press.

Stacey, J. (1988). Can there be a feminist ethnography? *Women's Studies International Forum, 11,* 21-27.

Staggenborg, S. (1989). Stability and innovation in the women's movement: A comparison of two movement organizations. *Social Problems, 36,* 75-92.

Taylor, V., & Rupp, L. (1991). Researching the women's movement: We make our own history, but not just as we please. In M. M. Fonow & J. A. Cook (Eds.), *Beyond methodology: Feminist scholarship as lived research* (pp. 119-132). Bloomington: Indiana University Press.

Van Maanen, J. (Ed.). (1983). *Qualitative methodology.* Beverly Hills, CA: Sage.

Van Maanen, J. (1988). *Tales of the field: On writing ethnography.* Chicago: University of Chicago Press.

Zald, M., & Ash, R. (1973). Social movement organizations: Growth, decay and change. In R. Evans (Ed.), *Social movements: A reader and source book* (pp. 80-102). Chicago: Rand McNally. (Original work published 1965-1966)

10. Modeling Theory From Fiction and Autobiography

SUZANNE E. ENGLAND

This chapter describes a study of stories about the experience of living with and caring for someone with Alzheimer's disease. Preferences of families about what would be helpful are poorly comprehended by service systems. Part of the reason is that most research on caregiving neglects such focal issues for families as the history and quality of relationships, the meanings that families attach to care and dependency, and how families judge the quality of home and family life. Questions of utilization and access are too often framed in terms of motivation and choice about services, such as home help, day care, and respite, that are assumed to be organized to meet families needs. But when assessed according to criteria other than providing assistance with care tasks, or giving a caregiver "time off," families may not consider services to be adequate and appropriate. Despite a commitment on the part of many agencies to respect client and family preferences, without a conceptual framework that appreciates how families view issues, it is difficult to plan appropriate and relevant services.

The study design was the result of a collaboration between a social worker and a humanist specializing in literature and illness, and it reflects a growing trend in the social and psychological sciences to base inquiry on interpretation of narratives rather than freeze-frame data. I chose stories—five novels, two plays, and three autobiographical accounts—for review because my purpose was to cultivate multiple perspectives about

AUTHOR'S NOTE: The research for this chapter was supported by the Alzheimer's Association.

how the problems of caregiving are defined and addressed by those experiencing them. I also chose stories because the complexities and shifts in ethical reflection and decision making are better apprehended through stories (Brody, 1987) than through hypotheses constrained by rules of falsifiability and generalization. By generating concepts and hypotheses from literary and personal stories, I hoped to gain a more critical perspective on how services fit or don't fit into people's lives. I studied the narratives initially to see whether current theories of moral reasoning were applicable to understanding decisions about caregiving and using assistance.

I began by looking for themes or expressions that might relate to Carol Gilligan's (1982) concepts of two types of moral reasoning, one based on an ethic of care honoring human connection and contextual thinking and the other stressing abstract principles such as autonomy, rights, and justice. However, I did not find in these works simple depictions of psychological states such as stress or burden, nor did I find straightforward statements of intention, rationalization, and decision for our inspection and categorization. Instead of evidence of an essence I could call the "care ethic," I found, as Lionel Trilling (1967) has observed, "a literature so shockingly personal [that] it asks every question that is forbidden in polite society." I found what we sought as well: alternative ways of thinking about care.

Account Making

We don't, we never did, go about making statements of fact to other people, or in our internal dialogue with ourselves. (LeGuin, 1980, p. 44)

My account of a research project that relied on stories for its data and on a group for its insights is itself a story, a version constructed to emphasize the process and to encourage others to journey along similar paths. The story is personal—told from the point of view of only one participant. And, to the extent possible, I try to convey the web of events in a plot, so that you the reader can get a sense of my experience of discovery. What follows is a story about two scholars from very different traditions who share a feminist perspective and a group composed mostly of practitioners who taught us a great deal about the power of stories, both read and told. Teaching and learning form the moral of the story.

A Political Question

For several years before this project began, I had been studying policies affecting families with infirm and disabled elderly members. Current policies, driven by ideologies of austerity and family self-sufficiency, view informal care—care provided by family and friends—as critical to preventing or forestalling dependence on public community care programs or costly Medicare and Medicaid funded nursing home placements. Fears that caregivers were eager to use formal services to substitute for their own care have failed to find empirical support (Bass & Noelker, 1987; U.S. Congress, 1990), but the idea that caregiving is heavily influenced by such cost-benefit calculations continues to exert considerable influence on thinking about long-term care policy.

Despite growing awareness that utilization of available services is tied to quality and acceptability, a policy concern with the mechanisms of maintaining family effort has tended to set the research agenda. Most of the questions on formal care are asked from the point of view of one set of stakeholders—policymakers and service planners. Part of the problem of using only the policy/provider perspective is that it tends to project onto the other major stakeholders, the caregivers and receivers, a utilitarian or instrumental view of care composed of tasks, activities, and motivational factors (burden and stress). As a result, research on how policies affect those for whom they were designed treat the elderly and their families as responders to stimuli. This is partly because the major research funder, the United States government, encourages research leading to better cost control, and partly because the dominant theories are psychological or psychoeconomic. A combination leads to what I term "dis-incentive" questions such as, "How much of what kind of stress leads families to place relatives in nursing homes?" Or, "What services are necessary and sufficient to keep families caring for their own kin?" A great deal is known, as a result, about how caregivers and receivers respond to what is available, but little is known about how they judge the usefulness or acceptability of what is available, or how they would fulfill their needs if they had a variety of resources from which to choose. To address questions of access we clearly need to ask caregivers about their experience and desires and, in the tradition of advocacy research, help make these previously hidden issues "thinkable" and "speakable" (Aronson, 1990).

Caregiver Voice

You have asked me all of your questions, but you still don't know the real me.
(Bloom, 1986, p. 129)

The purpose of our study was to develop strategies for listening to caregivers tell their own stories with their own voices. In order to pursue research that would put aside existing policy and service objectives to ask, "What would help? or "What ought to be?" we needed methods that would elicit the voice of caregivers, as unfettered and uncensored as possible by expectations of service providers and policymakers. With this in mind, I began a review of the existing findings on caregiver use of services for signs of caregiver voice and for clues to alternative concepts. We surveyed the existing research and found at least 18 studies. Most, but not all, were based on the predominant model of Alzheimer's caregiving.

The model focuses on patient and caregiver characteristics as factors in placement and service use decisions. Typically, questions have to do with factors such as the extent of symptoms and sequelae of dementia (e.g., confusion, irritability, wandering, inability to bathe, dress, or feed oneself) or with caregiver characteristics (particularly stress and burden). To overgeneralize somewhat, the findings from studies based on the dominant model of caregiving indicates that the more difficult and demanding the caregiving situation, the more likely families are to consider using outside services or nursing home placement. In the corpus of the research was a recurrent finding: caregivers and frail elderly often don't "take advantage" of services when they are offered (U.S. Congress, 1990). Despite the overwhelming evidence that most caregivers experience some level of burden and stress, that so few avail themselves of community services seemed paradoxical.

I began to think that perhaps too much scholarly attention had been paid to testing concepts and theories that treat the caregiver as a "reactor" rather than as a "transactor" who brings her own relevancies to the question of what constitutes useful help. What is it about services and programs that the elderly and their families find wanting? Are they discouraged by the relative lack of availability of supports? Are there characteristics of certain services that serve as barriers to use? Or do families and their elderly members perceive a dissonance between their own values and concerns about care and dependency, and the values and actions of the representatives of formal helping systems with whom they come in contact? One fact is certain: Caregivers themselves have rarely been provided the opportunity to construct their own versions of their experience. Like the woman quoted above, they had answered many questions but most research had not given them a voice (see Rojiani, this volume).

The handful of qualitative studies paying attention to how persons give meaning to the care experience (Bowers, 1987; Gubrium & Lynott, 1987; Lewis & Meredith, 1988; Rubinstein, 1989) reveals the conceptual and methodological inadequacies of measuring impairment, burden, and institutionalization decisions as though caregivers were responding to behavioral cues and stimuli. Bowers (1987), for example, found that caregiver definitions of care priorities differed markedly from those of nurses, particularly in the importance for the caregiver of protecting the care-recipient's dignity and self esteem. Miller (1987) found the same; one of her respondents worried about "demeaning" the care-recipient by having someone come in to care for him in her absence. These studies relied on concepts compatible with social work practice.

Family members are actively defining their experience, negotiating pathways of caregiving, constructing "meaning maps" from their perceptions of the environment, continually defining and redefining their actions and what is offered or available as help. The elements of each individual map includes cultural and subcultural mores of filial responsibility, gender and family roles, direct experience or knowledge of the experience of others, and qualities of relationships. Taken as a whole, the studies suggest dimensions neglected by the prevailing psychoeconomic perspective. One such dimension of potential importance to social work practice theory, is moral reasoning.

Moral Reasoning

Carol Gilligan's influential early work (1982) challenged then-current psychological theories of moral development not only on the grounds that they were developed from studies on men, but also because the resulting theories posed a hierarchy: Reasoning based on universal rights and abstract principles of justice sat at the pinnacle. Moral reasoning based on the maintenance of relationships—thought by Gilligan to be more characteristic of women than men—occupied a secondary and inferior position. Gilligan argued that reasoning based on preserving human relationships was different, not inferior.

Predominant theories of caregiving also favor explanations using abstract rules of behavior; motivation for caregiving could be classified as adherence to principles of filial responsibility, evidence of expectations of role reversal, or an example of exchange, that is, behavior explained in terms of economics. According to these theories, a typical caregiver statement, "My mother cared for me, now I will care for her," could be taken to indicate any or all of these concepts. Even if we wished to categorize the statement according to theory, without contextual information, it is impossible to decide whether it is evidence of exchange, filial responsibility, or commitment to a relationship. The abstract rules approach wrings the life out of words and closes off discovery of alternative ways of thinking. The abstract rules approach treats utterances as responses—end points in communication rather than the beginnings they are probably intended to be—and fails to question the ideologies from which the rules have sprung.

Despite the common view that Gilligan's original critique was primarily about gender differences, it was more fundamentally about the disparity between human experience and the ways in which theory has represented that experience. She recognized and demonstrated how unacknowledged ideologies underlying theory created hierarchies by which nonconforming experiences or responses could be judged inferior. Gilligan (1982) refocused onto the failure of theory (and method), and her concept of voice is not only about the possibility of a female voice but about *different* voices: "My interest lies in . . . different voices and the dialogues to which they give rise, in the way we listen to ourselves and to others, in the stories we tell about our lives" (p. 2).

With the exception of a study by Lewis and Meredith (1988), Gilligan's concepts have not been applied in research on caregiving of the elderly. Lewis and Meredith use a narrative approach and Gilligan's framework to develop the concept of the "caring matrix" and find that the moral ethics of caregiving do influence use of services. Other investigators, using qualitative and interpretive methods (Aronson, 1990; Lustbader, 1991; Miller, 1987; Rubinstein, 1989) also report statements by caregivers about the right or fair thing to do—provide care themselves, use paid or outside help, or place a relative in the nursing home.

Aronson (1990) interviewed caregivers and those being cared for to explore their thoughts and feelings about themselves, ideas about family ties, and the place of public services for the elderly. Her study reveals some of the ways women's own values and attitudes toward dependent care are shaped by public ideologies of independence and self-sufficiency.

Lustbader (1991), using clinical interviews, literature, and autobiography, finds eloquent reflections on the personal meanings of dependency. Rubinstein (1989) discerns statements in caregiver stories about the meaning of caregiving that describe axioms of their personal systems of understanding and beliefs. In one interview a caregiver, explaining her commitment to continuing to care for her mother and her presumption that organized care is neglectful, says: "I couldn't live with myself if my mother was in a home . . . why should she have to suffer the pain of bedsores because of poor care . . . I have control over her care" (p. 128). Rubinstein finds moral reasoning to be a major theme and identifies several crucial dilemmas expressed as questions: What does my caregiving behavior say about what kind of person I am? What is the moral value of my actions? In the quote above, the caregiver is expressing a moral judgment both about nursing home care—it is poor, it will result in bedsores, and it is not subject to family control—and about herself if she were to give up care.

Gubrium's (1989) research suggests another avenue for further exploration of moral reasoning. In a field study of the Alzheimer's experience, one part of which focuses on what Gubrium terms the "domestic meaning of institutionalization," he finds that when caregivers assess the acceptability of a nursing home, they often express concerns about whether it is "homelike." To quote Gubrium:

> The question of whether [nursing homes] provided homelike atmospheres and loving care had two facets: whether a facility's amenities would serve merely to house the patient or be a home, and whether the patient would be in the company of strangers or "family." Both facets were points of the placement decision. (p. 92)

When Gubrium's caregivers speak further about what was homelike or family-like to them, preferences that stem from moral values are hinted. These included whether strong personal preferences would be responded to, whether hands-on care would be done lovingly or "just going through the motions," and whether strangers would put up with a patient's abusive behavior. Caregivers assess their own homes according to the same values, and a decision to institutionalize could stem from a perception that the caregiver could no longer maintain a homelike atmosphere for the family or the patient.

In most of the studies—traditional as well as more interpretive—moral concerns are most often expressed in relation to nursing home placement. But moral judgments are also evident in decisions regarding having someone come into the home while the caregiver was out, or leaving the relative at a day care center. The whys and hows of relationships between caregivers and those cared for warrant conceptualization and study. To investigate access and barriers to organized helping (policy and services), we sought to understand both objective and subjective realities.

Gilligan's concepts provide an entry point for research, but we did not use them as a scheme for classification.[1] The various caregiver quotes provided by other investigators make it clear that taken out of context, few, if any, caregiver statements can be easily classified as care-based or rights-based. Most could be interpreted both ways or be ambiguous. Take a fairly typical statement, "She's my mother, of course she would come live with me, what else would I do." This could be interpreted as expressing adherence to a principle, filial responsibility, or could be a statement of commitment to a relationship. To study moral reasoning and caregiving, we wanted to avoid questions of *either-or* but instead search for when and how morality is expressed, how the narrator relates it to her perceptions of "choices and chances" in the environment. We sought evidence of moral reasoning—using personal relationship, abstract principle, or both—in relation to perceptions of formal care. A question guided the research: How do caregivers express the moral and ethical basis of their caregiving and how do they relate perceptions of organized helping to that ethic?

The Evolution of a Method

Serendipitously, while I was attempting to design a study that would address the question, I happened upon a subplot in a mystery novel that spoke of both the personal and political side of elder care. In P. D. James' novel, *A Taste for Death* (1986), Kate Miskin struggles with the conflict between her ambitions for a career in law enforcement and a sense of responsibility for her grandmother who raised her. Early in the novel Kate reflects, "She would take any trouble, spend any money, to avoid taking her grandmother to live with her. . . . But that, she knew, was what the old lady, in alliance with her social worker, was inexorably pressing her to accept" (p. 174). Her grandmother's social worker fosters in Kate "a confusion of guilt, resentment and depression" as the social worker's "controlled professional patience gradually [gave] way to frustration and, finally, an irritation that was close to hostility" (p. 173).

Later, when her grandmother has been mugged and it is clear that she is not able to live alone, Kate tells her grandmother that she is coming home with her, thinking, "There had been no hesitation and no choice. She couldn't look into those eyes and see for the first time real fear, real despair and say no . . . it had been as simple and inevitable as that" (p. 462-463). A few pages later, Kate makes a discovery about herself, "Nothing is more important to me than my job. But I can't make the law the basis of my personal morality. There has to be something more if I'm to live at ease with myself" (p. 464). Kate is also aware that she and her grandmother were now "locked together" and her grandmother would no longer be considered eligible for certain services. "And when she was too old to be left during the day, what then? . . . She knew what officialdom would say, 'Can't you ask for three months' compassionate leave, or find a part-time job?'" (p. 466).

Here in a novel was a clear expression of how a caregiver experienced the choices and agents of the formal system. Here too was a reminder that a caregiver may not so much *decide* about caregiving, but rather "find herself" doing it because of who she is, that is, who she considers herself to be in relationship with the dependent person. In conversations I had with caregivers, few, if any, defined themselves as such. Similarly, they tended to view their commitment and activity as stemming from a relationship rather than as a matter of choice and rational decision. Kate too says that there "had been no hesitation and *no choice*" (p. 462). She speaks of personal morality, but also makes the connection between her definition of "who I am" to judgments about the formal system. In Kate's story we find an expression of moral reasoning that transcends personal psychology to include the social environment, specifically the social welfare system. Kate links the personal with policy, which suggested to me that given the opportunity to reflect on the kinds of choices about caregiving that the social environment provides, real life caregivers may also make those connections. Choice about caregiving may involve not only personal morality and social role (both influenced by public meanings) but may also be a response to the opportunities—or lack thereof—in the environment. For social workers and others concerned with *how these opportunities are constructed* as well as the personal impacts of caregiving, the theme could be of great interest.

What if other personal accounts and existing research yielded additional examples? Gilligan's theory was built from interviews that elicited statements of moral reasoning around some dilemma. If there were more Kate Miskins in literature, how might Gilligan's or others' constructs be applicable? What would happen to a theory challenged by "found" narratives, where no interviewer was posing an artificial dilemma? Kate's story illustrates how the statement of "who I am" may often contain the answer to the question, "who am I as a moral person?" An expanded view of reasons for caregiving seemed intuitively right. Kate's story suggested a layering or interweaving of the personal and the political. Might other narratives depicting caregiver perceptions enlighten us about these dimensions? If so, they would help to counterbalance the current overreliance on one-dimensional psychological-economic explanations and provide a foundation for new concepts and theories. They would provide an alternate vocabulary—one that would focus on the social as well as personal responses to the burdens of caregiving. This focus and vocabulary would give us a way to move from questions of how much can caregivers bear, to questions about how the burden can be shared.

Searching for Funding

Knowing already of several nonfictional accounts of caregiving, and full of optimism that there were more stories like Kate Miskin's in literature, I sought help from Suzanne Poirier, a specialist on literary narratives and illness. We discovered our mutual interest in Gilligan's theories and caregiving and began to collaborate on proposals for funding our unconventional idea for research. I tried at first to "nest" the study of novels and journals within a study using in-depth interviews. But funders (in this case two foundations specializing in research on aging) were reluctant to fund a concept-generating project. Alternately, Suzanne Poirier took the lead on a proposal to the National Endowment for the Humanities that was well received by reviewers but turned down by the agency as not sufficiently theoretical! We continued to work on proposals, each time using reviewers' comments to sharpen our arguments. Among the proposals we sent was one to the Alzheimer's Association in response to a call for studies of access of families to formal services. Because the proposal outline seemed to assume a traditional methodology, I wrote the proposal more to continue to think through and articulate the concepts and methods than with any serious hope of getting funded. Much to our surprise the Alzheimer's project was funded. Although we have no information about the review process, it is conceivable that because the Association was funding a special initiative with 11 projects, our study was seen as having potential for adding another dimension to the overall effort.

Best-Made Plans

The study design as originally proposed included (a) a systematic review of research on access to formal care; (b) hermeneutic analysis of literary narratives to challenge current theories about the ways in which people reason care and dependency related to Alzheimer's Disease; and (c) implementation of software for using literary sources as data for research on moral reasoning. We had one year to conduct the review, recruit and "train" a narrative study group, and implement the software application. The methods spelled out in our proposal were ambitious and, as it turned out, somewhat naive in terms of what could be accomplished in one year. The review of the research was intended both to compile an exhaustive database of relevant findings and to provide a description of the structure and boundaries of current thinking on the question.

A collaboration between a humanist and a social-science-oriented social worker is unusual and a major strength of the study. What we couldn't anticipate when we were planning the project was how different our backgrounds and perspectives really were. Initially, Suzanne and I were more focused on what we had in common than our differences, but as will be described, the process did not follow the path I had planned or anticipated. I had approached the material as if the narrative study group could come to a consensus about meanings. I knew of course that each person would read and react to the whole work differently, but I had expected the group to be able to extract from each work statements and phrases that could be identified and classified according to emerging themes that we would then enter into a computer program for sorting and linking. However, the group was soon to teach me some lessons about stories and readers.

To put this part of the story in perspective, I'll give a flavor of how different our views were at first (although I didn't realize it at the time) by quoting Suzanne and then myself from the original proposal.

From Suzanne Poirier:

> Because ideas in fiction (not so different from real life) are often conveyed indirectly—by seemingly contradictory words and actions, metaphor, irony or satire—a hermeneutic analysis can be most successfully applied here. Hermeneutics asks that readers attempt to discover the motives and values that underlie a writer's work through recognizing the historical, biographical, and geographical context of the knowledge as well as plumbing the language, tone, and characterizations in the work to discover a writer's commentary on the "broader world" represented in the work. This combination of attention to the particular instances portrayed, the broader commentary

on human nature, and the personal viewpoint of the work's creator, demands that a reader be aware of a work's uniqueness while at the same time looking for generalizable themes. In social scientific terms, the hermeneutic process factors in a sense of "controls" that acts as a constant check on its search for "significant findings" that span the literature.

From Suzanne England:

> The specific process is similar to content analysis in that we break the narrative into parts by first identifying all statements relating reasons for caregiving and use our preliminary theoretical frameworks to type and categorize the statements, paying particular attention to lack of fit, ambiguity and anomalies. However, unlike classic content analysis, we attempt to view these statements in context and look for connecting statements about what alternatives these caregivers considered, rejected, or accepted and on what basis. Then we seek links between those considerations and moral voice.

Clues to the crucial differences in our views can be found in Suzanne's repeated reference to the "work" and my emphasis on the content of the texts. More detail from the original proposal reveals how I envisioned the "nuts and bolts" of the process:

> The Narrative Study Group (NSG) meets monthly for two hours and functions as an expert panel, reviewing classification schemes, data analysis and written reports. During these meetings they are provided with readings, excerpts and results of the work of their previous meeting. *Hermeneutic analysis recognizes that each reader reads from a time and place unique to him or her.* Therefore, each member of the NSG will independently read each piece to assure a negotiation of interpretations. All members of the NSG read the novels and literary pieces in their entirety and identify statements related to the questions for study. Non-conforming recurring themes or patterns— and unresolved issues among readers—will provide the more specific, concrete items by which the actual text material will be coded. Throughout the study, interpretations will be subjected to deliberate reconsideration. Thus there is a "hermeneutic loop"—a constant moving between not only caregiving, dependency, and the social dimensions of the separate narratives, but among all the narratives.

As the project began, I did not realize the import of the statement, "Hermeneutic analysis recognizes that each reader reads from a time and place unique to him or her," or how that fact precluded the possibility of coming to a group consensus about classifying the content of the narratives.

Making Sense With Stories

During the first quarter of the year-long project, we recruited and oriented the narrative study group and began to read and discuss the works, about half chosen in advance and the rest selected according to group preferences and whether we could obtain them in quantity. Members were recruited for the narrative study group from faculty at the university and included a physician-geriatrician, social work scholars specializing in aging and/or Alzheimer's, and clinical social workers from the university hospital and clinics. We were joined about halfway through by another social work educator from a nearby college. Our two part-time research assistants, one of whom holds a Ph.D. in creative literature and is a social work student, were members as well. Not everyone who began in the group was able to continue, but a core group of about 10 people regularly attended the monthly meetings.

The group was guided by Suzanne Poirier, who introduced the members to some of the relevant theories and methods of literary study. Over the year we read and discussed: *The Other Side* by Mary Gordon; *Diary of a Good Neighbor* by Doris Lessing; *Memento Mori* by Muriel Spark; *Dad* by William Wharton; *Memory Board* by Jane Rule; *Painting Churches* by Tina Howe; *Driving Miss Daisy* by Alfred Uhry; *Living With Alzheimer's: Ruth's Story* by Art Danforth; *Stolen Mind* by Myrna Dorenberg; and *The Summer of the Great Grandmother* by Madeline L'Engle. We began our study of literature with general questions that would guide our reading:

- How does the narrator or character express a "particular core sense of who he or she is and how events . . . have contributed to that core sense? (Rubinstein, 1989)
- How does the narrator or character present/judge others, for example, the person for whom they care, other caregivers, potential caregivers, and formal care agencies and staff?
- How is the notion of "burden" defined and regarded by characters? What is said about the sources of burden? Likewise, how is help or relief defined and regarded?
- Under what circumstances do narrators or characters consider, seek and/or use outside support? What supports have they used or considered? How do they judge outside supports and services?
- How does the narrator or character voice the reasons for caregiving? How are characteristics of the relationship expressed in relation to reasons for care? What connections, if any, are made between judgments about outside support and reasons for caregiving?

Top-Down Meets Bottom-Up

The narrative study group began with a novel, Muriel Spark's (1959) *Memento Mori*, which firmly resisted our questions and any easy definitions and classification. The whole work challenged my early views of how the narratives could be used. Here is what I wrote recently about the novel in relation to Gilligan's theory:

> *Memento Mori* is not simply a depiction of psychological states or a series of character studies, although it has these elements. Nor is it a memoir or diary that conveys personal knowledge or presents a self for others to understand or appreciate. *Memento Mori* is an example of how art can transcend what is incomprehensible—one's own death and the loss of self when a mind falters or fails. The story conveys volumes about possible motivations for caregiving, ranging from the most base to the spiritually inspired. What the story does not do is lay out statements of intention, rationalization and decision for our inspection and categorization. We do not find in its pages an essence we can identify as the "care ethic."

To convey some of the ambiguity about motivation to use help, a quote from the novel is illustrative. Here is an exchange between two characters in *Memento Mori*. Charmian is showing signs of dementia; Godfrey is her husband. Her sister-in-law, Dame Lettie, is visiting Jean Taylor, who used to be Charmian's maid/companion but is now in a nursing home because of severe arthritis. Dame Lettie says:

> I feel Charmian needs a firm hand if we are to keep her at home. Otherwise she will have to go to a nursing home. Taylor, you have no conception how irritated poor Godfrey gets. He tries his best. . . . And then, Taylor, there is the lavatory question . . . he isn't used to it, Taylor, he's not used to that sort of thing. (Spark, 1959, pp. 31-32)

In the context of the novel, Dame Lettie is a self-centered person who has harbored some jealousy of her sister-in-law Charmian, who was in her prime, a popular and probably gifted author. "Poor" Godfrey has likewise resented Charmian's popularity over the years, and seems to feel good about himself only in relation to the weaknesses and failings of others. In the conversation, Dame Lettie is promoting the idea that a manipulative (and as it turns out malevolent) woman, Mrs. Pettigrew, be hired to take care of Charmian at home. Dame Lettie is saying, in effect, that it is to be Mrs. Pettigrew or the nursing home; and although she views herself as acting out of compassion for Charmian and Godfrey, she is hoping that Mrs. Pettigrew will give Charmian her comeuppance.

The novel as a whole demonstrates that human motivation and moral reasoning are not always as benign or altruistic as theories would suggest. What the passage demonstrates is that context is critical to "explaining" motivation. In this particular instance, the passage could be used to illustrate the moral dilemma faced when what may be good for the caregiver may not be good for the dependent person. But that only touches the surface here because Dame Lettie's seeming concern for Godfrey is merely a socially acceptable rationale for a different set of calculations. In spite of the appearance of cost-benefit reasoning here, history of the relationships among persons is more telling.

As a testing ground for my methods, *Memento Mori* was ideal in that the artfulness of the work provided an early warning that the approach might not work as planned. I had originally expected that we could approach the stories much like an anthropologist approaches field study, thinking that the storytellers would be fluent field informants. Based on some of my own preliminary readings, I had also anticipated that we would find and read stories with more or less realistic depictions of how caregivers respond to Alzheimer's. My plan was that the group would generate common themes and patterns from these stories, but by the time we finished the third book, several members of the group expressed their unwillingness to take statements and passages out of context for analysis.

We had set out as a group to listen to the voice of caregivers and dependent persons through narratives; the novels, plays, and autobiographies provided ample opportunity for listening. What we didn't anticipate was how differently each individual would listen and how difficult it would be to reconcile these differences or find some common ground. This was partly due to the points of view of our respective professions and disciplines and partly due to differences in views of how theory would be used in relation to the narratives. In the first phase of the study, when we were reading the narratives and expressing our personal reactions, differences were muted. We were about a third of the way through the project when I attempted to implement my plan for analysis. It was then that the extent of the differences in our perspectives became evident. At least half the members of the group challenged my proposal for analysis, gently refusing, in effect, to break up the texts into statements or passages and to categorize them in relation to the theory. They made it clear that they thought we should treat each text as a whole. I found it difficult to imagine how we could analyze *across* the materials without identifying and using the common "data" that each text held. Bruner (1986) describes my approach to the text as "top-down":

> Armed with an hypothesis, the top-down partisan swoops on this text and that, searching for instances (and less often counter-instances) of what he hopes will be a right "explanation." In skilled and dispassionate hands, it is a powerful way to work . . . but it instills habits of work that always risk producing results that are insensitive to the contexts in which they were dug up. (p. 10)

Most of the group members, however, were approaching the text from the "bottom-up" in Bruner's terms: "To *read* a text for its meanings . . . not to prove or disprove a theory, but to explore the world of a particular work" (p. 10). When we began to realize the seriousness of our differences and their implications for the original plan, which had included using a microcomputer-based program to sort and re-sort the categorizations that the group generated, I decided to abandon it—at least to abandon the idea of using the group for this part of the analysis. I realized that, in general, the volunteers in the study group wanted to be readers, not theory builders. They were not averse to trying to apply Gilligan's concepts, but discussions usually moved away from theory rather quickly and on to discussions of context, plot, and character. Their resistance to uncoupling the characters from the stories was heeded, and we put off analysis until we could agree on a strategy.

To assure that we were using some system to discover what might be significant in the stories, I continued to use the series of questions with which we began the study as attention flags, the method I used to locate excerpts such as the one discussed earlier from *Memento Mori*. Particularly with the novels and plays, however, I found the original questions too direct and specific: it was more helpful to go through the works looking for passages about motives and then follow those aspects of character and plot throughout the work. By the close of the project it was apparent from discussions that some of the group members were using similar methods.

Our readings of the texts suggested that Gilligan's conceptualization— at least as we understood it—was difficult to apply to the narratives. The characters and plots were too rich and complex to be classifiable because *context*, including family history, ethnicity, and social class, shaped the way morality was reasoned. The narratives couldn't demonstrate the theory, but they did challenge us to expand upon it. We were gaining from the sum of the process what I had, at one time, given up hope for—alternative conceptualizations of the experiences and accounts of caregivers.

The plays and novels in particular evoked complex and diverse reactions from each of us. I gradually came to realize how central the interaction of text and reader is, and how, in this type of study, at least as much attention must be paid to responses of the readers as to the text itself. In our group, reactions to the works and characters were always strong, often emotional. Our group held no rules about how to read or react, and it was not at all unusual for one participant to dislike a writer, work, or character that another participant loved. When expressing these reactions each of us would try to explain what it was that evoked these feelings, which often led to revelations about personal history and, occasionally, to reflections on the cultural and social contexts that shaped the stories and our reactions to them.

Thinking back on the group, I'm struck by how strong the impulse is among those us of trained in the traditions of the social sciences to decontextualize and reduce in order to attain some reliability and validity in our observations. But equally compelling was the impulse to try to "fill in" a story or character with information from our theories, professional practice, or personal experiences. The separation of the self from what is being observed through standard techniques is the ideal when the investigator seeks one "true" interpretation (Mishler, 1986). However, observation of the self-as-observer is called for when we are concerned with a number of possible truths. In observing readers and texts, the criteria for believability (or validity, if you will) is not falsification or generalization, but verisimilitude to possible human experience (Bruner, 1986). The test of verisimilitude was our response as readers, co-creators, with the texts, of virtual worlds. How were we to learn to observe ourselves? We had to learn to communicate with one another about our personal experiences of the text and then learn to communicate with others who had not been part of the study.

Individual and Collective Pathways to Theory

The idea of co-operative inquiry starts with a paradox: the label implies equality and a democratic process in which we can all engage; yet it is not a casual and unstructured process, and to do it well requires intense commitment and subtle skill of those who undertake it. (Reason, 1988, p. 19)

In order to move from the unstructured and democratic process that characterized the project in the first half, we decided to focus in more systematically on Gilligan's theory and to discuss its applicability to the stories we had read. In the fourth quarter of the project, we completed the readings and selected four works to review in more depth: *Memento Mori, Memory Board, Diary of a Good Neighbor,* and *The Other Side.* Members of the group volunteered to work together in small groups to write an interpretation using Gilligan's framework as a starting point. Suzanne Poirier took the lead in bringing the short papers together into one paper that we agreed would be authored as a collective. Suzanne suggested rewrites for each of the small group papers and drafted an introduction, a closing, and transitional sections.

The Collective

Reflecting on how our intertwining of individual, small group, and group-as-a-whole interpretation worked, I make the following observations. The free-wheeling group-as-a-whole process opened up a multitude of possible interpretations but was uncritical and unscientific; we were not required to support an assertion by using any rules of evidence. For example, I could and, in fact, did make a statement about a writer's motive as follows. "He was writing his journal to deal with his feelings of guilt." In the group meetings I was not expected to cite the text for evidence of my assertion. Another member of the group could counter or support the statement, perhaps citing a scene or passage, but we did not systematically pursue the question. Although the group-as-a-whole process was highly stimulating, it was not accountable in ways that systematically build knowledge.

Small Group Papers

The specific task of examining one work in light of Gilligan's theory and then supporting our interpretations in an individual paper did force us to be accountable. We could not make generalizations or interpretations without evidence from the text to support them. That is not to say that our interpretations could be judged as more or less "accurate," but they had to have some basis in the narrative. The following excerpt from my contribution to the small group paper on *Memento Mori* illustrates how I was able to reach a level of abstraction in my individual interpretation. However, the excerpt is deceiving in that it doesn't reveal how demanding it was for me to find evidence in the text to support my assertions:

Reflecting on Gilligan's conceptualization of moral reasoning in relation to the caregiving of Mrs. Pettigrew, Jean Taylor, and the Maud Long Ward (a public nursing home), we find several variations on her theories. One is that motives for caregiving may be colored by inequalities in status. Another is that caregiving is nested within a series of social constructions so that individual behavior (for example, how nurses treat patients in a nursing home) is shaped by organizational practices (and ultimately by social policy). What Muriel Spark's novel allows us to see is how a caregiver (the malevolent Mrs. Pettigrew mentioned earlier), chafing at her lower status, uses her advantage over a dependent person for personal gain; how care can be organized in ways that burden those dependent on care; how a supposedly dependent person, Jean Taylor, does everything in her power to care about and for those around her.

The importance of the discipline imposed by having to write first an individual, then a small group, then a collective paper cannot be underestimated. In the small groups we had to defend our ideas with others who were themselves on intimate terms with the text. *Memento Mori* was insistent that I return to verify every speculation; constantly returning to the book (by now extremely worn) to reread every section referring to a particular character or plot line. What was surprising to me was how often my hypotheticals were dead wrong, considerably off the mark, or oversimplifications. Used to interpreting data that I had generated myself, and to which only I and a few others were privy, I learned to appreciate the power of commonly held data (a widely available paperback book) to keep one accountable. The experience of returning constantly to the text also brought home to me the need to keep my reasoning wary. The interplay between reading-in-common, writing, critical discussion, and rewriting contributed greatly to that end.

Personal Interpretation

In addition to the interpretations and pathways that emerged from the group processes, I was developing a perspective based on my own review of related empirical and theoretical work on Alzheimer's caregiving. My goal was to develop a conceptual approach that could be applied to both research and clinical interviews, and to my practice, the narratives provided a proxy for the kind of real life stories that a social worker might encounter in the field. Existing research using traditional social science methods had little to offer for direct practice and, on the whole, ignored the issue of the social construction of access to care. Our study of narratives, in combination with the research of Aronson (1990), Rubinstein (1989), Lustbader (1991), and Gubrium (1989) suggests conceptual pathways and possible connections to practice.

In contrast to Gilligan's theory, which we "tested" by the large and small group processes, the perspective I'm developing is personal. It resembles in some respects the informed intuition that prompted me to study moral reasoning in the first place, but in important ways it disputes the earlier formulation. The difference, of course, is that the initial hypotheticals (including those about method) were challenged by experience, by evidence, and by alternative explanatory constructs.

Prosaics

It is difficult in the confines of a chapter on method to summarize the alternative pathways and concepts that I've discovered, and it may be some time before the discoveries gel into something coherent enough to be a theory. As I write this, one concept is coming into focus, which I've termed *prosaics*[2] to convey attention to the small, everyday aspects of family life. In fiction and autobiography the most meaningful events are the homely, taken-for-granted details of daily life which, under the onslaught of disability, become troubles. When the demented person does not respond in old accustomed ways, moral dramas are played out, as family members attempt to reorder and reinterpret everyday domestic life .

Writers of fiction or drama often use small events or domestic scenes to evoke recognition and empathy in the reader. In *Driving Miss Daisy*, for example, most of the play takes place in the car and occasionally in the kitchen. It is there amidst the seeming trivia of life—shopping lists, cups of coffee, packed lunches, and errands—that we observe the unfolding of the relationship between Hoke, the black chauffeur, and Miss Daisy. In *Dad*, the anguish of family members trying to help two disabled parents maintain some semblance of a home life and marriage is played out in bedrooms and in living rooms with the television on—all punctuated with soiled laundry and lunches of cheese sandwiches and beer.

Focusing on everyday domestic life—such common elements as where one lives and with whom, feeding, toileting, doctor's appointments, decisions about property, and maintenance of personal preferences within patterns of relationships and intimacy—we find some elements charged with moral meaning. When a family member becomes demented, such elements become matters of conscious concern and deliberation. In *Driving Miss Daisy*, for example, Miss Daisy's driving becomes a question of personal autonomy versus risk of harm—a poignant issue for many families when disability strikes.

In the works we studied we saw how daily routines could be subtly choreographed by caregivers to preserve the dignity and autonomy of the elderly person, or could be manipulated in a struggle for control and power over the dependent person. We saw how eating, familiar objects, and places could become the source for reminiscence and rethinking, how frequently something as simple as getting around was fraught with moral conflict. Journal writers, too, focused on daily living, often describing scenes in the home where the usually smooth flow of life was drastically upset by dementia. Normalcy was gone and with it the small assumptions we make every day about good manners, safety, eating, and personal hygiene. Assumptions make events prosaic rather than poetic or dramatic, and when small assumptions are challenged or removed, larger ones about self and relationships are called into question. When we examine the larger assumptions, prosaics is a method not unlike what literary analysts refer to as reading the "margins" of a text—those aspects not obvious at first but which nevertheless form the basis for examining behavior and motivation.

In his interpretations of caregiver stories, Gubrium (1989) refers to larger assumptions as the public meaning of care. In interviews with Alzheimer's support group members, he observes an apparent consensus about what constitutes quality care but, when individuals spoke further, any easy consensus is revealed to be false. The works we studied allowed us to see similar layers of meaning, or contradictory truths. In every story, social expectations shape personal interpretations and expectations about care. We, too, find private thoughts and feelings that make us wary of concepts about caregiving derived from unquestioned social expectations.

In and of itself, prosaics does not connect the everyday small bits of life to moral reasoning and access to support but rather suggests a pathway for privileging the voice of caregivers and locating the impact of social context in the text. Instead of theory-driven concepts about internal psychological processes or behaviors of the demented person, what this emergent method provides is attention to the ecology, if you will, of family and communal life within the context of social values. It speaks the language of everyday life—a consideration of interest to those who try to help—and, by illuminating the contrast between public and private meanings, addresses the opportunity structure of care and support for caregiving. We start not with calculations about the performance of activities of daily living, but on the ground floor—how each person experiences dependency.

Our study does not have definitive "findings" but rather discoveries. Yes, we found evidence that moral reasoning is an aspect of motive for caregiving and using outside services, but moral reasoning is itself multidimensional and inextricable from social ideology. Have we been able, as we had wished, to discover how the personal is political? We are just now beginning to sort out how to use stories and our emerging method to do that. By reading the margins and focusing on domestic life, the social construction of care is coming more clearly into focus.

Truth Finding and Truth-Making

Sometimes the truths we see in personal narratives jar us from our complacent security as interpreters "outside" the story and make us aware that our own place in the world plays a part in our interpretation and shapes the meaning we derive from them. (Personal Narratives Group, 1989, p. 261)

Looking back on the project, we were not seeking truth in the sense of believing in one best or right answer, that by accumulating "objective" knowledge we could predict and control events. Rather, by recreating a "virtual world that stands against, and comments upon, the qualities of life-at-hand" (Barone, 1990, p. 317), we were attempting to *make truth*—to introduce or uncover voices that we suspected were suppressed.

One lesson I learned from the study is that there *are* two "natural kinds" of knowing, and they are incommensurable in the sense of sharing no common measure. Before the study, I thought that what is usually termed qualitative analysis (e.g., content analysis or field study) could be applied to narratives. Now I'm inclined to think that narratives, if they are studied respectfully, force us to confront issues of evidence, induction, and interpretation in wholly different ways; materials cannot be reduced to categories through consensus. Bruner (1986) observes the difference: "The one, science, is oriented outward to an external world; the other [narrative], inward toward a perspective and a point of view toward the world. They are in effect, two forms of an illusion of reality—very different forms" (p. 52).

Incommensurability has major implications for social work because it helps us understand difficulties we encounter when attempting to promote inquiry-based practice. One criticism of research is that it is rarely relevant to those working for social change. Traditional empirical study, whether quantitative or qualitative, begins with what is already named. Yet advocacy may call for naming what is, in Aronson's (1990) terms, not yet thinkable or speakable, what might in fact be suppressed in discourse. Narrative inquiry directly challenges received concepts and is language building. When studying at the margins we seek to hear what may not yet be speakable but is implied by the context; when observing ourselves as readers, we are seeking change in ourselves.

Our failure to embody the ideal of the social work practitioner-researcher is yet another indication that we should heed the differences between traditional science and narrative study. Because the norms of traditional inquiry treat narratives, and by extension the narrator, as reducible to codes or as anecdotal and therefore inadmissable, the practitioner, who works and thinks in a world of narratives, is expected by the traditional paradigm to selectively forget his or her tacit practice knowledge, and, in the name of objectivity, to put aside the desire to envision more humane possibilities. Voice-centered, collaborative, truth-making inquiry can be a kind of conspiracy to break down barriers between social workers and researchers, and help raise the voices of our constituencies. We must rethink how to do research that can be the basis for advocacy. We could begin by returning the human voice to our research, welcoming pluralism in experience, method, and interpretation.

Notes

1. In this study I put aside the question of gender, assuming that caring for someone with Alzheimer's can be so profoundly life-altering that it could easily override more superficial aspects of gender socialization.

2. I am indebted here to Howard Goldstein for introducing this idea to me and for his all-round intellectual generativity and nurturing.

References

Aronson, J. (1990). Old women's experiences of needing care: Choice or compulsion? *Canadian Journal on Aging, 9*(3), 234-247.

Barone, T. E. (1990). Using the narrative text as an occasion for conspiracy. In E. W. Eisner & A. Peshkin (Eds.), *Qualitative inquiry in education: The continuing debate* (pp. 305-326). New York: Columbia University, Teachers College Press.

Bass, D., & Noelker, L. (1987). The influence of family caregivers on elder's use of in-home services: An expanded conceptual framework. *Journal of Health and Social Behavior, 28,* 184-196.

Bloom, H. (1986). *The experience of research.* New York: Macmillan.

Bowers, B. (1987). Reconceptualizing intergenerational caregiving: A grounded theory analysis of middle aged women caring for their aging parents. *Advances in Nursing Science, 9*(2), 20-31.

Brody, H. (1987). *Stories of sickness.* New Haven, CT: Yale University Press.

Bruner, J. (1986). *Actual minds, possible worlds.* Cambridge, MA: Harvard University Press.

Danforth, A. (1984). *Living with Alzheimer's: Ruth's story.* New York: Howarth.

Dorenberg, M. (1986). *Stolen mind.* Chapel Hill, NC: Algonquin Books.

Gilligan, C. (1982). *In a different voice: Psychological theory and women's development.* Cambridge, MA: Harvard University Press.

Gordon, M. (1989). *The other side.* New York: Viking.

Gubrium, J. (1989). The domestic meaning of institutionalization. In L. E. Thomas (Ed.), *Research on adulthood and aging* (pp. 89-106). Albany: SUNY Press.

Gubrium, J., & Lynott, R. (1987). Measurement and the interpretation of burden in the Alzheimer's disease experience. *Journal of Aging Studies, 1,* 265-286.

Howe, T. (1988). Painting churches. In B. McNamara (Ed.), *Plays from the contemporary American theater* (pp. 350-388). New York: Mentor.

James, P. D. (1986). *A taste for death.* New York: Warner Books.

LeGuin, U. K. (1980). *Dancing at the edge of the world: Thoughts on words, women, places.* New York: Harper & Row.

L'Engle, M. (1974). *The summer of the great grandmother.* New York: Harper & Row.

Lessing, D. (1983). *Diary of a good neighbor.* New York: Knopf.

Lewis, J., & Meredith, B. (1988). *Daughters who care; daughters caring for mothers at home.* London: Routledge, Chapman & Hall.

Lustbader, W. (1991). *Counting on kindness.* New York: Free Press.

Miller, B. (1987). Gender and control among spouses of the cognitively impaired: A research note. *The Gerontologist, 27*(4), 447-453.

Mishler, E. (1986). *Research interviewing: Context and narrative.* Cambridge, MA: Harvard University Press.

Personal Narratives Group. (1989). *Interpreting women's lives: Feminist theory and personal narratives.* Bloomington: Indiana University Press.

Reason, P. (Ed.). (1988). *Human inquiry in action: Developments in new paradigm research.* London: Sage.

Rubinstein, R. (1989). Themes in the meaning of caregiving. *Journal of Aging Studies, 5*(2), 119-138.

Rule, J. (1987). *Memory board.* Tallahassee, FL: Naiad Press.

Spark, M. (1959). *Memento mori.* New York: Avon.

Trilling, L. (1967). On the modern element in modern literature. In I. Howe (Ed.), *The idea of the modern in literature and the arts* (pp. 164-165). New York: Horizon Press.

Uhry, A. (1986). *Driving Miss Daisy.* New York: Theater Communications.

U.S. Congress, Office of Technology Assessment. (1990). *Confused minds, burdened families: Finding help for people with Alzheimer's & other dementia* (OTA-BA-403) Washington, DC: Government Printing Office.

Wharton, W. (1981). *Dad.* New York: Avon.

Index

Societal impact, of chronic illness, 6
Sociodemographics:
  chronically ill elderly and, 11-14
  population aging, 6
Sociohistorical context, chronically ill eld-
    erly and, 6
Sociolinguistic approach, physical abuse
    in marriage and, 70
Soldo, B. J., 141
Solomon, C., 136, 153-168
Spark, M., 202, 203
Spence, D. P., 114, 131
Stacey, J., 185
Staggenborg, S., 172
Stanley, L., 50
Stark, E., 115
Starr, P., 30
Status, social work/physician collaboration
    and, 30
Stelling, J., 30
Stepfather, sexual abuse by, 84
Stivers, C., 133, 135
Stories:
  core, 103
  deceptive, 182
  elders' caregiver and, 202
  identity constructed through, 145-146
  telling about experiences, 114, 115
Strain, L. A., 148
Stratified sampling, chronically ill elderly, 7
Straus, M. A., 109, 115
Strauss, A., 1-2, 7, 9, 14, 18, 29, 32, 36,
    38, 43, 50, 56, 143, 172
Street-level bureaucracy, 155-156, 165
Stress:
  caring for elderly and, 192, 193
  social workers in health settings and, 31
  welfare workers and, 156
Subjectivity:
  as source of knowledge, 3
  importance of, 133-136
Subjects:
  emotional proximity to, 10-11
  friendships with, 53-55, 149
  negative responses to, 177
  power relationships and, 147-149
  relationship with, 139-140

social work/physician collaboration, 33-
    34, 43-44
traditional interviewing and, 53
Subsample, chronically ill elderly and, 11
Suicide attempts:
  chronic illness and, 17-18
  sexual abuse and, 74, 82, 87, 88
Sullivan, W. M., 67
Summaries, 175
Survival, crimes of, 79
Suspicion, hermeneutics of, 130
Sweden, societal changes in, 95-96

Target population, perspectives of, 50
Tarule, J. M., 83
Taylor, V., 176, 177, 184, 185
Teenage pregnancy, 75
Temporality, narratives and, 101
Text:
  reading margins of, 210
  unpacking, 70
Theme identification, 175
Theoretical coding, social work/physician
    collaboration, 38
Theoretical memos, 56
Theoretical sampling, 172
Theory:
  chronically ill elderly and, 10
  cooperative inquiry and, 206-209
  modeling from fiction and autobiogra-
    phy, 190-212
Thomas, W. I., 80
Tracy, S., 78-79
Transcriptions, 70, 115, 145, 157
Travis, S., 139
Triangulation, 183-184
Trilling, L., 191
Trost, J. E., 7
Truancy, 73, 74
Trust:
  client/welfare worker exchanges and,
    155
  researching feminist organizations and,
    176, 178
  revealing information and, 140
  sexual abuse by family member and, 83

About the Authors

Julie S. Abramson is Associate Professor at the School of Social Welfare, State University of New York at Albany, She has her MSW from Columbia University School of Social Work and her Ph.D. from Bryn Mawr College Graduate School of Social Work and Social Research. Prior to her academic positions, she worked for many years in psychiatric and medical settings as a direct practitioner and administrator. Her research and publications have related to collaboration between physicians and social workers, team work, program development in medical settings, and discharge planning. She is currently evaluating the impact of a clinical intervention to enhance control by elderly hospitalized patients over discharge planning decision making. She also is a consultant to hospital social work departments and to interdisciplinary teams.

Denise Burnette, Ph.D., MSSW, is Assistant Professor of Social Work at the Columbia University School of Social Work. She has extensive direct practice experience in medical and geriatric social work and has served as a practice and research consultant to numerous health and social services agencies. She is a faculty affiliate of the Center for the Study of Social Work Practice, a joint endeavor of the Columbia University School of Social Work and the Jewish Board of Family and Children's Services in New York City. She is also a consulting editor for *Social Work Research and Abstracts*. Her research interests include the mental health of older women, living arrangements in late life, changing roles of grandparents in American families, and combining qualitative and qualitative methods in the study of social work problems.

Suzanne E. England is Associate Professor in the Jane Addams College of Social Work and also holds an appointment in the Department of Occupational Therapy in the College of Associated Health Professions, University of Illinois at Chicago. She directs the Project for the Study of Families, Health and Social Policy, which conducts research on how social policy and the organization of health care affects families with ill or disabled members. Recent studies include analysis of the interaction of state-level, community-care policies with the gender structure of family care of dependent elderly persons, analysis of policies and programs to address elder employees, and an investigation of subjective aspects of caregiver decisions to use formal services. She is an author of a book, *Wages for Caring* (with Linsk, Keigher, & Simon-Rusinowitz) and has published a number of articles on policies related to elder care. Currently she is collaborating with humanities scholars, gerontologists, and practicing social workers to analyze literary and clinical narratives on illness, disability, and caregiving.

Robin Gregg is a Research Fellow at the Divison of Social Science, Ethics and Law, Shriver Center, Waltham, Massachusetts, where she is con- ducting qualitative research about the ethical attitudes of genetic counselors and physicians who provide genetic services. Her current research is supported by a post-doctoral fellowship from the Ethical, Legal and Social Implications Program of the National Center for Human Genome Research, National Institutes of Health. She has an interdisciplinary social work and social science background: BA, Political Science, Drew University; MSW, University of Kentucky; and Ph.D., Social Welfare, Brandeis University. Following college, she worked as a social worker in a women's prison in New Jersey. After obtaining her MSW in Kentucky, she lived and worked for 10 years in Central Appalachia (Kentucky, West Virginia, Tennessee, and Virginia), as a medical social worker, community organizer, adult educator, and college teacher. She has taught undergraduate and graduate courses in social work and sociology, at Davis and Elkins College, Virginia Intermont College, Virginia Commonwealth University (Bristol MSW Program), and Wesleyan University. Her research interests include women's health, genetics and ethics, feminist theory and methods, and health care services and policy. A book, *Pregnancy in a High-Tech Age: Paradoxes of Choice* is in press.

Cheryl Hyde is Assistant Professor of Human Behavior in the Social Environment at the Boston University School of Social Work, where she also coordinates the sequence on Racism and Oppression. She received her Ph.D., MSW, and Certificate in Labor and Industrial Relations from the University of Michigan, Ann Arbor. Her areas of interest include cultural diversity in social work education and praxis, organizational culture and transformation, feminist and progressive models of social change, the women's movement, and the New Right. She currently is working on a book about the grassroots feminist movement in the 1980s and she is the editor of the *Journal of Progressive Human Services.*

Margareta Hydèn received her Ph.D from Stockholm University in 1992 in social work. Her research has been supported by a 3-year fellowship from the Swedish Commission for Social Research, and a 2-year fellowship from Stockholm University. Her book, *Woman Battering as Marital Act: The Construction of a Violent Marriage* is in press. She has been teaching psychotherapy and family issues at Stockholm University School of Social Work since 1983. Over the years, she has lectured on domestic violence to student groups, social workers, police staff, volunteers at women's shelters, and other practitioners working in the field of family violence. She is a licensed psychotherapist and serves as a consultant for All Women's House in Stockholm, and has conducted a program of psychotherapy for battered women.

Terry Mizrahi, Ph.D., is a Professor at the Hunter College School of Social Work, CUNY. She is Chairperson of the Social Health concentration and Director of The Education Center for Community Organizing at HCSSW. She is secretary of the National Association of Social Workers (1992-1994) and columnist for the "National Health Line" of *Health and Social Work* (1991-1993). She has authored numerous books and articles on health advocacy, patients' rights, health policy, physician training and practice, community organizing, and collaboration and coalition-building. She is author of *Getting Rid of Patients: Contradictions in the Socialization of Physicians* (1986) and co-editor (with John Morrison) of *Community Organization and Social Administration: Advances, Trends and Issues* (1993). She chaired a national work group on National Health Care Reform for NASW in 1983. She has received numerous training and research grants to further her work. She is currently principal investigator on the first grant ever awarded to a school of social work under the Department of Health and Human Services' Health Careers Opportunity Program (HCOP). Her article is one of several works emanating from funded research, with Julie Abramson, on collaboration between social workers and physicians.

Catherine Kohler Riessman is Professor of Social Work and Professor of Sociology at Boston University. Both a social worker and a sociologist, she directs a Ph.D. program that connects disciplines. She is the author of *Divorce Talk* (1990), *Narrative Analysis* (1993), and numerous academic articles. Research and publications examine the relationships between women and health, social class and health service use, gender and divorce, and the emergent field of narrative studies. She teaches family theory, medical sociology, and research methods (including a course on qualitative analysis at the doctoral level). Recently embarking on a study of infertility, the first phase of her project will involve participant observation and interviewing of infertile women in India (Kerala state), and is supported by the Council for the International Exchange of Scholars. She is active in the Group for the Advancement of Doctoral Education in Social Work (GADE), and the American Sociological Association.

Robin A. Robinson is an Assistant Professor at Rutgers University in the School of Social Work, New Brunswick. She received her Ph.D. in social welfare policy from Brandeis University, Florence Heller School for Advanced Studies in Social Welfare. Before undertaking her doctoral work, she was employed for many years as a public services librarian in inner-city neighborhoods in Massachusetts, where she coordinated interagency efforts to provide social services. Her current research interests include the relationship between sexual abuse history and deviant behaviors, correctional control of women, classification of prisoner risk and need, and community-based mental health services. She is currently at work on a book on changing perceptions of female deviance and crime.

Rhoda Hurst Rojiani is a 3rd-year doctoral candidate at Virginia Polytechnic Institute and State University. She received her MSW from Virginia Commonwealth University and a Bachelors in Anthropology from San Diego State University. Her social work practice experience includes home health, Hospice, nursing home, juvenile and domestic relations family counseling and directing a Big Brother/Big Sister program. Her research interests currently focus on applications of attachment theory to late life caregiving and social support, and implications for physical and mental health. In January 1994 she will assume a faculty position with joint appointments in the Departments of Gerontology and Social Work at the University of South Florida.

Cate Solomon is an Assistant Professor at Rhode Island College, School of Social Work. She received her MSW from Smith College and her Ph.D. from Brandeis University Florence Heller School for the Advanced Studies in Social Welfare policy. After receiving her MSW she worked at the Chelsea Memorial Health Care Center of the Massachusetts General Hospital providing mental health and child protective services. Her interest and studies focus on low-income populations.